The
Persistence
of
Modernity

The
Persistence
of
Modernity

Essays on Aesthetics,
Ethics, and Postmodernism

ALBRECHT WELLMER

Translated by David Midgley

The MIT Press
Cambridge, Massachusetts

First MIT Press edition 1991

Translation © 1991 Polity Press

These essays are drawn from two collections of the author's work: *Ethik und Dialog* and *Zur Dialektik von Moderne und Postmoderne*, both © Suhrkamp Verlag, Frankfurt am Main, Germany.

Library of Congress Cataloging-in-Publication Data

Wellmer, Albrecht.
[Selections. English. 1991]
The persistence of modernity : essays on aesthetics, ethics, and postmodernism / Albrecht Wellmer ; translated by David Midgley.— 1st MIT Press ed.
    p. cm. — (Studies in contemporary German social thought)
    Essays selected and translated from: Ethik und Dialog and Zur Dialektik von Moderne und Postmoderne.
    Contents: Truth, semblance, reconciliation — The dialectic of modernism and postmodernism — Art and industrial production— Ethics and dialogue.
    ISBN 0–262–23160–3
    1. Aesthetics, Modern. 2. Ethics, Modern. 3. Critical thought.
    4. Postmodernism. I. Title. II. Series.
    BH151.W44213   1991   90–45286
    190'.9'045—dc20   CIP

Printed in Great Britain.

This book is printed on acid-free paper.

190
W 452

Contents

Introduction

The essays collected in this volume explore various aspects of
what might be called the spirit of modernity and its vicissitudes.
I argue for a conception of modernity which is wider than that
of many postmodernists, a conception according to which the
critique of metaphysics or, to use Adorno's phrase, the 'explosion
of metaphysical meaning' does not signify the end of modernity,
but the deepest concerns and the most difficult tasks of the
modern spirit itself. If there is one single thread running through
the four essays of this volume, it would be the thesis that modernity is for us an unsurpassable horizon in a cognitive, aesthetic
and moral–political sense. This thesis, not surprisingly, entails
the further thesis that the critique of modernity has been part of
the modern spirit since its very inception. If there is something
new in postmodernism, it is not the radical critique of modernity,
but the redirection of this critique. With postmodernism, ironi-
cally enough, it becomes obvious that the critique of the modern,
inasmuch as it knows its own parameters, can only aim at
expanding the interior space of modernity, not at surpassing it.
For it is the very gesture of radical surpassing – romantic utopianism – that postmodernism has called into question.

Consequently I shall argue that postmodernism at its best
might be seen as a self-critical – a sceptical, ironic, but nevertheless unrelenting – form of modernism; a modernism beyond
utopianism, scientism and foundationalism; in short, a post*metaphysical* modernism. A modernity beyond metaphysics would be

a new 'Gestalt' of modernity; perhaps we are witnessing the emergence of such a 'Gestalt'. A postmetaphysical modernity would be a modernity without the dream of ultimate reconciliations, but it would still preserve the rational, subversive and experimental spirit of modern democracy, modern art, modern science and modern individualism. In its moral and intellectual substance it would be the heir and not the end of the great tradition of European Enlightenment. A second modernity, perhaps, with a memory and a new understanding of the temptations and perversions that have haunted the modern spirit – totalitarianism, nationalism, scientism, 'instrumentalism' – and, at the same time, with a new, non-identitary understanding and practice of the democratic universalism and pluralism that is part of the modern tradition itself.

In the essays collected here I have explored various aspects of such a 'postmodern', non-identitary rethinking and recapturing of the modern spirit. The first three essays explore internal relationships between aesthetic modernism and the critique of identitary reason as well as what I have called the dialectics of the modern and the postmodern. The first essay, on 'Adorno's aesthetic redemption of modernity', is a critical reinterpretation of Adorno's aesthetics. I suggest a 'stereoscopic' reading of Adorno which aims at 'translating' the basic parameters of his thought into the conceptual framework of a post-utopian philosophy of communicative reason. In the essay 'The dialectic of Modernism and Postmodernism', a critical examination of Adorno's and Lyotard's accounts of aesthetic modernism provides the starting-point for a metacritique of the postmodernist critique of identitary reason and its subject. Drawing on arguments from Wittgenstein and Habermas I try to show that a 'non-identitary' moment is already inherent in the structure of ordinary communication and reasoning. The critique of identitary reason – exemplified again by Adorno's critique of 'identifying thought' – is then turned into an argument for a non-formalistic, 'plural' conception of rationality which would correspond to a 'postmodern' conception of democratic pluralism *and* universalism. The essay on 'Art and Industrial Production' explores the dialectics of modernism and postmodernism in the narrower field of architecture and industrial design. Finally, in the last essay, 'Ethics and Dialogue', I try to delineate the contours of a post-foundationalist dialogic ethics which would transcend the false opposition between universalism and contextualism. This essay was inspired by, but has turned into a critique of, Habermas's discourse ethics as well as of the so-called consensus theory of truth.

In spite of the common thread running through the four essays in this volume, they are in another sense, i.e. as to their topics and the occasions of their writing, quite heterogeneous. In particular, there is a dividing line between the first three essays, all of which deal broadly with various problems in modern/postmodern art and aesthetics, and the fourth essay, which is an essay in moral philosophy. Perhaps instead of speaking of a common thread connecting the four essays with each other I should rather speak of an overlapping of themes and motifs – particularly with respect to the first three essays – and a similarity of perspective which links all the essays together. It is this common perspective which I have tried to articulate in the first part of this Introduction.

1

Truth, Semblance, Reconciliation:*

Adorno's Aesthetic Redemption of Modernity

It is Theodor W. Adorno above all others who has explored the ambiguities of modern culture, ambiguities which reveal not only possibilities for unleashing aesthetic and communicative potential, but also the possible death of culture itself. Not since Schopenhauer and Nietzsche (with whose aesthetics and epistemology, incidentally, Adorno's thought secretly communicates) has a philosophy of art had so lasting an impact on artists, critics and intellectuals as that of Adorno, at least as far as Germany is concerned. The traces of his influence on the consciousness of those concerned with modern art, whether in a productive, a critical or merely a receptive capacity, cannot be overlooked. This is true above all of music criticism where, as Carl Dahlhaus says, it was really only Adorno who 'defined the very level on which

---

*Translator's note: The word 'semblance' has been used consistently to translate the German 'Schein' in the sense it denotes in the context of Adorno's aesthetics. 'Semblance' is used frequently in the English translation of Negative Dialectics, though not in that of Aesthetic Theory.

The page references incorporated in the text relate in each instance first to the standard German edition, and second to the available English translation, as follows: DoE = Max Horkheimer and Theodor W. Adorno, Dialektik der Aufklärung, Amsterdam 1955; Dialectic of Enlightenment, translated by John Cumming, London 1973. AT = Theodor W. Adorno, Ästhetische Theorie (Gesammelte Schriften, vol. 7), Frankfurt 1970; Aesthetic Theory, translated by C. Lenhardt, London 1984. ND = Theodor W. Adorno, Negative Dialektik (Gesammelte Schriften, vol. 6), Frankfurt 1973; Negative Dialectics, translated by E. B. Ashton, New York 1973. PhdNM = Theodor W. Adorno, Philosophie der neuen Musik (Gesammelte Schriften, vol. 12), Frankfurt 1975 (no English translation).

it is possible to talk about modern music at all'.[1] In recent music
criticism, Adorno's authority can be felt even where music has
gone beyond the boundaries that Adorno had drawn for it; I am
thinking here of H.K. Metzger's defence of the 'anti-authoritarian'
music of John Cage, for example.[2] On the other hand, while
Adorno's mode of thought, indeed the entire cast of his intellectual response to art, has left its mark on the consciousness of
artists, writers and intellectuals, his *Aesthetic Theory* has fared
less well in the spheres of academic philosophy of art and literary
theory. After some ten years of critical response to Adorno's
aesthetics, it appears that only fragments and remnants of his
work in this area live on in philosophical, literary and musical
scholarship. It is not the esoteric nature of the *Aesthetic Theory*
that has hampered its reception. The problem lies rather in its
systematic aspects: Adorno's aesthetics of negativity has revealed
its rigid features; something artificial has become visible in his
aporetic constructions, and a latent traditionalism has become
apparent in his aesthetic judgements. As so often happens in
philosophy, the critics (or at least those who do not regard the
matter as over and done with) have divided the booty amongst
themselves; fragments of that complex interrelationship of negativity, semblance, truth and utopia, in terms of which Adorno
conceived artistic phenomena, are to be found for instance in
Jauss's reception theory, in Bürger's sociology of literature, or in
Bohrer's aesthetics of the 'abrupt' (*'Ästhetik der Plötzlichkeit'*). But
this is not simply the result of an eclectic appropriation of Adorno's ideas, as is apparent from the philosophical critique of
Adorno, particularly those critiques of the systematic aspect of
Adorno's aesthetics which have been undertaken by Bubner, and
by Baumeister and Kulenkampff.[3] It seems to me indisputable
that these criticisms of Adorno's work are at least partially correct.
They nevertheless leave a sense that the conclusions arrived at
are not commensurate with the object of their inquiries, as if the
actual substance of Adorno's aesthetics eluded them. This is the
danger inherent in any partial critique, i.e. one which does not
tackle the object in its entirety. It might be possible to avoid this
danger in the case of Adorno's aesthetics if one could release its
central categories from their dialectical stasis and set them in
motion from within the system itself, as it were. The necessary
precondition for achieving this is not the attenuation of criticisms
which have been made of Adorno, but the focusing of their

combined energies. This is the direction in which I shall try to proceed in this essay.

I

The *Dialectic of Englightenment* by Adorno and Horkheimer remains a fundamental text for understanding Adorno's aesthetics. It is there that the dialectic of subjectivization and reification is developed and the dialectic of aesthetic semblance at least intimated. The mutual interpenetration of these two sets of ideas is the dynamic principle at work in the *Aesthetic Theory*.

As far as the *Dialectic of Enlightenment* is concerned, the extraordinary character of the book is derived not simply from the concentrated literary quality of its prose with its lightning-flashes of illumination, but from the extraordinary audacity of the attempt to merge two disparate philosophical traditions, one which leads from Schopenhauer, via Nietzsche, to Klages,[4] and another which runs from Hegel, through Marx and Max Weber, to the young Lukács.[5] Lukács had already integrated Weber's theory of rationalization into the critique of political economy; the *Dialectic of Enlightenment* might be understood as an attempted Marxist appropriation of Klages' radical critique of civilization and reason. Thus the progressive stages of emancipation from nature and the corresponding phases of class domination (Marx) are both interpreted as stages in the dialectic of subjectivization and reification (Klages). For this purpose the epistemological triad of subject, object and concept has to be reinterpreted in terms of a process of repression and subjugation in which the repressor – the subject – also appears as the victim. The repression of inner nature with its anarchical lust for happiness is the price paid for the formation of a unified self, which was itself necessary for the sake of self-*preservation* and the control of external nature. The notion that concepts are 'ideational tools' in the service of a subject conceived essentially as a will to self-preservation, which uses them to control and subdue reality, is one which goes back not only to Klages, but to Nietzsche and even Schopenhauer. Formal logic, according to this view, is not an instrument of truth, but merely the mediating link between the unity of the subject – the 'ego principle that founds the system' (ND 36/26) – and the concept, that 'prearranges' and effectively 'truncates' reality (cf. ND 21/9). From the outset, the spirit that brings about conceptual objectivation and systematizes according to the principle of non-contradiction acquires the character of instrumental reason by virtue of its very origins in the 'splitting of life into the mind and its object' (DoE 279/234). This instrumental spirit, which is itself a part of the living world, is ultimately capable of articulating itself only in categories of a *dead* nature; as an objectifying principle, the instrumental spirit is in its very origins *oblivious* of itself, and being oblivious of itself, establishes itself as a universal system of delusion, a closed universe of instrumental reason.

As good Marxists (and Hegelians), however, Adorno and Hork-heimer cleave to the notion that civilization is a process of *enlightenment*; 'reconciliation', 'happiness' and 'emancipation' are for them only conceivable as the *result* of this process (cf. DoE 80/63). A return to Klages' archaic world of images is thus precluded as a merely illusory path to reconciliation. Reconciliation is conceivable only in terms of sublating the 'disunion' of self and nature, something which can only be achieved through the historical self-constitution of the human species by means of labour, sacrifice and renunciation (cf. DoE 71/55). It follows from this that the process of enlightenment would only be able to transcend and perfect itself within its own medium, that of the spirit controlling nature. The process of enlightening enlightenment about itself (the 'mindfulness [*Eingedenken*] of nature in the subject') is only possible within the medium of conceptual thought, the necessary condition being that the concept itself is turned against the reifying tendency of conceptual thought, as Adorno will go on to postulate in *Negative Dialectics* when he speaks of philosophy striving, 'by means of the concept, to transcend the concept' (ND 27/15).

In his *Negative Dialectics*, Adorno attempts to characterize this self-transcendence of the concept as a process by which conceptual thought acquires a 'mimetic' quality. Rationality must combine with a mimetic principle in order to be released from its own irrationality. Mimesis is the name given to those forms of behaviour which are sensually receptive, expressive and communicative. It is in art that mimetic forms of behaviour have been preserved as spiritual ones in the course of the development of civilization. Art is a form of mimesis that has become spiritualized; that is, it has become transformed and objectified by rationality. Art *and* philosophy thus constitute the two realms of activity in which the spirit breaks through the crust of reification by means of the close interaction of rationality with mimesis. Of course, this interaction takes a contrasting form in either case: in art it is the mimetic principle which assumes the appearance of the spirit, while in philosophy the rational spirit becomes muted to a mimetic and conciliatory force. The 'reconciling' spirit is the common medium of both art and philosophy; but it also constitutes the common meeting point of their endeavours, the common element in their relationship to truth, their utopian goal. Just as the concept of the instrumental spirit denotes not only a cognitive relationship, but also a structural principle in the relations between human beings, and between humanity and the natural world, in the same way the concept of the reconciling spirit stands not only for the 'non-violent synthesis of the disparate' both in the beauty of art and in philosophical thought, but at the same time it stands for a non-violent unity of the diverse in the reconciliation of relations between all living things. This reconciliation of all living things is prefigured in the cognitive modes of art and philosophy, where a non-violent resolution is achieved between intuition and concept, between the particular and the universal, between the part and the whole. And *only this manifestation of the spirit*, which in its own form prefigures a state of reconciliation, is capable of true cognition (*Erkenntnis*); it is in this sense that we should understand the line from the *Minima Moralia* that 'cognition has no light to see but that which shines down onto the world from redemption'.[6]

Viewed in terms of an utopian ideal, then, art and philosophy both have an antithetical relationship to the world of the instrumental spirit; that is the origin of their inherent negativity. But whereas art and philosophy, each in its own way, seek that non-violent resolution of the hiatus between intuition and concept, they remain nonetheless separate fragments of a non-reifying spirit. Their relationship to each other parallels once more the disparity between intuition and concept – and this relationship is incapable of resolution into an articulated unity of cognition. The presence of a reconciling spirit in an unreconciled world is something that can only be conceived in terms of an aporia.

And the aporia is this: discursive and non-discursive cognition both aim at the entirety of knowledge; but precisely this division of knowledge into discursive and non-discursive modes means that each can achieve only a partial apprehension of the truth, as refracted through its own medium of presentation. The two modes complement each other, and the fusion of them into a total, untrammelled perception of the truth would be possible only if the division between them were eliminated, i.e. if reality were 'reconciled'. In art, truth becomes manifest in the sensual domain; that is where art has the advantage over discursive knowledge. But it is precisely *because* it is sensually presented in art that truth is inaccessible through aesthetic experience: because the work of art is incapable of formulating the truth that it is presenting, aesthetic experience cannot truly know what it is experiencing. The truth that displays itself in that momentary flash of aesthetic experience is concrete and immediate; as we try to grasp it, it fades away. It was in order to clarify this aspect of the aesthetic manifestation of truth as something immediately 'evident' but at the same time ineffable, that Adorno compared works of art with riddles and pictures puzzles. The work of art resembles a picture puzzle in that 'what it conceals appears, like the letter in Poe's story, but through its very appearing, hides itself' (cf. AT 185/178).* If we try to grasp the ineffable by seeking to penetrate its aesthetic appearance it eludes us like the end of the proverbial rainbow (AT 185/178). But if the truth content of works of art were entirely enclosed in the moment of aesthetic experience, then it would be lost to us forever and aesthetic experience itself would be in vain. It is because of this that works of art are dependent on 'interpretive reason', on the 'production of their truth content' through interpretation (AT 193/186) – for the sake of that something in them which points beyond the fleeting moment of aesthetic experience. For Adorno, interpretation means *philosophical* interpretation; when he speaks of the 'need' that art has for interpretation (AT 193/186), he means that aesthetic experience has a need for philosophical illumination. 'Genuine aesthetic experience must become philosophy or it fails to exist at all.' (AT 197/190) On the other hand, philosophy, whose utopia it is 'to unseal the non-conceptual' by means of concepts, but without reducing it to conceptual categories (ND 21/10), remains tied to conceptual language (what Adorno calls *'die meinende Sprache'*[7]) in which the immediacy of the aesthetic

---

Translator's note: The quotation here is an exact rendering of Adorno's original German (*Gesammelte Schriften,* vol. 7, Frankfurt 1970, p. 185).

presentation of truth cannot be reconstituted. Just as a moment of blindness adheres to the immediacy of aesthetic perception, so does a moment of emptiness adhere to the 'mediacy' of philosophical thought. Only in combination are they capable of circumscribing a truth which neither alone is able to articulate. 'Truth lies unveiled for discursive knowledge, but for all that, it does not possess it; the knowledge that is art has it (truth), but as something incommensurable to it.' (AT 191/183) In his 'Fragment on Music and Language', Adorno describes this mutual insufficiency of aesthetic and discursive knowledge like this: 'Discursive language wishes to express the absolute in a mediated way, but the absolute eludes its grasp at every turn, leaving each attempt behind in its finiteness. Music expresses the absolute directly, but the very moment it does so, the absolute is obscured, just as excessively strong light dazzles the eye so that it can no longer register what is clearly visible.'[8] The language of music and discursive language appear as the separated halves of 'true language', a language in which 'the content itself would become manifest', as we read in the same fragment.[9] The idea of this 'true language' is 'the figure of the divine name'.[10] In the aporetic relationship between art and philosophy, a theological perspective is sublated: art and philosophy combine to form the two halves of a negative theology.

II

The antithetical relationship between artistic beauty on the one hand and the world of the instrumental spirit (i.e. empirical reality) on the other arose from a utopian concept of art. This is also the basis for Adorno's inversion of the theory of imitation, according to which art does not imitate reality, but at most that aspect of the real world which itself points beyond reality, namely natural beauty (cf. AT 113/108). Adorno sees in natural beauty a cipher of nature as it does not yet exist, of nature in a state of reconciliation, which has thus developed beyond the splitting of life into the mind and its object, reconciling and 'sublating' this splitting within itself; a nature which would be the non-violent 'togetherness' of the diverse, with the particularity of each individual entity remaining unharmed. The work of art, as an imitation of natural beauty, thus becomes the image of a nature which has found its speech, a nature redeemed and liberated from its muteness, just as it becomes the image of a reconciled humanity. This extension of the utopia of reconciliation to nature as a whole is accounted for by the radical character of the antithesis between the instrumental spirit and the spirit that pursues aesthetic reconciliation: both the instrumental and the reconciling spirit signify an order of living nature as a whole.

The interrelationship between truth, semblance and reconciliation, which is fundamental to Adorno's aesthetics, similarly aims to connect the negativity and the utopian purport of artistic beauty. But just as the interrelationship betweeen art and philosophy turned out to be aporetic, so the interrelationship between truth,semblance and reconciliation in artistic beauty turns out to be antinomial; this is the dialectic of aesthetic semblance.

This dialectic of aesthetic semblance is already hinted at in the *Dialectic of Enlightenment*, where the splitting off of artistic beauty from the praxis of life appears in a dual perspective. On the one hand we have the *relegation* of beauty to the status of mere semblance, demonstrated with reference to the Sirens episode; on the other hand we have the *release* of beauty from functional connections of a magical nature, allowing it to be *liberated* as an organum of cognition. The truth and untruth of beauty are interwoven. In order to understand more precisely the dialectic of semblance as Adorno expounds it above all in his *Aesthetic Theory*, we first have to give precise definition to his concept of the 'truth' of art. The point at issue here might be expressed like this: what is made manifest in art is not the 'light of redemption' itself, but *reality* in the light of redemption. The truth of works of art is concrete, the truth of art is a plural phenomenon bound to the concrete manifestation of individual works. Or rather, it is a single truth which, however, can only become manifest as a *particular* truth; each work of art is a unique mirror of reality, like a Leibnizian monad. The truth content of works of art, as a *specific* one, resides in the non-falsification of reality, in the fact that reality as it is is made manifest in the work of art. If we wished to separate analytically the elements which are dialectically connected in Adorno's thinking, then we might distinguish truth$_1$, as aesthetic rightness or validity (*Stimmigkeit*), from truth$_2$, as representational truth. The unity of these two moments would then mean that it is only by virtue of aesthetic synthesis (truth$_1$) that art can represent cognition of reality (truth$_2$), and conversely that aesthetic synthesis (truth$_1$) can only succeed if it helps to make reality (truth$_2$) manifest. Now, since art is the sphere of seeming reconciliation, it is by definition the Other, the negation of an unreconciled reality. Art can thus only be true in the sense of being faithful to reality to the extent that it shows reality *as* unreconciled, antagonistic, divided against itself. But it can only do this by showing reality in the light of reconciliation, i.e. by the non-violent aesthetic synthesis of disparate elements which produces the semblance of reconciliation. This means, however, that an antinomy is carried into the very *heart* of the aesthetic synthesis – which can by definition only succeed by turning against itself and questioning its own underlying principle, for the sake of the truth which nevertheless cannot be extracted except with recourse to this very principle.

> Art is true to the extent to which it is discordant and antagonistic in its language and in its whole essence, provided that it synthesizes those diremptions, thus making them determinate in their irreconcilability. Its paradoxical task is to attest to the lack of concord while at the same time working to abolish discordance. (AT 251/241)

This antimonial structure of art is present from the very outset in the historical separation of image from sign, of non-conceptual from conceptual synthesis, even if the conscious awareness of it only becomes apparent in the art of the modern world, i.e. under conditions of fully developed instrumental rationality. It is inherent within the idea of art that it must turn against its own principle and become a rebellion against aesthetic semblance.

I have said that the mutual interpenetration of both dialectics – the dialectic of subjectivization and reification and the dialectic of aesthetic semblance – is the dynamic principle of Adorno's aesthetics. It could be shown in detail how the antinomies and aporias of modern art – the ambivalence of the construction principle, the aporias of open form, and the antinomy of the nominalistic principle – result from the interweaving of these two dialectic systems as Adorno depicts them. Let us simply remind ourselves that for Adorno, the dialectic of subjectivization and reification is itself inscribed within the concept of subjectivization as a dialectical constellation. On the one hand, the concept signifies a strengthening of the subject both in relation to the compulsions of external and internal nature, and towards the power of objectively binding meaning, and thus towards the institutions, norms and conventions of society as they have acquired validity through a quasi-natural process of historical development. And on the other hand, the same concept signifies the price that has to be paid for these successful advances towards emancipation, namely the growth of 'subjective', which is to say instrumental rationality, and progressive reification leading to self-destruction. Now, Adorno tries to show that the emancipation of aesthetic subjectivity, in which a release of art into an aesthetic 'state of freedom' appeared to announce itself, is also overtaken by this dialectic. As he represents the situation, reification enters the pores of modern art, so to speak, from all directions. It enters from society, whose technical rationality leaves its mark on the constructive procedures of art (Adorno's standard example of this is the degeneration of the twelve-tone principle into a compositional *procedure*); it enters from the weakened subjects, which show themselves to be inadequate to the potential for freedom which art embodies; and finally it enters from the aesthetic material itself which, through its own development, causes the individualization of language to become transformed into a disintegration of language. But these tendencies towards aesthetic disintegration, which penetrate art from without and from 'beneath', as it were, are only brought to a head by the force from within which compels art towards the destruction of aesthetic meaning. For the sake of its truth, art must turn against the principle of aesthetic synthesis. 'Negation of synthesis became a principle of artistic figuration.' (AT 232/222) What this paradoxical formulation is saying is that art can only survive and remain authentic if it succeeds in articulating the negation of synthesis as its aesthetic meaning, and in bringing about aesthetic synthesis in the very process of negating it. The modern work of art must, in a single pass, both produce and negate aesthetic meaning; it must articulate meaning as the negation of meaning, balancing, so to speak, on the razor's edge between affirmative semblance and an anti-art that is bereft of semblance.

What Adorno says, at the end of the Schönberg chapter of his *Philosophie der neuen Musik*, about the most advanced modern music implicitly refers to the authentic art of modernism as a whole: 'It has taken upon itself all the darkness and guilt of the world. All its delight is derived from the recognition of misery;

all its beauty from the renunciation of the semblance of beauty.' (PhdNM 126) But the antinomy of modern art is expressed in the fact that there is no concept available with which to describe the success of the balancing act we are talking about here; in the strict sense, such success is not conceivable. For where art succeeds in articulating the negation of meaning in an aesthetically meaning-ful way – for Adorno, the most important examples of such success in the field of literature are the works of Beckett – it transpires that art which is capable of surviving as art, i.e. art which has taken upon itself the darkness and guilt of the world, cannot escape the antinomy; the token by which it remains art is also the mark of its untruth; its aesthetic success, which is to say its truth and authenticity, is inseparable from a remnant of aesthetic semblance, and thus of untruth:

> Art is illusion [semblance] in that it cannot escape the hypnotic suggestion of meaning amid a general loss of meaning. (AT 231/222)

For the sake of the hope of reconciliation, however, art must take this guilt, too, upon itself: this is what the 'defence of semblance' means as Adorno understands it.

III

Walter Benjamin had argued in his 'Theses on the Philosophy of History' that the 'puppet of "historical materialism"' needed to enlist the services of theology.[11] Adorno's philosophy could be understood as the attempt to fulfil this postulated need. There is, however, a fissure between messianic–utopian and materialistic motifs in Adorno's thought, which cannot be overlooked; more-over, the same fissure is repeated within the elements of material-istic theory, running between historical materialism and utopian sensualism. Adorno's aesthetics thus come closer in some respects to an eschatological and sensualistic modulation of Scho-penhauer than to a theologically enlightened Marxism. The light of redemption which, according to Adorno, should be cast upon reality through the medium of art, is not only not of this world; it issues, in Schopenhauerian terms, from a world that lies beyond space, time, causality and individuation. But at the same time

Adorno cleaves to a sensualist concept of happiness as the epitome of sensual fulfilment. The theological motif interacts with
the sensualist one to produce a utopian perspective in which the
hope of redemption is nourished by the yearning for a lost
paradise. In a certain sense we might say that Adorno has
invested the entirety of his powerful intellectual energy in the
effort to dignify this dream of reconciliation, if not as a philosophical concept, then at least as a philosophical idea in which
all truth is encompassed. Only in this context could aesthetic
synthesis become for Adorno a preview of a reconciled relationship among people, things and natural beings.

The eschatological–sensualist utopia puts such an immeasur-
able gap between historical reality and the condition of reconciliation that the task of bridging it can no longer constitute a
meaningful goal of human praxis. As Adorno says, the gap grows
into a 'chasm between praxis and happiness' (AT 26/17f). There
can be no concepts in which we might *conceive* the condition of
reconciliation; the idea of such a condition appears, as it were,
only *ex negativo* on the horizon of art and philosophy – as
something which can most readily be grasped when, seized by
the tremors of aesthetic experience, the ego looks 'beyond the
walls of the prison that it is' (AT 364/347). Thus Adorno, like
Schopenhauer, conceives aesthetic experience in ecstatic terms
rather than as a real utopia; the happiness that it promises is not
of this world.

On the other hand, the immeasurability of the gap between
reality and utopia means that reality becomes fixed transcen-
dentally, so to speak, prior to all experience, in negative terms.
If truth can only be accorded to us if we see the world 'as it shall
be revealed, distorted and deprived, in the messianic light',[12]
then the murderous character of world history is ensured even
before the experience of it can lead us to despair. The fact that
the necessity of such despair is built into the fundamental categories of Adorno's philosophy explains, if anything does, the
peculiar way in which the question of truth in Adorno's interpretations of modern art is decided in advance.

It cannot be overlooked, of course, that elements of genuinely
materialistic theory lead a powerful independent existence within
the utopian–messianic perspective of Adorno's philosophy. An
external reference to social praxis survives within these elements,
in the light of which the theological perspective might once
again be reinterpreted: only then would the puppet of 'historical

materialism' have put theology to work. What this would require would be a form of critique which set the system of Adorno's categories as a whole in motion and thus made it possible to decode his aesthetics in materialistic terms.

Jürgen Habermas has laid the foundations for such a critique of Adorno in his *Theory of Communicative Action*, taking the break between materialistic and messianic motifs as his starting-point.[13] Habermas's basic argument is as simple as it is persuasive: the attributes of a spirit that is bound to language include the intersubjectivity of mutual understanding as well as the objectivization of reality in the context of instrumental action, the symmetrical communicative relationship between subject and subject as well as the asymmetrical distancing relationship between subject and object. But the paradigm of a philosophy of consciousness which is obliged to take an asymmetrical subject–object model of cognition and action as the basis for explaining the function of language in achieving knowledge of the world, leaves no room for the communicative moment of the spirit, which becomes exiled, so to speak, from the realm of conceptual thought. This is what happens in Adorno; his name for the realm of communicative behaviour that exists outside the territory of conceptual thought is *mimesis*. Reflexion on the foundations of the instrumental spirit in terms of a philosophy of language, by contrast, requires us to acknowledge a 'mimetic' moment within conceptual thought itself, for a mimetic moment is sublated in everyday speech, just as it is in art and philosophy. This is something which must remain concealed from a philosophy which understands the function of the concept in terms of the polarity between subject and object; it is incapable of recognizing communicative performance behind the objectivizing functions of language as a precondition of the possibility of those functions. That is why it can only conceive mimesis as the Other of rationality, and the coming-together of mimesis and rationality only as a negation of historical reality. In order to recognize the *prior* unity of the mimetic and the rational moment in the foundations of language, we need to change the philosophical paradigm:

> The rational core of mimetic achievements can be laid open only if we give up the paradigm of the philosophy of consciousness – namely a subject that represents objects and toils with them – in favor of the paradigm of linguistic philosophy – namely that of

intersubjective understanding or communication – and put the cognitive–instrumental aspect of reason in its proper place as part of a more encompassing *communicative rationality*.[14]

But if the intersubjectivity of understanding – communicative action – is constitutive of the realm of the spirit in the same measure as is the objectivation of reality in the context of instrumental action, then the utopian perspective which Adorno tries to explain by means of the philosphical concept of a 'non-violent' synthesis migrates, so to speak, into the realm of discursive reason itself. If we think of unimpaired intersubjectivity as a condition which permits a multiplicity of subjects to come together without coercion, making it possible for individuals to exist at one and the same time in proximity and distance, in identity and diversity, then this represents a utopian projection, constructed by discursive reason out of elements which are rooted in the nature of language. This utopian projection is not the Other of discursive reason, but the idea which discursive reason has of itself. Since this utopia is rooted in the conditions of language, the utopia in question is of this world, and in this sense a 'materialistic' one.

The consequence of acknowledging a communicative moment in conceptual thought is that the dialectical connection constructed by Adorno and Horkheimer between subjectivization and reification is dissolved *as* a dialectical one. Habermas demonstrates this point in *The Theory of Communicative Action*. The main point of his argument could be clarified by comparing two statements by Adorno. In his *Aesthetic Theory*, Adorno speaks at one point of the epistemological insight that 'the input of subjectivity and that of reification complement each other' (AT 252/242). This formulation is highly ambiguous; it would be possible to reconcile it with Habermas's thesis that 'communicative rationalization' on the one hand, and 'system rationalization' and scientific or technical progress on the other stand in a 'complementary' relationship in the modern world. This thesis is concerned with the differentiation of two types of rationalization and their *possibilities* of influencing each other's structure in the modern world. It leaves open the question of the way in which the structures of communicative and instrumental–functionalistic rationality, which are certainly conceived as *conceptually* complementary, will interpenetrate each other within the over-arching structure of the living context of society at large. This question is an empirical and historical one; Habermas's own explanation of the threat to the structures of communicative rationality and of the hypertrophy of systemic rationality in the modern world is ultimately a Marxist one. In Adorno, by contrast, the two levels of analysis tend to coincide, as is shown by the second statement, also from his *Aesthetic Theory*, namely that subjectivity works towards its own 'extermination . . . by virtue of its own logic' (AT 235/225). Since the communicative input of the subject becomes invisible in the subject–object model, the only complement to the increasingly powerful subject that remains visible is, by virtue of *conceptual* logic, the tendency to reification. This is why in Adorno (and Horkheimer) the *complementarity* of subjectivization and reification has to become a *dialectic* of subjectivization and reification. But even if Habermas on the one hand and Adorno and Horkheimer on the other did not draw such very different consequences when it came to interpreting the times in which they are living, the crucial point remains this: that the conceptual differentiations with which we are concerned here enable history *itself* to retrieve a degree of freedom which it had lost through the choice of fundamental categories exercised by Adorno and Horkheimer, and without which the idea of a potential for freedom *immanent in* history becomes null and void. The direct consequence of this for aesthetics is that the transition from the 'negation of objectively binding meaning' to the 'meaninglessness' of late capitalist reality can no longer be derived dialectically from the impossibility of 'meaning posited by the subject' (AT 235/224), a mode of derivation which is, however, central to Adorno's construction of the antinomy of modern art. The related question of the aesthetic meaning of 'open forms' in modern art is one to which I shall return.

IV

The first question we have to answer is how the categories of truth, semblance and reconciliation can be set in motion if they are no longer bound up with the thesis of a dialectical relationship between subjectivation and reification. As I have shown, the sense of these categories in Adorno is inseparable both from the idea that art exists *a priori* in a polemical relationship to reality, and also from the perspective of a 'redeemed' world of nature. If we abandon either one of these assumptions, then the connection which Adorno constructs between truth, semblance and the utopian purport of a work of art can no longer hold. This point can be clarified with reference to three examples drawn from critiques of Adorno, each of which highlights a different aspect of the problem.

1   H. R. Jauss cites the *communicative* functions of art in evidence against Adorno.[15] There is a good reason why Adorno does not refer to these, namely that it is only possible to pose questions about reception and communication in connection with art if we first question the unequivocal interrelationship that Adorno constructs between reality, utopia and the work of art. But where this interrelationship is presupposed, problems of reception and communication are reduced to the problem of adequately apprehending this interrelationship itself, and all that matters there is genuinely experiencing works of art and deciphering them philosophically. When we start to speak of communicative functions in art, the constellation reality/art/utopia is effectively replaced by the constellation reality/art/receiving subject, which can no longer be conceived as a linear relationship, but only as a circular one in which art is accorded a function in living praxis; art is conceived as something which *actively affects* reality.

2   P. Bürger criticizes Adorno's way of linking the categories of truth, semblance and reconciliation from another angle.[16] Bürger interprets Adorno's defence of aesthetic semblance as a paradigm of reconciliation as an attack on the attempts of the avant-garde to mobilize the relationship between art and living praxis.[17] And indeed, Adorno's 'defence of semblance' is directed against tendencies towards a false sublation of art which, in his view, accompany the development of avant-garde art in the twentieth century like a shadow. However, Bürger is no more inclined to take Adorno's linking of the categories of truth, semblance and reconciliation seriously than Jauss is, otherwise he would have been bound to notice that Adorno's reservations about a *false* sublation of art were grounded in his idea of the *true* sublation of art as the realization of its promise of happiness. The truth of the matter is that the notion of a historically changing constellation between art and living praxis, which Bürger perceives as the true productive core of avant-garde aspirations to sublate art,

is in practice scarcely compatible with Adorno's 'reconciliation paradigm' of art. That is why Bürger replaces the constellation of reality, art and reconciliation with a constellation of reality, art and living praxis – but he creates new problems as he does so by privileging the significance of this constellation for artistic production over its significance for reception. This becomes apparent, not least in the fact that Bürger wishes to eliminate the category of aesthetic semblance entirely, and replace it with that of 'rupture' (Bruch).[18] The only part of the edifice of Adorno's aesthetics that he tries to defend – given that as a whole it is now indefensible – is its foundations, i.e. the claim of art to express truth. From the point of view of a philosophical aesthetic, however, the attempt to occupy these foundations appears peculiarly pointless if access upwards to the utopian splendour of aesthetic semblance is blocked.

3   In contrast to Bürger, who wants to downplay the category of aesthetic semblance in favour of that of truth, K. H. Bohrer has made the attempt, following Nietzsche, to defend the category of aesthetic semblance by severing its connection with the concept of truth entirely.[19] His aim is, so to speak, an emancipation of aesthetic semblance in the sense that it comes to absorb into itself the other pole of Adorno's central constellation truth/semblance/utopia, with the utopia coming to be located within the instant of aesthetic experience, and the utopian dimension of that experience losing its reference to any real future. Bohrer, we might say, pursues an aestheticist resolution of an inherent ambiguity in Adorno which results from the tension between Schopenhauerian and Marxist aesthetics: the promise of happiness that art offers is redeemed in the ecstatic moment of aesthetic experience. Bohrer does admittedly retain the idea of a subversive function of aesthetic experience. For this reason it would be possible to understand what he says about the 'allegorical' role of 'messianic–eschatological metaphors' in the writings of Benjamin and Musil as also constituting a demystification of Adorno: 'They invoke, out of a sense of awe, the inexhaustible allegorical force that a cultural or religious mental image from the past possesses for a "now" which cannot logically and psychologically exist as something totally present, but which nevertheless has to be dramatized as such a presence if we do not wish to succumb to the compulsion of cultural norms and written history, or of outmoded ideas.'[20] Of the three authors cited here, Bohrer is the

only one who resolutely holds on to the utopian valency of aesthetic semblance. But in doing so, he emphatically rejects all attempts to 'expand the boundaries' of art, whether these be 'political and moral', 'surrealistic and destructive', or 'utopian and sentimental' in nature.[21] That is why he negates not only the claim of art to express truth, but with it also the real future sense of its utopian element. Without really having Adorno in mind, Bohrer is defending the strategically important middle storey of the structure of Adorno's aesthetics, but he has abandoned the access routes to the upper and lower storeys as untenable.

In the case of all three of these authors, the interrelationship between the aesthetic categories of truth, semblance and reconciliation has been dissolved. This is indeed unavoidable if one abandons the polemical utopian perspective of Adorno's aesthetics or no longer takes it literally; and this is the point on which all three authors agree. Each of them is defending only fragments of Adorno's aesthetics: Jauss and Bohrer defend the subversive character of aesthetic experience as the 'negation of objectively binding meaning'; Bohrer the utopian lustre of aesthetic semblance;. and Bürger the claim of art to express truth. Now, I think that it would be perfectly possible to reunite these fragments of Adorno's aesthetics into a whole, but in doing so, one would have to convert the linear, one-dimensional relationship between the categories of truth, semblance and reconciliation into a complex and, as it were, multi-dimensional constellation of categories. If we could achieve this, then we should have set Adorno's dialectically frozen categories in motion from within. I shall try to indicate what this would look like, although the outcome of the experiment can as yet only be surmised.

V

I shall begin with Bohrer's reduction of the utopian purport of art to the instant of aesthetic experience. I see this as a legitimate way of clarifying a thought that remains ambiguous in Adorno to the extent that he interprets the ecstatic moment of aesthetic experience as also constituting a real utopian moment. But the idea that aesthetic synthesis points to a possible form of social 'synthesis', which is part of Adorno's meaning, does not simply become redundant when the connection between semblance and utopia is demystified. It is possible, rather, to reconstruct it in a new sense if we abandon the thesis of a dialectical connection between subjectivization and reification, and with it the polemical utopian burden placed on the concept of aesthetic synthesis.

For Adorno, the 'negation of objectively binding meaning' had represented the epitome of the emancipatory potential of modern art. What he meant was the questioning of traditional norms, conventions, syntheses of meaning, and forms of life, in which enlightenment discovered something unreflected, illegitimate and violent. In retrospect, the formal categories and aesthetic norms of tradition which provided unity and meaning also turn out to be unreflected and violent syntheses of meaning. And this is true not only of *specific* formal categories and aesthetic norms; it is rather a *type* of unity and meaningful whole that becomes questionable, a type which was represented in the era of great bourgeois art by the unity of the closed work of art as well as by the unity of the individual ego. Aesthetic enlightenment discovers something violent, unreflected and inauthentic in the unity of the traditional work, as in the unity of the bourgeois subject, namely a type of unity which is only possible at the price of suppressing and excluding that which is disparate or cannot be integrated, that which remains unarticulated or repressed. It is the inauthentic unity of a fictitious totality of meaning, one which has remained analogous to a divinely created cosmos. According to Adorno, the open forms of modern art are a response of emancipated aesthetic consciousness to the inauthentic and violent aspect of such traditional totalities of meaning. It is the moments of *inauthenticity* and *violence* in traditional syntheses of meaning that Adorno has in mind when he characterizes modern art on the one hand as an 'action against the work of art as a constellation of meaning', and on the other hand claims for modern art a principle of individuation and of an 'increasing elaboration-in-detail'. The relation between these two claims can be thought of as follows: as modern art incorporates those aspects of reality that are senseless, alien to the subject, and not integrated into his universe of meaning, so a higher degree of flexible and individual organization of the work becomes necessary. The 'opening-up' or 'expansion of the boundaries' of the work of art is conceived as a correlative development to the increasing capacity for the aesthetic *integration* of all that is diffuse or has been split off. Adorno himself saw a strengthening of aesthetic subjectivity as a precondition for such an open-ing-up of art towards the 'refuse of the world of appearance'. To this extent, Adorno himself set the open forms of modern art in relation to a form of subjectivity which no longer corresponds to the rigid unity of the bourgeois subject, but which displays the more flexible organizational form of a 'communicatively fluid' ego-identity. What prevented Adorno from taking this thought one step further was that he did not concede to modern society what he had conceded to modern art, namely that enlightenment has liberated possibilities of 'extending the limits of the subject' (G. Schwab) as well as unleashing possibilities of reification, so that the fate of enlightenment in this context, too, is as yet undecided.

But if this point is taken, the way is open to making a connec-tion – not only in historical, but also in *functional* terms – between the reflexively opened forms of modern art and the 'expanded boundaries' of the *receiving* subject. It is in this spirit that G. Schwab has recently undertaken a major study which focuses on Virginia Woolf, James Joyce, Samuel Beckett and Thomas Pynchon.[22] Schwab's idea is that the reflexive opening-up of literary forms of representation triggers a playful to and fro between identification and differentiation on the part of the reader, which effectively works towards a genuine expansion of subjective boundaries. In this sense one might also say that new forms of aesthetic synthesis in modern art point towards new forms of psychic and social 'synthesis'. This is the *emancipatory* potential of modernism: a new type of 'synthesis' comes into view – in an aesthetic, moral–psychological, and social sense – in which that which is diffuse and unintegrated, that which is 'meaningless' and split off could be gathered together in an arena for non-violent communication which would encompass the opened forms of art as well as the open structures of a no longer rigid type of individuation and socialization. But of course we can only talk in these terms if we no longer treat the notion of the art form 'in itself' as primary and as the scheme for reconcil-ation. Only as a medium of communicative mediation, as a medium that is both produced and received, can the work of art come to correspond formally to the changing forms of individu-ation and socialization.

I am now able to clarify why Adorno gives a one-sided interpretation of the 'negavity' he ascribes to the 'shattered unity' of the modern work of art. What Adorno saw in great works of art, in theory as well as in his interpretations of modern art (such as his brilliant interpretation of Beckett's *Endgame*), was a faithful reflection of the disintegration of meaning and the subject in reality; to this extent his views are not dissimilar from those of his opponent, Lukács. But the 'path of progressive negativity' that art follows also encompasses that other moment expressed in the 'negation of objectively binding meaning', namely the growing capacity for aesthetically *processing* those aspects of reality which, by virtue of their aesthetic articulation, are *no longer* merely negated, i.e. excluded from the realm of symbolical communication. But if this point is conceded, then the 'action against the work of art as a constellation of meaning' can no longer straightforwardly be attributed to the disintegration of meaning in capitalist reality, an objection which could be made against Lukács no less than Adorno. Clearly we would have to distinguish between an increase in the disintegration of meaning and of the subject in reality (to be conceived as taking place in the horizontal plane of historical time) on the one hand, and an aesthetic appropriation of experiences remote from the subject and 'meaning' (taking place in the vertical plane of psychic organization) on the other. It seems to me unquestionable that modern art has to do with both these processes; but the fact that Adorno neglected the second of them does not mean that he was blind to it (as his interpretations of Schönberg's Expressionist phase show), it is rather a consequence of his philosophical premises.

The connection between the expansion of the boundaries of the work of art on the one hand and of the subject on the other shows that what Adorno called 'aesthetic synthesis' can after all be ultimately linked up with a real utopia of non-violent communication. But this is true only if we acknowledge that art has a *function in connection with* forms of non-aesthetic communication or of a real change in ways of understanding ourselves and the world. In so far as the work of art relates to a real possibility of reconciliation, it is not the illusory presence of a condition that does not yet exist, but the provocative latency of a process which begins with 'the transposition of aesthetic experience into symbolic or communicative action' (Jauss).

If the work of art is no longer related to 'reconciliation' in a substantial sense, but in a functional one, then the relationship

between art and philosophy is also changed. Under these circumstances, aesthetic experience still needs to be illuminated by
interpretation and criticism, but it no longer stands in need of a
philosophical enlightenment which tells it what the 'semblance'
of beauty is really about. For works of art which point towards
an expansion of the boundaries of communication by virtue of
their *effect* and not their *being* do not fulfil their enlightening,
cognitive function at the level of philosophical *knowledge*, but on
that of the subjects' relationship to themselves and to the world,
where works of art intervene in a complex network of attitudes,
feelings, interpretations and evaluations. It is through this intervention that what we might call the cognitive character of art is
fulfilled. The fact that the cognition that is achieved through art
cannot be expressed in words is not attributable to the inad-
equacy of the concept, but to the fact that the enlightenment of
consciousness signified by the term 'cognition' here encompasses
cognitive, affective, and moral and practical aspects in equal
measure. To this extent, 'cognition' means an end result which
comes closer to being a capability rather than abstract knowledge,
something more like an *ability* to speak, to judge, to feel or
perceive than the result of cognitive effort.

  We can now try to decode Adorno's concept of the truth of art,
at least up to a certain point. Like Koppe, I proceed on the basis
that we can only speak of the truth of art if we already know
what is meant by truth independently of this specific context.[23]
I should like to take Habermas's pragmatic differentiation of the
everyday concept of truth as my starting point. In Koppe's terms,
what we are dealing with here is a distinction between 'apophantic' truth, 'endeetic' truth (truthfulness), and moral and practical
truth. These three concepts of truth represent the dimensions of
validity for everyday speech, and thus a preconception of 'truth'
which is available to every speaker. If we proceed on the basis
of an *everyday* concept of truth that is differentiated in this way,
then the concept of the truth of art seems at first to take on an
enigmatic character. It transpires, however, that art is *involved* in
questions of truth in a peculiar and complex way: not only does
art open up the experience of reality, and correct and expand it;
it is also the case that aesthetic 'validity' (i.e. the 'rightness' of a
work of art) *touches on* questions of truth, truthfulness, and moral
and practical correctness in an intricate fashion without being
attributable to any one of the three dimensions of truth, or even

to all three together. We might therefore suppose that the 'truth of art' can only be defended, if at all, as a phenomenon of interference between the various dimensions of truth.

Now in his way, Adorno also emphasized the moment of interference between various dimensions of truth in his discussion of the truth of art; this is apparent in his notion of an interconnection between the mimetic–expressive and the rational moments in the work of art, as well in his construction of the relationship between truth, semblance and reconciliation. The interpretation of the truth of art as a phenomenon of interference between various dimensions of truth thus represents in the first instance merely a reformulation in terms of linguistic pragmatics of one of Adorno's central ideas. The question of the consequences resulting from this reformulation is therefore of greater importance than the reformulation itself. Some of these consequences have already been adumbrated above, at the point where I drew a distinction between a 'functional' and a 'substantial' relation between the work of art and 'reconciliation' and emphasized the *practical* character of aesthetic cognition in this connection. If we apply this to our earlier analysis of Adorno's concept of the truth of art, then what we are doing is separating two aspects of this concept of the truth of art which Adorno integrates dialectically, namely 'truth$_1$' (aesthetic rightness) and 'truth$_2$' (objective truth). This is not intended to mean that aesthetic rightness (*Stimmigkeit*) has nothing to do with aesthetic truth, but rather that aesthetic rightness does not in itself *mean* reconciliation. The substantialization of the relation between the work of art and reconciliation means that, for Adorno, this relation becomes a central moment of the truth *content* of art. For this reason, Adorno is only able to conceive of the act of appropriating the truth of art in terms of a transformation of aesthetic experience into philosophical insight. For Adorno, the attempt to decipher the truth content that is encoded in the work of art is nothing other than the attempt to retrieve the truth of art, which would otherwise be lost, by putting it into words. *What* is retrieved by conceptual articulation in this way, however, is the polemical and utopian concept of art as such, the relation of art to reconciliation as something that can be known. It is a truth *about* art, and not the truth content of any individual work of art. For Adorno, the two planes of analysing the *concept* of art on the one hand and appropriating the specific, concrete truth of art on the other coincide; and it is only because this is so that he is bound to conceive of aesthetic cognition as philosophical insight, and of the truth of art as philosophical truth. In this way it is the apophantic dimension of the truth of art which ultimately comes to dominate the picture: Adorno's aesthetics becomes an apophantic aesthetic of truth.

The interpretation of the truth of art, in terms of a pragmatic philosophy of language, as a phenomenon of interference between the various dimensions of truth clearly carries a greater significance than a mere reformulation of Adorno's insights. For only now does it become possible to arrive at a conceptual distinction between the truth content of works of art and their relation to reconciliation. Between these two poles of the relation of art to truth, which are dialectically integrated in Adorno, the receiving subject enters the picture as a mediating instance. But in the process, the sense in which we speak of the truth content of works of art must itself also change. In view of what was said earlier it is reasonable to suppose that the truth of art will have more to do with a *potential* for truth in works of art than with truth in the literal sense. The truth content of works of art would then be the epitome of the potential effects of works of art that are *relevant* to the truth, or of their potential for *disclosing* truth. Such an interpretation of the truth of art as the epitome of *effects* relevant to the truth admittedly remains unsatisfactory as long as we are not in a position to say what it is about aesthetic products that makes them *bearers* of truth potential. In other words we would still have to explain the connection between aesthetic *validity* (*Stimmigkeit*) and the truth of art.

Since no philosopher from Kant to Adorno has been able to clarify entirely the complex relationship between beauty and truth, the prospects for reconstructing this central element of Adorno's aesthetics in terms of a pragmatic philosophy of language are admittedly not very bright. I think it is nevertheless possible to indicate a direction in which we might look for a solution to this problem.

I would formulate the problem like this. There is something about art which leads us to view works of art themselves – or at least many of them – as vehicles of truth-*claims*; and these claims to *truth* that are made by works of art are connected with their *aesthetic* claim to validity. In what follows I shall confine myself to the discussion of apophantic and endeetic truth, i.e. to the apophantic and endeetic 'truth-claims' of art.

Let us take as our starting-point the intuitive core of the apophantic concept of the truth of art, which might be characterized by means of such metaphors as the 'disclosing', 'revealing' or 'showing' of reality. The idea is that art 'discloses', 'reveals' or 'shows' reality in an outstanding fashion. Such metaphors are interesting because they are, in certain aesthetic contexts, as unavoidable as they are notoriously misleading. They are unavoidable because reality can only be shown, and not put into words. They are misleading because, in the case of art, *what shows itself can only be shown (in this way) in the medium of showing*, which is to say in the work of art itself as something sensually present; it cannot show itself as an aesthetically unmediated presence. Therefore what shows itself in the work of art can only be recognized as something showing itself on the basis of a familiarity with it which did not before have the character of perceptual evidence. It is as if a mirror had the capacity to show the 'true' face of human beings: we should only be able to know *that* it was their *true* face on the basis of a familiarity with them which only assumed the form of an unveiled sensual presence when the image of them appeared in the mirror. We can only recognize the 'essence' which appears in the apparition if we already *know* it as something which does not appear.

With the help of the metaphors of 'appearing' and 'being shown' we can clarify the connection between aesthetic validity and the capacity of the beautiful to disclose reality, even if we cannot clarify the connection between aesthetic validity and *truth*. In an aesthetic construct (in the traditional sort, at least) every detail is important; just as a minute alteration of the facial features would change the expression of a face, so too would the reality that is shown in an aesthetic construct be altered if the sensual configuration of that construct were changed. Alternatively we might say that an aesthetic construct is more or less appropriate, more or less faithful, more or less 'authentic' in making manifest what appears in it. It may not be a simple matter, of course, to decide whether reality has been made manifest in an adequate fashion. Or rather, if the intuitive judgements are controversial, then the corresponding (aesthetic) discussions might be endless.

Such aesthetic discussions are concerned with the correct understanding, the correct perception of the aesthetic phenomenon. They refer back to the aesthetic experience itself, both correcting and expanding it. The aesthetic sense of 'rightness' must, in the final analysis, be *perceived*; and in so far as the aesthetic rightness is connected with the showing of reality, the work of art must also be perceived *as* a reality being shown in the medium of showing, and reality must be *recognized* as showing itself. It must be recognized not in the sense that the truth of a statement, but in the sense that a face is recognized, only with this difference: when we 'recognize' reality in an aesthetic experience (and for Adorno the gesture of showing embodied in the work of art is represented by the expression 'that's how it is'), then what we have known diffusely, experienced vaguely and apprehended implicitly acquires the firm outlines of a sensual experience for the first time. What was always present in diffuse fashion, at a pre-conscious or sub-conscious level, comes together into the manifestation of an image, something which can be 'grasped' – or to use a semantically related term, which can be *'comprehended'*. To put it another way, the uncomprehended experience is illuminated by becoming condensed into an experience of a higher order: experience becomes experienceable.

So far I have been using a Platonic model, as it were, in which 'being acquainted with something' has an ontological precedence over the 'recognizing' of it. But art clearly works in *both* directions: art also *transforms* our experience of the thing we are acquainted with, so that it only becomes the thing we recognize *in retrospect*. Art does not merely disclose reality, it also opens our eyes. This opening of eyes (and ears), this transformation of perception, is the healing of a partial blindness (and deafness), of an incapacity to perceive and experience reality in the way that we learn to perceive and experience it through the medium of aesthetic experience. We might say that in modernist art, this moment of the *transformation* of perception through aesthetic experience becomes increasingly dominant.

Now, what has all this to do with aesthetic *truth*? Clearly the temptation to expand the concept of truth into the realm of aesthetics is based on the power of beauty to disclose reality. This power *manifests* itself in those *effects* of art which are relevant to questions of truth; at the same time it *confronts* us as an aesthetic *validity*-claim. In the light of what we have said so far it is possible to explain in what sense we can speak of a truth-*claim* which corresponds to the truth-*potential* of works of art, and which is inseparable from an *aesthetic* validity-claim. It is evidently not possible to explain what this truth-claim is by reference to an apophantic concept of the truth of art; when we tried to capture this concept in metaphorical terms it eluded our grasp. But we can try, as M. Seel has suggested,[24] to understand the connection between aesthetic validity-claim and truth-claim by reference to the structure of aesthetic discourse, which is a realm in which the question of the 'authenticity' of 'representation' is dealt with at the same time as the question of aesthetic rightness. Aesthetic discourse is the mediating instance between the apophantic metaphors from which we started out, and questions of aesthetic rightness. That is why we can only understand the truth-*claim* of art if we start by looking at the complex relationship of interdependency between the various dimensions of truth in aesthetic discourse. In any dispute over the truth or falsehood of aesthetic constructs which is also to be a dispute over the aesthetic quality of those constructs, the participants have to bring their own experience to bear on the discussion. However, their own experience can only be mobilized for discussion and transformed into arguments within the three dimensions of truth, truthfulness, and moral and practical rightness *simultaneously*. Both the truth-*potential* and the truth-*claim* of art can thus only be explained with recourse to the complex relationship of interdependency between the various dimensions of truth in the living experience of individuals, or in the formation and transformation of attitudes, modes of perception, and interpretations.

Truth can thus only be ascribed to art in a metaphorical sense. But this metaphorical ascription has a firm basis in the relationship between aesthetic validity and the truth-potential of works of art. If we pursue this idea further, we can see that the interweaving of the various dimensions of truth in the *effects* of art and in aesthetic discourse can be related to the metaphorical interweaving of the dimensions of truth in the work of art itself. For it is no coincidence that the metaphors of 'showing' and 'revealing' can be easily linked to those of 'saying' and 'expressing'. Reality is manifested in art, to borrow a phrase from F. Koppe, in a 'mode of being affected'; the processes of 'revealing' and 'expressing' are intermeshed. As something that speaks, as something expressive, art converts what has been diffusely experienced into the presence of a sensual phenomenon; as something that reveals, it becomes eloquent and expressive. Which is why it would also be possible to see the immanent utopia of aesthetic semblance in the overwhelming experience that it can be said, and that – as Adorno once put it – art 'objectifies the ephemeral, thus citing it into permanence'.[25] In so far as the metaphors of 'saying' and 'expressing' dominate the way we think about art, we shall tend to explain what is authentic in a work of art, not in concepts of apophantic truth, but in terms of endeetic truthfulness; this is the tendency I notice in Habermas and – up to a point – in Koppe. But both attempts at an explanation, whether on the basis of apophantic truth or of endeetic truthfulness, share a common weakness in that they have to interpret the work of art by analogy with a special type of speech-act. In a work of art, however, the artist does not (literally) *say* something; and the authenticity of a construct is therefore not decided by the question whether the artist was being truthful. It is rather the other way around: the truthfulness of the artist, in so far as we can speak of it at all, is *shown* by the authenticity of the construct. Neither truth *nor* truthfulness can be ascribed to the work of art in a *non-metaphorical* sense if we are understanding 'truth' and 'truthfulness' in terms of a pragmatically differentiated everyday concept of truth. The *metaphorical* interweaving of truth and truthfulness – and even of normative correctness – in the work of art is, on the contrary, something which we can only explain by the fact that the work of art, as a symbolical construct that carries an *aesthetic* validity-claim, is at the same time the object of an *aesthetic experience* that refers back to our ordinary experience in which the three dimensions of truth are interwoven in a *non-metaphorical* sense.

If we reconstruct the concept of the truth of art in the way that has been indicated here, then it is also possible to combine Kantian insights with motifs of an aesthetic of truth. In his critical account of the aesthetics of truth, R. Bubner has tried to *oppose* Kant's concept of beauty to the aesthetics of truth.[26] I do not believe that this presentation of the matter in terms of stark alternatives is convincing, as indeed is already indicated in Kant's aesthetic by the transition from the analysis of beauty to a theory of the beautiful in art. Kant's idea of characterizing the experience of beauty in terms of an indefinite and free interplay of imagination and understanding is certainly irreconcilable with an apophantic aesthetics of truth, because the free play of the *faculties* is precisely *not* supposed to become fixed as a determinate relationship between concept and intuition. But precisely the *expansion* of the faculties which results from the pleasurable and free interplay of imaginative and intellectual–reflexive moments in aesthetic experience could be related to the notion of truth. We only have to apply the character of potentiality, which is contained in the term 'faculties', to the concept of truth in order to see that the truth-content of the work of art is really its truth-*potential* – in the sense I have outlined above.

If aesthetic semblance can be understood as the arena of that pleasurable and free interplay of imaginative and intellectual–reflexive activities, in the Kantian sense to which we have just alluded, then the utopian 'lustre of semblance' would not in the end be totally isolated from truth and a real utopia. For the ecstatic moment of aesthetic experience, in which the continuum of historical time is exploded, can be understood as the 'point of entry' for forces which, in their non-aesthetic usage, might restore a continuity between art and living praxis. This is presumably also what Jauss means when he forges a connection between 'aesthetic enjoyment' and the 'conversion of aesthetic experience into symbolic or communicative action'.[27] But if this 'conversion' of aesthetic experience into communicative action indicates that works of art are closely involved in questions of truth, as we have just seen, then the emancipation of semblance cannot be total: semblance communicates secretly with truth and reconciliation, as Adorno believed, and yet in a sense that differs from what Adorno believed.

VI

I have tried to show in what sense the relationship between Adorno's categories of truth, semblance and reconciliation can be developed into a complex constellation of categories such that the philosophical potential and the critical purpose of Adorno's aesthetics can be preserved. If we add a dimension of 'communicative rationality' to Adorno's concept of rationality, then it becomes possible to expand his aesthetics of truth in a pragmatic way. If the receiving, communicating and acting subjects are incorporated into the relationship between art, reality and utopia, this produces an effect of 'multi-dimensionality' by contrast with Adorno's own dialectically one-dimensional constructions. It would be worth while discussing issues of actionist, aleatoric, and popular art (towards which Adorno, almost *a priori*, adopted a critical attitude), as well as the issue of the 'dissolution of the concept of the work' about which we have heard so much recently, from this point of view. I believe that, on these issues too, we should have to give a new slant to Adorno's central arguments, which are frequently criticized today – and not without cause – as 'traditionalist'. But for present purposes I should like to limit myself to two partial aspects, namely the question of the mutability of the relationship between art and living praxis, which has been given prominence by P. Bürger in particular, on the one hand, and the question of the aesthetic valency of popular art forms on the other.

1   In my discussion of Habermas, I have interpreted the process of differentiation between the spheres of validity of science, law and morality, and art, in which problems are dealt with according to the special logic appropriate to the particular type of validity-claim in question, as the expression of an irreversible cultural learning process. If we keep to this interpretation, on the abstract level of dimensions of validity, then it is no longer possible for slogans like the 'sublation of art in the praxis of life', if we take them literally, to point the way towards a possibility of escaping from a condition in which art is ideologically *separated* from the reality of life. Those avant-garde movements that Bürger has analysed tried to convert the aesthetic *directly* into the practical,[28] and their failure was therefore rooted in a self-deception about the nature of their own activities, *amongst other things*. Bürger rightly points to the fact that 'what had become historically split off as the realm of aesthetics' cannot be made into 'the organizing centre of a liberating and liberated praxis of life'.[29] But nevertheless we can – and Bürger insists that we should – think of the *relationships* in which art and living praxis stand to each other as changeable. The process of differentiation between spheres of validity must be distinguished from particular forms of *institutional* differentiation. Bürger says of the bourgeois 'institution of art' that 'art as fully individuated subsystem is, at the same time, one whose individual products no longer tend to assume a social function'.[30] It is consistent with this view when Bürger demands a *transformation* of the institution of art, or at least of the norms that regulate it,[31] in order that art should regain its social relevance. Bürger's utopia of an avant-gardist transform-

ation of the institution of art so that 'all can freely develop their productive potential'[32] seems to me to represent an interpretation of the 'praxis of art', of its social function, that is weighted too heavily towards the aesthetics of production. It is only for this reason that he can play off the praxis of art against Adorno and against the idea of the (great) work of art.[33] If, on the other hand, we take the reception side into account, then it is not clear why a change in the function of art that is related to a democratic opening-up of society should exclude the idea of the great work of art. The opposite seems to me to be the case: without the paradigmatic productions of 'great' art, in which the imagination, the accumulated knowledge and the skill of obsessively special-ized artists is objectivized, a democratically generalized aesthetic production would presumably decline into an amateur arts-and-craftism. A similar case might be made here as for the elements of improvisation in recent music. Boulez and Dahlhaus have pointed out that music would suffer a regression if the moment of improvisation were to be treated as something absolute: improvisation is as a rule only an activation and variation of what is laid down in memory or, as Boulez says, it is 'manipulated recollection'.[34] John Cage hit upon the same problem when he said, 'I must find a way of liberating people without them going silly.'[35]

I argue on the assumption that a transformation of the 'institu-tion of art' cannot mean the abolition of the 'culture of experts',[36] but that it would amount rather to the establishment of a tighter network of connections between the culture of experts and the life-world on the one hand, and the culture of experts and popular art on the other. Barriers to such a rapprochement between aesthetics and the practical sphere, between high and low culture, have been identified by Adorno and Horkheimer in their critique of the culture industry. But if we allow the course of history such a degree of ambiguity that we can still see it as possessing a potential for emancipation, then it is also possible to discover traces of a transformation of the relationship between art and the life-world in reality. On the basis of these traces we can defend the idea of an altered relationship between art and the life-world in which a democratic praxis would be able to draw productively on the innovative and communicative potential of art. My reflec-tions on the truth of art were intended to show, amongst other things, that the perspective of *this sort* of 'sublation' of art in the praxis of life really is present in the concept of artistic beauty. In this connection, too, it would be possible to fetch an idea of Adorno's back from the realm of the inconceivable into the realm of the conceivable.

2   As we come to the end of this essay, it is only possible to take a cursory glance at a theme which is of great importance for Adorno, that of popular art. Adorno's critique of Benjamin is well known; his work on jazz can be understood as a reply to Benjamin's optimistic appraisal of modern mass culture in the essay on the 'Work of Art'. In connection with that essay, Adorno writes in a letter to Benjamin that Schönberg and the American film are the 'torn halves of an integral freedom'.[37] But in the same letter he makes it clear that he is *only* able to discern reification and ideology in mass culture, *not* freedom. What Adorno means with his phrase about the torn halves of freedom is basically, yet again, the polarity in art between the sensual, mimetic dimension and that of intellectual construction; the phrase should be read in conjunction with a passage from his *Dissonanzen* where Adorno emphasizes the liberating role of the sensual, expressive and superficial for the emergence of Viennese classicism, and thus for all the great music that comes after Bach:

> Thus these deplored moments became part of great Western music: sensual stimulation as gateway to the harmonious dimension and finally to the coloristic one; the unrestrained individual as bearer of the expressive and humanizing dimensions of music; 'superficiality' as critique of the dumb objectivity of forms . . .   [38]

Mozart's *Magic Flute* is, for Adorno, a moment of perfect coincidence between serious and light music; but it is also the last such moment. 'After the *Magic Flute*, serious and light music could no longer be forced into a common framework.'[39] For Adorno, the 'light' music of the present day is nothing but ideology and trash, a product of the culture industry just like film. Adorno utterly condemns jazz.

It seems to me that where Adorno passes judgements such as this, what is being expressed is not only a legitimate criticism of the culture industry, but also a traditionalist prejudice which similarly prevented him from recognizing the productive elements in Benjamin's interpretation of mass culture. There were, of course, powerful *theoretical* arguments behind Adorno's objections: the fundamental theses of the *Dialectic of Enlightenment*, for example, do reserve a certain degree of ambivalence in their treatment of 'great' art, but none for mass culture – which appears as fitting perfectly into the universal system of delusion. But in this case it seems to me that Benjamin's exploratory approach, which is theoretically less secure and unafraid of contradictions, is more productive. For whereas Adorno measures the products of the new mass culture by standards which can only make them appear primitive, inane or cynical, Benjamin sees something *aesthetically* new arising out of the interference of new technical procedures and new modes of reception; he sees new ways of processing reality aesthetically, which are aimed at producing an 'equilibrium between the human subject and the technical apparatus'.[40] Benjamin argues, for example, that the American grotesque film brings about a 'therapeutic exploding of the unconscious' which finds its expression in 'collective laughter'.[41] Under the impact of technology, art becomes a vaccine against those collective psychoses in which the enormous tensions that technological innovations generate in mass populations would otherwise vent themselves.[42]

In technologized mass culture, Benjamin sees elements of an antidote to the psychic destruction of humanity by industrial society, whereas Adorno regards it above all as a medium of conformism and psychic manipulation. It is only the antithesis as such that is interesting: it appears to me that Benjamin's analysis at least points towards a *positive potential* in modern mass culture – from film to rock music – which Adorno was unable to see because of his traditionalism and his theoretical preconceptions. Rock music as the 'folk music of the industrial age' would be a test case.[43] I think that there is just as much positive potential for democratization and the unleashing of aesthetic imagination as there is potential for cultural regression in rock music and in the attitudes, skills and modes of perception which have developed around it. It is *ambivalences* such as these, as in the case of jazz, that we ought to defend against Adorno.

An analysis of modern mass culture based on Benjamin's approach would have to investigate, amongst other things, the explosive mixtures of aesthetic and political imagination which have become characteristic of the new brand of subversive behaviour on the part of protest movements since the Sixties. There is an argument of Benjamin's which might be extrapolated: he argued that it was in film that the Dadaist impulse had found its artistic medium, and in a similar way we might perhaps argue that it is only in the new political forms of action, and in the alternative and resistance movements, that artistic 'actions' and 'happenings' have found the context in which they can develop their aesthetic explosive force. And as Benjamin suggested, this politicization of aesthetics ought to be sharply distinguished from the aestheticization of politics that took place under fascism. The latter signifies a destruction of politics through the expropriation of the masses, who become degraded to mere extras in a cynically organized spectacle; but the former means, potentially at least, the appropriation of politics by a mass population grown conscious of its own power. In terms of ideal types, these two possibilities represent polar extremes. The fact that in the world of concrete phenomena the poles occasionally meet is a feature of a social condition which contains within itself the possibility of both political regression and a new potential for freedom.

VII

In various ways we have come closer to a new interpretation of the relationship between the categories of truth, semblance and reconciliation in Adorno's writings. In the process, the truth of art has come to appear as a phenomenon of interference between the various dimensions of the everyday concept of truth. This concept is associated with a utopian perspective, however, namely that of non-violent communication. Just as the three dimensions of truth interact in the concept of the truth of art, so too are they interconnected in the idea of non-violent communication. But the *specific* utopian aspect contributed by art is also present in every single authentic artistic production, whether in the overcoming of speechlessness, or in the sensual crystallization of a meaning that is dispersed in empirical experience. What non-violent communication means, however, is not the *sublation* of art. The beauty of art does not stand for reason in its entirety; it is rather the case that reason needs art to illuminate it, for without aesthetic experience and the subversive potential it contains, our moral discourse would necessarily become blind and our interpretations of the world empty.

At the end of his *Aesthetic Theory*, Adorno at least hinted at a similar way of looking at things. In the final passage of the book he emphasizes once more the communicative potential of emancipated art as opposed to its 'progressive negativity', commenting, 'Perhaps a pacified society will reappropriate the art of the past which at present is the ideological complement of an unpacified one; however, if newly evolved art were then to return to a condition of peace and order, to affirmative representation, this would be the sacrifice of its freedom' (AT 386/369). What is remarkable is not that Adorno, even here, defends modern art against traditional art, but that he finds a place in emancipated society for emancipated art. In statements such as this, the solidarity of Adorno the Marxist, the theoretician of modernity, and the artist, with his times breaks through the conceptual constraints of an overly narrow construction of history. The intention that has guided me in these reflections was to release the truth-content of Adorno's aesthetics and to develop it through critique and interpretation – in the fashion that Adorno postulated for works of art. In alluding to Adorno's conception of the interpretation of art here, I mean to offer more than simply an analogy: Adorno's writings on aesthetics themselves possess something of the qualities of a work of art, and thus may not be captured or surpassed by any process of interpretation. But interpretation and critique might nevertheless take on the function of a magnifying glass in relation to these texts; and if we read the texts with the aid of such a magnifying glass it might be that layers of meaning which appear fused to the naked eye would then separate out and distinguish themselves one from another. The image of a stereoscope would be better still: what would be achieved would be a three-dimensional image in which the latent depth of the texts became visible. By reading Adorno 'stereoscopically' in this way, we shall discover that Adorno's incomparable ability for the philosophical penetration of experience has permitted him, even within the limited medium of a philosophical dialectic of subject and object, to express, or at least to intimate, much that is actually resistant to presentation in that medium. My own reflections here were intended, apart from anything else, to promote just such a stereoscopic reading of Adorno.

2

The Dialectic of Modernism and Postmodernism:

The Critique of Reason since Adorno

I Introduction

In all the artistic, literary and social debates of the last decade, the concept of postmodernism has been one of the most elusive components. The term 'postmodernism' belongs to a network of 'postist' concepts and modes of thinking, such as 'post-industrial society', 'post-structuralism', 'post-empiricism', and 'post-rationalism'. All of these seem to represent the attempt to articulate the sense of a new age dawning, one whose contours are as yet unclear, confused and open to interpretation, but one in which the central experience of the 'death of Reason' appears to mark the definitive end of a historical project, whether that project is equated with cultural modernism, the European Enlightenment, or even the entire span of Western civilization since the Greeks. The network of 'postist' concepts and modes of thinking in fact has something of a picture puzzle about it. If looked at from the right angle, it is possible to discern in it also the contours of a radicalized modernism, of an Enlightenment that has acquired a higher consciousness of itself, and of a post-rationalist concept of reason. Looked at in this way, postmodernism takes on the appearance of a de-mythologized Marxism, a continuation of aesthetic avant-gardism, or a radicalization of language philosophy. As with a picture puzzle, it is possible to discern in 'postist' thinking both the pathos of the end of enlightenment and that of its radicalization.

But of course our image of a 'picture puzzle', useful as it might be to articulate an initial confusion about the ambiguous nature of postmodernist thinking, is also profoundly misleading. It is misleading because it suggests that a complex interplay of intellectual, aesthetic, cultural and social phenomena has the same properties as a picture in which the ambiguity inherently resides within the disposition of the optical phenomena themselves, and which the observer is therefore at liberty to interpret just as his angle of vision or a passing whim dictates. The attempt to understand a historical conjunction, even one in which the ambiguity resides within the phenomena themselves, is radically different from the process by which we peruse a visual image and discern its content. It is different for the simple reason that the observer himself belongs to the historical process and is therefore not capable of *observing* it in any strict sense. I wish to argue that it is not possible to say anything illuminating about postmodernism unless it be from a particular (theoretical, philosophical, intellectual or moral) *perspective*; that in so far as this perspective represents a view *of* the present it must also constitute a sense of one's own position *in* the present; and that this sense of position must necessarily be that of someone fully involved in his or her own time, in terms of intellectual awareness, emotional engagement, and practical commitment.

What follows is therefore not an investigation of two clearly defined phenomena called 'modernism' and 'postmodernism'. It is much rather the elucidation, tentative as yet, of a perspective in which the concepts of modernism and postmodernism are placed in a particular relationship to each other, and in which characteristic ambiguities become apparent in the 'modern' as well as the 'postmodern' consciousness. If I have chosen to use the term 'dialectic' to characterize these relationships and ambiguities (and the relationships between the ambiguities), then I do so without any strong desire to evoke traditional associations in epistemology or the philosophy of history. The term 'dialectic' should be understood here without the specific connotations of truth or history perfecting itself. It is open to readers to call this application of the term 'dialectic' postmodern if they will. But it is a use of the term which excludes one thing for certain, namely the dissolution of dialectics into a mere energetics such as Lyotard once postulated.[1] And with this point I have already embarked on the elucidation of my own understanding of postmodernism.

II Exposition

I should like to begin properly with a – more or less arbitrary – selection of descriptions of 'things postmodern'. What I have in mind is a kind of collage, the components of which, especially in the form of quotations, are so arranged that postmodernism can be perceived as a symbolic or conceptual field with distinct force-lines.

Ihab Hassan, a spokesman of American postmodernism, sees the chief characteristic of the 'postmodern moment' as a movement towards 'unmaking' – which seems to come close in meaning to the notion of 'deconstruction'.

> It is an antinomian moment that assumes a vast unmaking in the Western mind – what Michel Foucault might call a postmodern *épistémè*. I say 'unmaking' though other terms are now *de rigueur*: for instance, deconstruction, decentering, disappearance, dissemination, demystification, discontinuity, *différance*, dispersion, etc. Such terms express an ontological rejection of the traditional full subject, the *cogito* of Western philosophy. They express, too, an epistemological obsession with fragments or fractures, and a corresponding ideological commitment to minorities in politics, sex and language. To think well, to read well, according to this *épistémè* of unmaking, is to refuse the tyranny of wholes; totalization in any human endeavor is potentially totalitarian.[2]

The moment of postmodernism is a kind of explosion of the modern *épistémè* in which reason and its subject – as guarantors of 'unity' and the 'whole' – are blown to pieces. On closer inspection, this turns out to be a movement towards destruction – or deconstruction – of the *cogito*, of totalizing rationality, which has been under way in modernist art for a long time. For Hassan, the most radical impulses of modern art have been collected and subsumed within the postmodern consciousness.

> In the arts, we know, the will to unmaking began to manifest itself earlier, around the turn of the century. Yet from the ready-mades of Marcel Duchamp and the collages of Hans Arp to the autodestructive machines of Jean Tinguely and conceptual works of Bruce Naumann, a certain impulse has persisted, turning art against itself in order to remake itself . . . But the main point is this: art, in process of 'de-definition' as Harold Rosenberg says, is becom-

ing, like the personality of the artist himself, an occurrence without clear boundaries: at worst a kind of social hallucination, at best an opening or inauguration. That is why Jean-François Lyotard enjoins readers 'to abandon the safe harbour offered to the mind by the category of "works of art" or of signs in general, and to recognize as truly artistic but *initiatives* or events, in whatever domain they may occur'.[3]

The movement against totalizing reason and its subject is at the same time a movement against the autonomous work of art and its pretensions to unity and fullness of meaning. That is why the avant-garde impulse which foreshadows postmodern conscious-ness is bound to call into question the *concept* of art (or in sociological terms, the differentiation of art as a separate sphere in the modern world in contradistinction to the technological system, politics or science) at the same time as it challenges the unity of the subject and the unity of the work of art.

It is possible to develop Hassan's programmatic statements *both* in the direction of a neo-Marxist aesthetic (*post-Adorno*) *and also* in the direction of an 'affirmative' aesthetic in Lyotard's sense. Frederic Jameson sees the postmodernist repudiation of the violence of a 'totalizing' reason as the opportunity for a new, as it were, dialogic, postmodern concept of totality. In Adorno's terms, we might describe what Jameson has in mind as the 'non-violent unity of the many'; Jameson himself speaks of a 'relationship by way of differences'.[4] Another element that is reminiscent of the aesthetics of Adorno and Benjamin is Jame-son's characterization of the aesthetic of postmodernism as an aesthetic of the 'allegorical', 'which, an explicit repudiation of the aesthetic of the "symbol", with its organic unity, seeks a designation for a form able to hold radical discontinuities and incommensurabilities together without annulling precisely those "differences"'.[5] Once again, the attempt to characterize postmod-ernism reaches way back into the history of aesthetic modernism. The feature of Jameson's description that lends itself most readily to being termed postmodernist in a *specific* sense is the way he constructs a connection between aesthetics and *politics*: for Jameson, the aesthetic of postmodernism corresponds to the 'mic-ropolitics' of a decentred New Left.[6] In this connection, the repudiation of the organic totality of the 'symbolic' work of art corresponds to the repudiation of the practical and theoretical forms of a totalization from above that characterized traditional Marxist working-class movements. A similar connection between postmodernist aesthetics and a decentred, democratic micropolitics also occurs in Charles Jencks's description of postmodern architecture. One might say that postmodernism, in Jameson's perspective, represents a new, a post-rationalist form of aesthetical, psychic and social 'totalization' ('unity', 'synthesis'); it is not merely a negation of totalizing reason and its subject, but a movement of 'self-transcendence' (Castoriadis) on the part of reason and the subject.

Another line of development leads from Ihab Hassan's postmodernism to the affirmative aesthetic of Jean-François Lyotard. In Lyotard's case – the Lyotard of the early Seventies, that is – the critique of totalizing reason and its subject is compressed into a repudiation of the terror of theory, of representation, of the sign, of the idea of truth. Lyotard criticizes Adorno for retaining the category of the subject,[7] and Artaud for not going far enough down the 'path of a generalized de-semiotics'.[8] According to Lyotard, if I understand him correctly, in both instances there is only a half-hearted break with representational thought, with the terror of signs and meanings. Adorno remains committed to the notion of expression, Artaud to a grammar of gestures; Lyotard, by contrast, postulates the dissolution of 'semiology' into 'energetics'. For Lyotard, the subject, representation, meaning, sign, and truth are evidently links in a chain which has to be broken in its entirety: 'The subject is a product of the representation machine, and disappears with it.'[9] Neither art nor philosophy have anything to do with 'meaning' or 'truth', they are merely functions of 'transformations of energy' which can no longer be attributed to 'a memory, a subject, an identity'.[10] Political economy is transformed into a libidinal economy that is freed of the terror of representation.

This bizarre postmodernist conception of a transition from capitalism to socialism, which is presumably inspired by the *Anti-Oedipus* of Guattari and Deleuze, betokens both a regression from Adorno to Nietzsche, and in the same breath a sidestep from Adorno to Positivism. For in substituting the *will* ('in the sense of wanting what is possible') for an 'attitude which is regulated by the edifice and the artificiality of representation', and with the dissolution of semiotics into 'energetics', Lyotard's postmodernism becomes indistinguishable from behaviourism –

although this is not a behaviourism for social engineers as we find it in Skinner, but a behaviourism for the cultural furbishment of a social system that has itself become behaviouristic. At this point postmodernism becomes the ideology of *'post-histoire'*; it is not for nothing that Lyotard – the Lyotard of the Seventies – replaces the pathos of criticism with the pathos of forgetting.

There is, then, a sense of the term 'postmodern moment' in which the word 'moment' is to be taken literally. To express the point paradoxically, it is to be understood as the fundamental category of a post-historical sense of time which has thrown off the notions of past and future along with the burden of the Platonic heritage. From this point of view the 'revolution of postmodernism', as Jean Baudrillard has termed it, can then be presented as 'the gigantic process of loss of meaning' which has led to 'the destruction of all histories, references and finalities'.[11] Baudrillard seems to me to be more consistent than Lyotard, at least, when he discerns a parody of the already accomplished messianic moment in the unhistorical character of postmodern society:

> The future has already arrived, everything has already arrived, everything is already there . . . I mean that we can neither expect the realization of a revolutionary utopia, nor an atomic explosion. The explosive force has already entered things themselves. There is nothing more that we can wait for . . . The worst case, the imagined cataclysmic event upon which every utopia was founded, the striving of history after a metaphysical purpose, etc., any kind of ultimate goal now lies behind us . . . [12]

If this perspective is correct, then postmodernism represents a historically accomplished unhistorical reality, and the death of modernism is already with us. But this would also mean that postmodern society was an unlikely cross between the visions of system theory and the imaginings of Ludwig Klages – the rebirth of a world of archaic archetypes out of the spirit of modern electronics.

In the meantime Jean-François Lyotard has put forward a modi-fied version of postmodernism which is inspired on the one hand by Wittgenstein and on the other by the *Critique of Judgement*, and within which features of a post-empiricist epistemology (Feyerabend), a modernistic aesthetic (Adorno) and a post- utop-ian political liberalism are suggestively combined. In one sense

the break with totalizing reason now takes the form of an abandonment of 'great narratives' ('the emancipation of humanity, the
realization of the Idea'[13]) and of the foundationalism of ultimate
legitimations, as well as entailing a critique of the 'totalizing'
surrogate ideology of system theory. In another sense it is a
repudiation of the (complementary) projections of totalizing
thought, i.e. utopias of unity, of reconciliation, of universal harmony. Lyotard argues for an irreducible pluralism of 'language
games' and emphasizes the irreducibly 'local' character of all
discourse, all agreements and legitimations.[14] We might speak of
a pluralistic and 'punctualistic', a 'post-Euclidian' concept of
reason, in contrast to Habermas's consensual concept of reason,
for example, which appears from Lyotard's point of view as
a last supreme effort to cling to the 'totalizing' categories of
reconciliation characteristic of German Idealism (and the Marxist
tradition), including the idea of the unity of truth, freedom and
justice. In a typical passage, which bears more than an accidental
resemblance to Feyerabend's anarchistic epistemology, Lyotard
explains what 'justice' would mean in non-consensual terms,
namely 'recognizing the autonomy, the specificity of the various
untranslatable and mutually interconnected language games;
with one rule which would nevertheless be a universal rule: "let
play continue . . . and let us play in peace"'.[15]

As Lyotard sees it, postmodernism is the result of a huge
'delegitimation' movement in European modernity, for which
the philosophy of Nietzsche is an early and central document.[16]
It seems to me that it is in Lyotard's philosophy that the 'questing
movement' of postmodern thinking has found its most pregnant
utterance to date. I shall return to Lyotard's theses later, but for
the moment I should like to stick to the problem of aesthetics. It
is characteristic of Lyotard that he presents *aesthetical* postmodernism as a radical form of aesthetical *modernism*, as a modernism
that has become conscious of itself, so to speak. 'A work can
become modern only if it is first postmodern. Postmodernism
thus understood is not modernism at its end but in the nascent
state, and this state is constant.'[17] We already find aesthetical
modernism characterized in terms of a permanent compulsion to
innovation and subversion of form and meaning in the writings
of Adorno; in his eyes, these characteristics were closely associated with the unleashing of technical productive forces in capitalist society and with the destruction of traditional meaning sys-

tems that this brought with it: 'What guarantees the authentic quality of modern works of art? It is the scars of damage and disruption inflicted by them on the smooth surface of the immutable. Explosion is one of the invariable traits of modern art, whose anti-traditional energy becomes a voracious eddy that consumes everything.'[18] In much the same way, Lyotard now speaks of the 'amazing acceleration' which characterizes, in his view, the development of aesthetical modernism, with its permanent questioning of each new set of rules for literary, artistic or musical production as it is established. For Lyotard – and this is where an interesting parallel to Adorno presents itself, to which I shall return – the invariant element in this 'anti-traditional eddy' is an aesthetic of the sublime. Modernism develops 'in the withdrawal of the real and according to the sublime relation between the presentable and the conceivable'.[19] But *postmodernism* – and here lies the crucial difference between Lyotard and Adorno – would be the working-out of this aesthetics of the sublime without 'regret' and without any 'nostalgia for presence'.[20] Postmodernism would thus be a modernism without regret, without the illusion of a potential 'reconciliation between language games', without the nostalgia for 'the whole and the one', for 'the reconciliation of the concept and the sensible, of the transparent and the communicable experience',[21] in brief, a modernism which would cheerfully accept the loss of meaning, values, reality – postmodernism as a Nietzschean 'gay science'.

In the piece from which I have been quoting, Lyotard speaks of a 'period of slackening'. His defence of aesthetical modernism is directed, not least, against a variety – or view – of postmodernism which I have not yet mentioned. This is the postmodernism of a new eclecticism and historicism in architecture, of a new realism or subjectivism in art and literature, or of a new traditionalism in music.

This brings us to a further discovery about the picture puzzle that is called 'postmodernism'. It is not without plausibility when Charles Jencks, for example, describes the rediscovery of the language of architecture, its new 'contextualism', 'electicism' or 'historicism', as a specifically postmodern development. For at the basis of the postmodernist architectural aesthetic which Jencks advocates, an aesthetic which is directed against that of the Bauhaus tradition, there is again a renunciation of the 'rationalism' of modernism in favour of a play with fragments and signs, a synthesis of disparate elements, double codings and democratic approaches to planning.[22] The postmodernism of Jencks or Venturi is characterized by 'complexity and contradiction versus simplification; ambiguity and tension rather than straight-forwardness; "both–and" rather than "either–or", doubly-func-tioning elements rather than singly working ones, hybrid rather than pure elements, and messy vitality (or "the difficult whole") rather than obvious unity'.[23] There are indubitably correspon-dences between this postmodernism and that of Hassan or indeed Jameson. On the other hand, Eyck's idea of a 'labyrinthine clar-ity', which is conceived in polemical opposition to the ideal of mathematical or geometric clarity in modern architecture or town planning, points far back into the history of aesthetic modernism; we find an analogous figure of thought in Kandinsky or Schön-berg, for example, in the transitional phase between represen-tational and abstract painting, and between tonal and atonal music. Here too, then, the postmodern avant-garde turns out to be a continuation of aesthetic modernism, and not a break with it – as long as we conceive of the element of breaking with previously established 'rules' (and here we should be in agree-ment with Lyotard, Adorno, and also Barthes) as constitutive of aesthetic modernism itself.

It is true that in Jencks, to stick with the case of postmodern architecture, there emerges an ambiguity in postmodernism which has not been apparent in the statements I have quoted so far, at least not in *this* form. Or rather, Jencks is describing an extraordinarily ambiguous phenomenon, and the ambiguity duplicates itself in his postmodernist aesthetic because he scar-cely recognizes its existence. Such points might prompt us to protest, like Lyotard, against the misuse of the term 'postmodern-ism'; for my own part I think it is more correct to speak of an ambiguity in the 'postmodern field' itself, which also affects postmodernism.

In Jencks's case, the ambiguity is to be found above all in concepts like 'historicism' and 'eclecticism'. Jencks does recognize the connotations of lassitude, retraction, conservatism in these concepts; but he thinks that postmodern architecture contains a potential for an 'authentic' eclecticism and historicism which would be different from the eclecticism and historicism that existed at the end of the last century. If, however, we look at the products of postmodern architecture 'as it actually exists' – just as the postmodernists point to the products of functionalism as it actually exists – then alongside avant-garde elements we also find a lot of quaintness or mannerism, elements of mock-traditional or 'gemütlich' revival. What this shows is that the theoretician can never keep the social penumbra of his concepts under control; it is not possible to convert the eclectic, historicist and regressive tendencies of the times into manifestations of an 'authentic' eclecticism or historicism simply by redefining them, any more than it is possible to redefine the products of vulgar functionalism as manifestations of *authentic* functionalism. But if we dig deeper, then the ideas of contextualism or the preservation of the 'fabric of our cities' also display a neo-conservative or purely defensive aspect – as if it were merely a matter of preserving and enhancing stocks that modernism had almost destroyed. This is the point where the neo-conservatism of the dominant culture joins forces with the regressive and particularist elements of the counter-culture, and the cultural project of modernism ends in defensive gestures, while the technical modernization of society proceeds unimpeded.

What I want to say is that postmodernism – and this is simply borne out particularly clearly by Jencks – participates in an ambiguity which is deeply rooted in social phenomena themselves. It is the ambiguity of a critique of modernity – and by 'critique' I mean not only theoretically articulated criticism, but also a social transformation involving change of attitudes and orientations – in which we might detect a self-transcendence of modernity in the direction of a truly 'open' society just as much as a break with the 'project of modernity' (Habermas) – and this should not of course be confused with breaking out of the steely electronic casing of the modern world – i.e. a transformation of enlightenment into cynicism, irrationalism or particularism. Postmodernism, in so far as it is not simply the programme of the latest avant-garde movement or a mere theoretical vogue, is the as yet unclear sense of an ending and a transition. But an end of what? And a transition to what? Lyotard has provided a few suggestive answers to these questions which I believe it is worth trying to develop. The connections I shall make to Lyotard are admittedly in part only indirect. After some reflections on Lyotard's aesthetic of the sublime, I should like to present the theme of a critique of reason and language, which plays a part in all varieties of postmodernism, from a somewhat different perspective from

Lyotard's. I do, however, share Lyotard's belief that many of the problems, conjunctures and convulsions of our times are reflected in this theme. This alone, if anything at all, justifies us in seeing postmodernism as something more than a fleeting fashion that will soon be forgotten.

III Intermezzo (Stretto)

Let me return once more to Lyotard's remark about the 'slackening' tendency of the times. It is possible to agree with this comment without sharing Lyotard's *interpretation* of this tendency. My objection to Lyotard's interpretation is comparable with Peter Bürger's recent criticism of Adorno.[24] Bürger criticizes Adorno's thesis that there is always a state of the aesthetic 'material' that is most advanced, and from which one can thus determine what is (still) aesthetically possible at a given moment in time and what is not. Now, Adorno's thesis is blurred enough to be defended; Bürger sharpens the focus in such a way that it appears false – and I agree with him in this. Bürger refers not only to Adorno's polemic against the musical neo-classicism of Stravinsky in his *Philosophie der Neuen Musik*, but also to the following interesting Adorno quotation: 'While it may be true that abstract paintings today find their way into executive suites and city halls without causing a stir, this does not justify a return to representationality even when a *bona fide* radical like Ché Guevara is chosen to promote the cause of reconciliation with the object.'[25] Against this seemingly sweeping disparagement of all realist art today, Bürger defends neo-realist procedures in contemporary art. His thesis about the ageing of modernism is, amongst other things, a thesis about the ageing of Adorno's concept of modernism. Bürger's counter-thesis to Adorno's is that in fully developed modernism, there is no procedure and no material that is any longer taboo, and that only the individual work in the context of a concrete situation can decide what will be aesthetically possible.[26] Against Adorno's thesis of the 'most advanced' material for a given juncture, Bürger posits a pluralism of materials and ways of proceeding. I believe Bürger's thesis to be correct provided that we understand it – as Bürger does – as the expression of a *difficulty* as well as of a new *degree of freedom* in modern art. Both Lyotard *and* Adorno are correct to argue that there is no going back in aesthetical terms. Every new realism in painting, for example, can only be a realism *beyond* the academic art that has been surpassed and supplanted by photography and film – but in modern painting, precisely, we find productive interaction between photographic realism and the realism of painting which has nothing to do with a return to academicism. The thesis that Lyotard seems to advance against this argument is that experiment and realist procedures are mutually exclusive. At this point it emerges that Lyotard and Adorno share one element of common ground which is interesting and revealing: *both* might be said to conceive of the 'progressive negation of meaning' as *the* principle of modern art. But as Adorno presents this principle, it already carries several meanings: it means negation of *traditional* meaning, negation of the traditional form of *contextual* meaning (in the organic work of art), and negation of *aesthetic* meaning as a response to the meaninglessness of capitalist reality.[27] Lyotard alters the directional thrust, so to speak, of this negativism, but he still displays a multiplicity of meaning similar to what we find in Adorno. 'Negation of meaning' for Lyotard means negation of representation, negation of reality: 'Modernity, in whatever age it appears, cannot exist without a shattering of belief and without discovery of the "lack of reality" of reality, together with the invention of other realities.'[28] Realistic procedures – such as those of photography and the cinema – contradict this aesthetic tendency to strip reality of its reality, since their objective is 'to stabilize the referent, to arrange it according to a point of view which endows it with a recognizable meaning'.[29] This is realism as affirmation of 'the' meaning. But what is ultimately meant for Lyotard by 'stabilization of the referent' or affirmation of meaning is that aesthetic judgement becomes assimilated to cognitive judgement and that reflective judgement is supplanted by 'determinant judgement'.[30] But if we once accept the possibility of a close affinity between aesthetic representation and conceptualization, then we can summon Kant as chief witness for aesthetical postmodernism. What Kant says about the function of genius in providing aesthetic rules becomes tantamount to a principle of progressive negation of *representation*: 'A postmodern artist or writer is in the position of a philosopher: the text he writes, the work he produces are not in principle governed by pre-established rules, and they cannot be judged according to a determinant judgement, by applying familiar categories to the text or to the work. Those rules and categories are rather what the text or the work of art are looking for. The artist and the writer, then, are working without rules in order to establish the rules of what *will have been done.'*[31] The progressive negation of representation here becomes indistinguishable from the process whereby every work of art negates the rules established by preceding works.

Lyotard understands the non-conceptual, trans-discursive aspect of art as Kant analyses it in the sense of a negation of (aesthetic) representation. The idea behind this, if I understand it rightly, is that in every aesthetic representation of *something*, the thing that we recognize as being represented signifies a conceptual moment in the aesthetic object, so that a picture *as* a picture of an object, an interior or a landscape, for example, is not a pure picture in the sense of an aesthetic object. In so far as it is representative, art is still participating, so to speak, in a discourse which it is its purpose to overcome and leave behind it. In this way the concept of aesthetic representation comes to approximate that of conceptual statement, and the negation of representation becomes the true purpose of art. But in the process, Kant's concept of artistic beauty stands revealed as an untenable equivocation, an equivocation which necessarily was called into question by the very development of art. We are then left with a straight choice between an aesthetic of ornamentation and an aesthetic of the sublime; and faced with this choice, anyone who takes art *seriously* will opt, like Lyotard, for an aesthetic of the sublime. The parallel between Adorno and Lyotard now becomes clear: both define the 'progressive negation of meaning' – i.e. of representation – as the principle of modern art; but for both of them, too, it is precisely this movement of negation that makes art into the cipher of the absolute. For Adorno the work of art is the semblance, the sensual presence, of something that can be neither thought nor represented, namely reality in a state of reconciliation; for Lyotard, art becomes an allusive indication of something that can be thought but not represented. 'To make visible that there is something which can be conceived and which can neither be seen nor made visible: this is what is at stake in modern painting.' Its aim is to make 'an allusion to the unpresentable by means of visible presentations'.[32] The difference between Lyotard and Adorno here is obvious, but so is the common element. Lyotard eliminates the utopian valency of aesthetic semblance; but for him, as for Adorno, the absolute is that which is concealed in the moment of appearance.[33]

It is – perhaps – a profound thought that the work of art 'signifies' the absolute precisely in the movement of negation of meaning, of representation. My objection concerns the philosophical 'instrumentation', so to speak, of this thought by Lyotard – as indeed by Adorno. I should like to stress that, of course, there is something violent and inadmissible in equating negation of meaning (Adorno) with negation of representation (Lyotard). But I am concerned with a common *structural* feature in Adorno and Lyotard, which consists in the fact that for both of them, the concept of art is related in a negatory fashion to a concept of the concept (i.e. of 'identificatory thought', or of 'representation') which is derived from a Nietzschean tradition of criticizing language and reason, and which seems to me highly problematical from the point of view of a philosophy of language. The feature which the respective critiques of language and reason by Adorno and Lyotard have in common at the level of 'deep grammar' is voiced in structural homologies between the critique of identificatory thought and the critique of the representational sign. It is these common premises which prevent Adorno and Lyotard alike from naming that aspect of art which makes it into something *more* than merely a cipher of the absolute; which is to say, that which relates art in a complex way to *reality*.[34] Perhaps we may speak in either case of a hidden dogmatism at the depths of the theory. Just as, for Adorno, art is fixated for the sake of its own concept upon the negation of meaning, so too for Lyotard, it is fixated for the sake of its concept upon the negation of representation. Just as the critique of 'identificatory thought' is the key to Adorno's aesthetic of negativity, so too does the critique of representation become the key to Lyotard's aesthetic of postmodernism. These common premises of Adorno and Lyotard are problematic because they express a critique of the logic of identity which has not been thought through to the end. Where Lyotard is concerned, I can only state this as a hypothesis; with regard to Adorno, I shall return to the point.

IV Development (1): Modern Art and the Negation of Meaning

In a recent publication Lyotard has given us a further variation on the theme of an aesthetic of the sublime, in which Burke now stands alongside Kant as a principal witness for the aesthetic avant-garde.[35] Here Lyotard is above all concerned to develop the dimension of aesthetic impact or effect within his aesthetic of the sublime. And in a surprising way he thereby comes full circle and returns to his earlier theses about the need to replace 'semiotics' with 'energetics'. With reference to Burke, Lyotard connects the idea that art tries to show that there are things which can neither be seen nor represented to the idea that art presents the terror of nothingness, the threat that *all occurrence will cease,* in a way which simultaneously brings this thought to our attention and dispels it. It can then be argued that the effect of art – and also its *purpose* – is an intensification of our sense of living. 'By keeping this threat at bay, art creates an appetite for relief, for gaiety. Thanks to art, the soul is restored to a state of agitation, of movement between life and death, and this agitation is its health and its life.'[36]

Art, as the cipher of the absolute, simultaneously invokes and dispels the absolute terror of nothingness. This is how it serves the purpose of life-enhancement. 'The sublime . . . is not a matter of elevation . . . but of intensification.'[37] For Lyotard, as for Adorno, there is ultimately but *one* thing that art is capable of saying; but the conclusions that Adorno and Lyotard draw appear to be diametrically opposed. For Adorno, aesthetic experience stands in need of philosophical illumination in order that what it signifies, its truth content, is not lost. The purpose of art is not its emotional impact, but knowledge attained through the impact it makes. For Lyotard, on the other hand, the purpose of art is not that we should grasp what it signifies, but the generation of sublime emotions through those things that are sign-ified in it. Thus it appears that, despite his recourse to an aesthetic of the sublime, Lyotard's concept of avant-garde art does indeed replace 'semiotics' with 'energetics'.

In both cases, a radical segregation of semiotics and energetics is the price that is paid for a singular reduction in the semiotic dimension of art – in Adorno it takes the form of a pure aesthetic of truth, in Lyotard of a rigorous aesthetic of impact. The task we face in response to this segregation is to conceive of semiotics and energetics, of the significance and the impact of art, in such a way that none of these elements is posited as absolute, and by the same token their polar opposition would fall away. The aesthetic object could then be understood as a field of forces and tensions, but on the level of meaning – and the act of understanding it as a constellation of meaning would be tantamount to a radiation of energy. Art would then appear as a second nature, but as a nature that is beginning to speak. This mixing of metaphors might sound off-putting, but perhaps it will provide some helpful pointers for the route we shall be taking in the discussion that follows.

Let us begin with the semiotic dimension. When we speak of a semiotic dimension in art, we mean that there is something in art to be understood. But if it is a specifically *aesthetic* form of understanding that is at issue, then this cannot mean the (pragmatic) understanding of words or sentences in a literary text or the recognition of objects in a picture. Aesthetic understanding concerns the *configuration* of the elements in a construct, the 'logic' of their relationship. Now, in traditional art aesthetic understanding had a relatively secure basis in the comprehension of a 'language' – of a vocabulary, a syntax, of conventions for form and expression. But ever since modern art has set about demolishing, dissolving or exploding the very constituent elements of meaning in aesthetic production in the course of its 'progressive negation of meaning', aesthetic understanding has become an immense practical problem, while at the same time, the very *concept* of aesthetic understanding seems to have become increasingly questionable. We might be tempted to say, following the logic of Lyotard's arguments, that through the progressive 'negation of representation' the problem of aesthetic understanding has come to present itself in a pure form, and now it can be seen that we are not in fact dealing with a problem of *understanding* at all – at least, not where the *specific* purpose of art is concerned. This would mean that aesthetic constructs as such do not have a *meaning* which can only be grasped through understanding. The thesis I should like to advance against this is that to fend off any concept of aesthetic understanding in this way is just as untenable as the (complementary) thesis of the older school of Logical Positivism that traditional metaphysics is void of cognitive content and therefore either bad or disguised poetry. What might aesthetic understanding be, however, if it cannot be reduced to the understanding of 'semantic particles', the understanding of statements, or the understanding of an artist's intention? Adorno gave an answer to this question in which we already find an indication of a link between 'semiotics' and 'energetics'. He says of the concept of aesthetic understanding.

> If this is to convey something adequate, something appropriate to the matter in hand, then the kind of imagery in which we should have to conceive it today is likely to be that of travelling along the same route, of mentally tracing the tensions laid down in the work of art and the processes that have become objectified in it. We do not understand a work of art by translating it into concepts . . . , but by entering into its immanent dynamic – I would almost say that the way to understand it is for our ear to recompose it, for our eye to paint it, for our speech organs to speak it anew, according to its own particular logic.[38]

Adorno describes understanding as part of a consummated aesthetic experience. Aesthetic experience confronts us with works which either open up to us or remain closed; which draw us into their dynamic or repel us; which engage us in the tracework of their tensions, or else reject our inquiring gaze. But the fact that this really is a matter of the 'logic' or 'meaning' of a construct, and not merely a matter of like or dislike that defies further explanation, is apparent from the way in which aesthetic understanding articulates and manifests itself: namely in explanation, criticism and commentary, in reproduction, performance or recital, and finally in the productive application of aesthetic experiences – which extends from very ordinary indications that our faculty of perception, conceptualization and communication has been expanded, to the creation of new works. Adorno's characterization of aesthetic understanding is thus phenomenologically correct, but incomplete; here as elsewhere, understanding should not be confused with the feeling that we have understood, rather it can ultimately only be grasped in its manifestations. And these are located in an arena of public communication – which is what makes it possible to have a dispute, with arguments, about aesthetic understanding or failure to understand, or (what amounts to much the same thing) about the success or failure of works of art or performances. The existence of literary and art criticism bears witness to this.

I spoke of an expansion of our *faculty* of perception, conceptualization and communication as a manifestation of aesthetic understanding. It is no coincidence that this is reminiscent of Kant. For already in Kant we find the attempt to frame the connection we have in mind between a 'semiotic' and an 'energetic' moment in aesthetic understanding; he does so in the concept of a reflexive aesthetic pleasure. If we translate Kant's insight into our way of looking at the matter, then he is saying that the expansion of the cognitive, perceptive and affective faculty is not merely an *effect* of aesthetic understanding, but also the precondition for it. The work of art breaks through the bonds of our accustomed ways of perceiving and thinking, and opens up a new dimension of meaning for us in doing so; only by shocking us, touching us emotionally, or setting us in motion, can it communicate to us. Aesthetic effect and aesthetic understanding are mutually interdependent; the one cannot exist without the other.

Looked at like this, the progressive negation of meaning – or of representation – should not be understood as an irreversible movement of art towards its pure concept which consigns it to a world beyond significative language or representational depiction. In such a world beyond language and representation, it would only be possible to conceive of the work of art in terms of higher meaning (Adorno) or of non-meaning, i.e. pure energy (Lyotard). But it is neither of these things. It would be truer to say that it expands the boundaries of meaning – of what can be said and represented – and that in doing so it also expands the boundaries of the world and of the subject. Even in the radical subversion of meaning in modern art – or precisely there – the work of art constitutes the potential for such an expansion of the boundaries of meaning and of the subject. For as aesthetic synthesis is pushed forward onto the plane of the semantic particles, the syntax and the grammar of language (in literature, painting and music), so the explosive energies immured within the seemingly solid housing of everyday meaning, which can otherwise only register themselves in dreams, jokes and psychoses, are also released and made available to the subject: they are, as it were, sublated into the world of meaning. It is commensurate with the logic of dreams, and thus with the logic of a dissipated archaic dimension of everyday meaning, if, for example, the separation of sound, word, image and script (i.e. the separation of expressive sound-articulation from conventional signification, or of speech recorded as writing from pictorial representation) is challenged. To be sure, audibility is a dimension of speech; but only children have to read out loud in order to understand the meaning of a text. For poetry alone has it always been the case that it had to be read aloud in order to be fully apprehended; the silent reading of a poem is like reading a musical score, in that only a highly developed auditive imagination can make listening in the literal sense redundant. Novels, on the other hand, can be read in silence: for them the advantage of hearing the text over what the normal reader is capable of grasping in silence becomes negligible. Advanced literary works like *Finnegans Wake*, in contrast, need to be read (i.e. 'seen') *and* heard, for the internalization of the auditory faculty is not adequate to the demands they make; the text will not reveal itself to the silent reader because he is as if cut off from the sound dimension of language. But unlike the case of poetry, it is not sufficient to hear the text either: the associative ramifications are encapsulated in the print, much as in a rebus, and need to be discovered visually. Script thus becomes picture and musical score in one, and in the medium of a single art form – the novel – the separation of the arts into painting, music and literature (which is founded on the separation of sound, image and music) is virtually suspended.

In the case of *Finnegans Wake*, the departure from traditional limitations of art and the reception of art goes still further; even Adorno's characterization of aesthetic understanding can scarcely be applied here because it still presupposes a solitary recipient who immerses himself in the artistic object and creates it afresh by a process of reconstruction. There are many indications that such a linear and totalizing reception, so to speak, is no longer possible in the case of *Finnegans Wake*; it is as if even the clear distinction between recitation, aesthetic contemplation, and communication among the literary public can no longer be maintained in this instance. It is only in a polyphonic and communicatively loosened reading that the aesthetic energies of the text can be set in action. Robert M. Adams has recently put the point very nicely:

> The *Wake* is peculiar among literary books in being better read by a committee than by one person; it demands the kind of eclectic and polyphonic analysis recommended by Saint Paul in I

Corinthians 14:26. ['How is it then, brethen? when ye come together, every one of you hath a psalm, hath a doctrine, hath a
tongue, hath a revelation, hath an interpretation. Let all things be
done unto edifying.'] Studied in congenial company, it imposes
its own direction and pace, alternatively groping and tentative, then
explosive. Thought moves through and around the text in loops,
streams, eddies, pools, and abrupt, careening leaps. The book
harrows our habits, too; layers of long-settled and apparently
stratified verbal convention are shaken and fractured.[39]

In works like *Finnegans Wake*, the concept of an aesthetic totality
of meaning tends to become inapplicable; the 'whole' of the work
becomes an ideal horizon which can only be apprehended in
fragmentary fashion. As Klaus Reichert has observed, it thus
becomes a multiple 'whole'.[40] We might well call the work 'postmodern' in the sense of those characterizations of postmodernism
which were cited at the beginning of this essay. And yet Ezra
Pound's dictum that 'great literature is simply language charged
with meaning to the utmost possible degree'[41] is applicable here,
too. The work is charged with meaning to the utmost – a formulation incidentally, which already contains the sense of interrelationship between 'semiotic' and 'energetic' moments of the
aesthetic.

This interrelationship between semiotic and energetic
moments in aesthetic experience means, amongst other things,
that it is possible for works of art to sustain 'energy loss', to fade
or go cold, at least temporarily. This is the form of mortality
peculiar to works of art. The closer art comes to the nature of
pure event, the easier it is to grasp this type of mortality. But
the work of art in the traditional sense also has something of
this character of an event, as becomes clear from the repeatability
of performances and aesthetic experiences. Thus it is possible for
the work itself to fade in the process of its reception, and to
remain only as a burnt-out shell. It would live on in the ways of
reacting and perceiving which it had itself first engendered,
above all in the production of new works; and it is possible that
a long-dead work can be revitalized only by the fresh perspective
which such new works cast upon it.[42] But then, this is only half
the truth because it is conceived entirely in energetic terms;
Benjamin had the other half of the truth in mind when he spoke
of criticism being the 'mortification of works of art'.

> Mortification of the works: not then – as the romantics have it –
> awakening of the consciousness in living works, but the settlement
> of knowledge in dead ones. Beauty, which endures, is an object
> of knowledge. And if it is questionable whether the beauty which
> endures does still deserve the name, it is nevertheless certain that
> there is nothing of beauty which does not contain something that
> is worthy of knowledge. . . . The object of philosophical criticism
> is to show that the function of artistic form is as follows: to make
> historical content, such as provides the basis of every important
> work of art, into a philosophical truth.[43]

Benjamin, like Adorno after him, conceives of the mortality of
beauty in terms of an aesthetic of truth. This too is only half the
truth, as we have said. The 'settlement' of knowledge in works of
art is only a moment in the process of receiving – or 'consuming' –
them. There is more to this than the appropriation of a philosophical truth-content. It could be understood as a process of
incorporation, of internalization in a somatic sense even, i.e. as
an internalization which involves eyes, ears, nerves and tactile
sensation, just as much as the intellectual faculty of understanding. In this way, when interested members of the public 'consumed' the sculpture that Joseph Beuys had built out of blocks
of basalt on the Friedrichsplatz in Kassel for Dokumenta 7 by
carrying away individual blocks 'in order to plant them in the
ground alongside newly planted oak trees,[44] then this might
present an allegory of art itself. 'Anyone who wishes to see the
pile of rocks [one angle of which pointed towards a newly planted
oak tree – A. W.] preserved as Beuys's work of art is preventing
it from achieving its effect. But whoever tries to help Beuys's
work achieve its effect, is also helping to make it disappear.'[45]
In this sense it would no doubt be possible to understand many
an avant-garde attempt to erase the boundaries between art and
life as provocative allegorical demonstrations of the ontological
status of art – reminders that the work of art has ceased to exist
as a neutralized cultural object.

I have drawn attention to the complex interrelationship
between the semiotic and energetic aspects of art, in order to
counter the hasty or one-sided fixation of modernist (or
postmodernist) aesthetics on a progressive negation of representation as the index of truth and falsehood in progressive art. Art
is not the Other of reason or of meaning, nor is it unadulterated
pure meaning or reason in its true shape; rather, art is meaning

that has been concentrated, set in motion, charged with new or previously unfocused energies. It is not against the terror of signs, meanings, representational thought, or truth, that it directs its polemical force, but against the terror of meaning as it has become established and petrified at any given time. Only from the perspective of the latter does it appear as non-sense. Concealed within the fixation of art upon a progressive negation of meaning, linear construction of progress in art lives on. But such a linear progress of art could only end in nothingness, as Adorno, incidentally, saw very clearly. An art that was purified of the last vestige of signification, of representation, of meaning, would be indistinguishable from pleasant ornament, senseless noise, or technical construction. What art amounts to in reality, however, is a *concentration* of meaning as much as a disruption or negation of devitalized meaning. This is as true of great modernist art as it is of traditional art. So that if we want to establish a connection between modernist art and a genuinely postmodernist impulse, we should have to construct it in a different way from Lyotard. *Finnegans Wake* was just one example; I shall return to the idea that I touched on in that connection. But first I should like to pick up the other end of the argument, and try to develop the basic theme of postmodernism, namely the critique of 'totalizing' reason.

V Development (2): The Critique of Reason and its Subject

I should like to distinguish between three forms of critique of reason and its subject; all three of them play a part in postmodernism, but the ability to *distinguish* between them is the prerequisite for clarifying what we might – perhaps – mean by 'modern' and 'postmodern' forms of knowledge. I have in mind (1) the psychological critique (unmasking) of the subject and its reason; (2) the philosophical, psychological and sociological critique of 'instrumental' or 'identitary' reason and its subject; (3) the linguistic critique of reason as transparent to itself, and of its subject as constitutive of meaning. It is far from the case that these are mutually independent forms of the critique of reason and its subject; but the line of *approach* is different in each case, and this is what I intend to show. I believe that the only reason why the concepts of reason and the autonomous subject appear to have been irresistibly drawn into the maelstrom of the critique of 'logocentrism' is that widely varied motives, insights and discoveries have become intermingled and stratified within that critique.

1 The psychological critique of the subject and its reason

I wish to mention this form of critique here merely as a preliminary step which provides the necessary background for the discussion of the philosophical critique of reason. The psychological critique – in which the central figure is, of course, Freud – consists in demonstrating the *factual* impotence or non-existence of the 'autonomous' subject, and in demonstrating *as fact* the irrational nature of its putative reason. This involves the discovery of an *Other* of reason within the subject and its reason. As embodied beings, as 'wish-machines' or even as 'will to power' (in the sense of Freud's great predecessor, Nietzsche), human beings do not know what they want or what they are doing. Their 'reason' is merely an expression of psychic forces or an imprint of social power relations, and the Ego – a meagre remnant of the philosophical subject – is at best a weak mediator between the demands of the Id and the threats of the Super-Ego. The philosophical subject, with the capacity for self-determination and for *logon didonai*, is unmasked as a virtuoso of rationalization in the service of alien powers; the unity and transparency of the I stands revealed as a fiction. In other words, the 'decentred' subject of psychoanalysis is a nexus of psychic and social forces, rather than a master of these forces; the arena of a sequence of conflicts, rather than the director of a play or the author of a story. Not only psychoanalysis, but the literature of the present century, too, has contributed a wealth of material to the phenomenology of this decentred subject. To be sure, in the experiments of the literary avant-garde which, as Axel Honneth has put it, 'aim at an aesthetic demonstration of the way subjects become inextricably involved in a chain of events that surpasses their individual horizon of meaning',[46] the motives of a psychological critique of the subject intersect with those of linguistic philosophy. Let us, therefore, stay with psychoanalysis for a moment. Freud himself was still a representative of European rationalism and the

Enlightenment, albeit a sceptical one; he shook our faith in the rationality of the subject and the power of reason, but with the intention of *strengthening* the power of reason and the power of the Ego. The normative horizon of his critique – and in this he remains an Enlightenment figure – was a disabused, disillusioned humanity that had *come to* its senses and gained *control* of itself within limits. Whatever view we might take on this, there is a particular question which the discoveries of psychoanalysis – which were in any case not as new as all that – leave unresolved, and that is what is to happen to the concepts of the subject, of reason, of autonomy as *normative* concepts. It is difficult to say in what sense Freud himself retains these. What is clear is that they *can* no longer be the concepts of a Cartesian or idealist philosophy of the subject – nor the idealizing assumptions of a will to truth as the intelligible alternative to the pleasure principle or the will to power, of a non-violent dialogue as the intelligible alternative to symbolic violence, or of moral self-determination as the intelligible alternative to the economy of the libido. For it was not the least of Freud's (or Nietzsche's) discoveries that desire (or the will to power) has always embedded itself as a non-intelligible force *within* rational argument and moral consciousness. Let it be noted that this is a *discovery* only if we *start out* with rationalist idealizations. The first point that remains to be resolved is what is to happen with the concepts of the subject, of reason, of autonomy, once they have been released from the rationalist constellations that psychoanalysis has disrupted.

2 The critique of 'instrumental' or 'identitary' reason

Here we are dealing in a certain sense with a *radicalization* of the psychological critique of rationalism. It is something which is already apparent in Nietzsche (and earlier), is radicalized by Adorno and Horkheimer, and continues to exert an influence in French post-structuralism. I should like to confine myself to the version that is sketched in the *Dialectic of Enlightenment* and subsequently developed by Adorno. This is undoubtedly one-sided, but I hope that this narrowing of our topic will also prove productive.

In the *Dialectic of Enlightenment*, following in the footsteps of Klages and Nietzsche, Adorno and Horkheimer interpret the epistemological triad of subject, object and concept as a relationship of suppression and subjugation in which the suppressing instance – the subject – is simultaneously the suppressed victim. The suppression of one's inner nature with its anarchical desire for happiness is the price to be paid for developing a unitary self which was necessary for the sake of self-*preservation* and the control of nature as an external and social phenomenon. The correlate of the unitary self is an objectifying and systematizing ('totalizing') reason, which is thus conceived as a medium of domination – domination over external and social nature as well as the nature within each of us. For Adorno and Horkheimer, much as for Nietzsche and Klages before them, this character of reason as a force which unifies and systematizes, which objectifies and exercises instrumental control is inherent in its discursive character, in the logic of the concept. Or rather, it is inherent in the intimate relationship between concept, linguistic meaning, and formal logic. As we read in the *Dialectic of Enlightenment*, 'The principle of contradiction is the system in a nutshell.'[47] At the heart of discursive thought we thus discover an element of violence, a subjugation of reality, a defence mechanism, a procedure for excluding and controlling, a prearrangement of phenomena for the purpose of controlling and manipulating them, and an incipient system of delusion. This objectifying, systematizing and instrumentalizing reason has found its classical expression in the natural sciences; but as Foucault has shown, the human sciences can also be viewed in the same categories. Ultimately the rationalization processes of the modern age – with its bureaucratization, its formal law, all the formalized institutions of modern societies and economies – are also manifestations of this unifying, objectifying, controlling and disciplining reason.

This brand of reason has its own image of history, namely that of progress as it presents itself in the unceasing technical and economic progress of modern society. Reason (in the person of its proponents) confuses this indisputable progress with the idea of progress to a better state of being; it holds that humanity as a whole is progressing – towards reason. As this play on words suggests, the expectations that the Enlightenment had of reason anticipated something other and something better than mere technical, economic and administrative progress. It looked for the abolition of tyranny and delusion through the abolition of ignorance and poverty. And we only have to look a little beyond the letter – not the spirit – of the *Dialectic of Enlightenment* in order to be able to add that even where the confidence of the Enlightenment has been exposed as a pious illusion (in the post-Kantian philosophy of German Idealism, and in Marx) this only led to the renewed entrenchment of the 'totalitarianism' of reason on a higher plane, namely in a dialectic of history whose rationality was revealed in the terror of Stalinism.

In Adorno and Horkheimer, as I have already indicated, formal logic no longer appears as the organum of truth, but only as a mediating instance between the 'ego principle that founds the system'[48] and the concept which 'prearranges' and 'truncates'.[49] The spirit that brings about conceptual objectivation and systematizes according to the principle of non-contradiction acquires from the outset the character of instrumental reason – by virtue of the very 'splitting of life into the mind and its object'.[50] The critique of identitary reason is thus also a critique of *legitimizing* reason. What is expressed in the closed nature of philosophical systems, just as in the pursuit of philosophical fundamental groundings, is the almost manic striving of 'identificatory thought' after certainty and domination. The legitimation systems of the modern age – from epistemology to political and moral philosophy – contain a remnant of mythical mania transmuted into discursive rationality.

It is, of course, a feature of the *dialectic* of enlightenment that together with myth it also successively destroys all those legitimations which enlightened reason has put in the place of myth, having first identified them as hallucinations. Reason ultimately becomes positivistic and cynical, a mere instrument of domination. In advanced industrial society, reason as an instrument of domination has become condensed into a system of delusion in which the subject, which was once the vehicle of enlightenment, itself becomes superfluous. The individual 'is reduced to the nodal point of the conventional responses and modes of operation expected of him. Animism spiritualized the object, whereas industrialism objectifies the spirits of men.'[51]

As we can see, for Adorno and Horkheimer the unified, disciplined, inner-directed subject is only the complement to instrumental reason in a *temporary* sense; their thesis is not so very different from Foucault's when he pronounces the subject to be a product of modern discourse.[52] For Adorno and Horkheimer, however, the disintegration of the subject in late industrial society signifies a *regressive* development.[53] It thus becomes clear that they do not see 'enlightenment' and 'reason' as entirely subsumed under the destructive dialectic they try to reconstruct. Adorno and Horkheimer cleave to an emphatic concept of enlightenment, which means for them a process of enlightening enlightenment about itself, which is to say, enlightening identitary reason about its own character as an instrument of domination, as well as the 'mindfulness [*Eingedenken*] of nature in the subject'. This in turn means, however, that it would only be possible for enlightenment to correct and transcend itself in its own medium – which is that of identitary reason. This is the sense in which Adorno, in his *Negative Dialectics*, has attempted to pursue the critique of 'identificatory' thought to its final conclusion. There he postulates a philosophy which turns against the reifying tendencies of conceptual thought while remaining within a conceptual medium; the 'striving of the concept' becomes a striving 'by way of the concept, to transcend the concept'.[54] Adorno tried to define this notion more closely in terms of the concept of 'configurative' thought, of a 'transdiscursive' philosophy in other words, of which the most impressive example in his own writings is perhaps the *Minima Moralia*.

It might seem that we have strayed far from the psychological critique of the subject, although I did point out that the critique of identitary reason constituted a radicalization of that critique. I should now like to provide the justification for that assertion. It appears to speak *against* my thesis that Adorno and Horkheimer cleave to the 'unity' of the self, and that they conceive the disintegration of this unified self in late industrial society as a process of *regression*. This objection disappears if we understand the expression 'unified self', not in terms of the autonomous subject which was destroyed by Freud, but – rather more in the manner of Foucault – as the correlate or product of the 'discourse of modernity', namely as a disciplined and disciplining form of the organization of humans as social beings. It is *violence* that stands at the origin of this unified self, and not an act of autonomous self-positing. 'Men had to do fearful things to themselves before the self, the identical, purposive, and virile nature of man, was formed, and something of that recurs in every childhood.'[55] This is a statement to which Freud might also have subscribed. But the radicalization of Freud's critique consists in the fact that

Adorno and Horkheimer call into question that constellation of norms of rationality to which Freud still adhered, namely 'the identical, purposive, and virile nature of man'. For Adorno and Horkheimer that constellation of norms represents a nodal point – like bourgeois society for Marx – through which it is necessary to pass, but which is destined to be sublated in a self-transcendence of reason. From the point of view of the *Dialectic of Enlightenment*, it thus transpires that psychoanalysis contains within its inner recesses something of precisely that rationalism which Freud had so assiduously dismantled in its idealistically reflected form.

It is a rationalism, but – it might be said – it is also a realism. And with regard to this realism of Freud's, Adorno and Horkheimer were unable to explain how it might be possible to conceive of a self-transcendence of reason (in the sense of enlightening enlightenment about itself) as a historical project, having themselves destroyed the Marxist conception of a self-transcendence of (bourgeois) reason with their critique of instrumental reason. If I understand the problem correctly, it was a similar difficulty that confronted Foucault. Adorno goes on to elucidate the self-transcendence of reason by showing how mimesis and rationality are interwoven in philosophy, as in the work of art. But he is only able to construct a connection to social change by interpreting the 'non-violent synthesis' of the work of art and the configurative language of philosophy – aporetically – as a glimmer of messianic light glimpsed in the here and now, an anticipation of reconciliation in the real world. The critique of instrumental reason cannot do without a philosophy of history based on the idea of reconciliation; it needs a utopian perspective because it would cease to be conceivable as a *critique* otherwise. But if history has to become the Other of history in order to escape the system of delusion that is instrumental reason, then the critique of the historical present moment turns into a critique of historical being – the latest form of a theological critique of the earthly vale of tears. The critique of identitary reason seems ultimately to result in a choice between cynicism and theology – unless we wish to argue for a cheerful acceptance of the regression or disintegration of the self without regard for the consequences. This is precisely the alternative direction in which Klages was moving, and which Adorno and Horkheimer wanted to avoid at all costs.

The critique of identitary reason ends in an aporia because it repeats once more that very 'forgetfulness of language' characteristic of European rationalism, which it had itself in a sense criticized. The critique of discursive reason as *instrumental* reason as conceived by Adorno and Horkheimer is still surreptitiously psychological, i.e. intentionalistic; without acknowledging the fact, it still draws on the model of a subject that is 'constitutive of meaning' and posits itself against a world of objects in transcendental singularity. But as I shall show, the critique of identitary logic acquires a different meaning if identitary logic is not only unmasked psychologically, but if we use the methods of linguistic philosophy to investigate it and question its premises. For then it turns out that there is a communicative praxis even at the foundations of instrumental reason which, because it is constitutive of the living existence of linguistic meaning, *cannot* be reduced either to the manifestation of a *self-preserving* subjectivity, or to that of a subjectivity that is *constitutive of meaning*. I should like to add that the *complementary* form of reduction, i.e. the reduction of the subject to the autonomous life of discourses or of linguistic meaning, cannot succeed either. I should like to call the third form of critique of reason and the subject – the form which was developed within the philosophy of language and to which I am now turning – 'Wittgensteinian reflection', because it was in the late writings of Wittgenstein that this approach was formulated in all clarity for the first time.

3 The linguistic critique of the subject-as-constitutive-of-meaning

What we are dealing with here is the philosophical destruction of rationalistic conceptions of the subject and of language, in particular the destruction of the notion that the source of linguistic meaning is the subject with its experiences and intentions. We might speak instead, as Wittgenstein does, of a critique of the 'name theory' of meaning, whereby the notion that is criticized is the one that linguistic signs acquire meaning as a result of someone (a sign-user) assigning a sign to something given (things, classes of things, experiences, classes of experiences, etc.) and thus assigning a name to a meaning that is somehow 'given'. A name theory of meaning such as this appears to be deeply rooted in the consciousness – or at least the pre-consciousness –

of Western philosophy. It is a theory which continues to exert its influence especially in the area of radical empiricism down as far as Russell. I call this theory of language 'rationalistic' because it is based – explicitly or implicitly – on the primacy of a subject that gives the name and is constitutive of meaning, and because it participates willy-nilly in idealizations characteristic of the rationalist tradition – especially the objectification of meanings as something 'objectively existing' – which extend beyond the customary distinctions between rationalism and empiricism. Of course, the philosophical critique of the rationalist theory of language neither begins nor ends with Wittgenstein, but I believe that in a certain sense Wittgenstein was the most important exponent of it in our century. Wittgenstein's way of doing philosophy incorporates a new form of scepticism which even casts doubt on the certainties of Hume or Descartes. His sceptical question runs, 'How can I know what I am talking about? How can I know what I mean?'[56] What is destroyed by the critique conducted by the philosophy of language is the subject as author and ultimate arbiter of its own intentions.

It might be objected at this point that the critique to which I am referring is an old topic of hermeneutics as well as structuralism. In a certain sense this objection is correct. But since the consequences which each of these schools has drawn from the critique of an intentionalist theory of meaning are so radically different from each other, I should like to base my argument here on the more rigorous form of critical reflection upon language as we find it in Wittgenstein. I shall also refer to the thoughts of Castoriadis,[57] which can be understood on several central points as reformulations and developments of Wittgenstein's insights, even if they are derived from a different tradition.

In order to avoid from the outset any positivistic reduction of the subject we are dealing with, I would stress that we have not expressed the really important thing about it if we merely point out that linguistic sign-systems have primacy over the speech and intentions of subjects and are what make them possible in the first place. This discovery, taken on its own, contains the germ of a new mystification of the 'signitive relation'. The crucial point is rather the clarification of the signitive relation inherent within linguistic codes or 'language games' – a 'relation' which philosophy before Wittgenstein appears hardly to have countenanced. Wittgenstein's most important concepts in this connection are those of the 'rule' and the 'language game'; or rather, what is important is the new philosophical use which Wittgenstein makes of these concepts. The rules in question must not be confused with what is commonly understood by rules, whether these be regulative or constitutive; and language games here are not games, but life-forms, ensembles of linguistic and non-linguistic activities, institutions, practices and the meanings 'incorporated' within them. The 'interweaving' of the concepts of 'rule' and 'meaning' is shown in the fact that rules signify an intersubjective praxis for which someone has to be *trained*, in the fact that meanings are essentially *open*, and that if we speak of *the* meaning of a linguistic utterance, then this 'identity' of meaning must be provided with an index of otherness, both with respect to the relationship between language and reality and with respect to that between speaker and speaker. Meanings thus become dissolved as objects in their own right, as given entities, whether in an ideal or psychological sense, or in reality. But even if we understand meaning in terms of a relation – 'x means Y' or 'x signifies y' – then it turns out that this is a singular kind of relation which, as Castoriadis has emphasized, does not have 'a place in inherited logic-ontology'.[58] For even the simplest 'designating relation' (such as that which 'links' the word 'tree' with real trees) does not only presuppose a system of semantic relation within a language, without which it would be totally unable to function *as* a designating relation; rather it is impossible to explain this designating relation unless one has already presupposed it. But what we are presupposing here is the command of a rule which is founded in nothing other than the praxis of its own application to a class of cases which is in principle open – so that the designating relation is in reality the very essence of this praxis and not a relation between two relata that are somehow 'given' independently of each other. Castoriadis expresses the point like this:

> This co-belonging, which can be termed signitive co-belonging to distinguish it from 'objective' or 'real' co-belonging, obviously cannot exist without (for it circularly implies) the operative schema of the *rule*: x *must* be used to designate y and not z, y *must* be designated by x and not by t. This *must* (*Sollen*) is a sheer fact: its violation, as such, entails no logical contradiction, no ethical violation, no aesthetic ugliness. . . . It cannot be 'founded' on

anything other than itself. Not only can no particular signitive relation be 'founded' (it can, at most, be partially 'explained' or 'justified' on a *second* level) but the signitive relation as such and the rule that it implies circularly can themselves be founded only on the necessities of *legein*: there must be an approximately univocal rule of designation if *legein* is to exist, and there must be *legein* if a rule such as this is to exist.[59]

The linguistic critique of the subject, like its psychological counterpart, leads to the discovery of an 'Other of reason' *within* reason itself. But it is a *different* 'Other of reason' in either instance. The psychological destruction of the subject was concerned with the discovery of libidinous forces (or social power) within reason, but the destruction of subjectivism by linguistic philosophy is concerned with the discovery of a quasi-fact which pre-exists all intentionality and subjectivity, i.e. the discovery of linguistic systems of meaning, of life-forms, of a world disclosed in a particular way through language. Here we are not dealing with a world without subjects, without a human self; rather we are dealing with a world in which human beings, in various ways, might or might not 'be themselves'. It is possible to interpret this prior commonality of a world disclosed through language as a prior 'accord', provided that we do not conceive this in terms of 'conventions', or of 'consensuses', which might be either rational or irrational. It is much rather an accord which is constitutive of the possibility of distinguishing between true and false, between reasonable and unreasonable. (Wittgenstein, *Philosophical Investigations*, paras 241 and 242: '"So you are saying that human agreement decides what is true and what is false?" – It is what human beings *say* that is true and false; and they agree in the *language* they use. That is not agreement in opinions but in form of life. – If language is to be a means of communication there must be agreement not only in definitions but also (queer as this may sound) in judgments. This seems to abolish logic, but does not do so.')

Neither structuralist objectivism nor neo-structuralist scepticism does justice to Wittgenstein's basic insight: the former fails because it ignores the pragmatic dimension of a signitive relation that is essentially open and not objectifiable; the latter because it relates the openness and non-objectifiability of linguistic meanings to the uncontrollable non-identity of each *individual* use of a sign. But the life of linguistic meaning can neither be reduced to the anonymous life of linguistic codes, nor can it be attributed to an indeterminate play of differences. The first half of this thesis is not something for which I can provide a justification here; as far as the second half is concerned, I shall content myself with a few indications of how it might be justified. The position I am criticizing might be expressed in the thesis that – as Manfred Frank has put it – 'on the basis of the structural possibility of repetition . . . the use of any linguistic type carries an index of indeterminate change'.[60] This is, of course, aimed at Derrida.[61] Now I find myself convinced by Derrida's critique of an objectivistic interpretation of linguistic meanings: the identity of meanings is first of all constituted in the chain of uses to which signs are put; both the possibility of an irreducible plurality of ways of using words, and also the infinite potential of linguistic sense to shift and expand, are features of the existence of linguistic meaning. But only if an intentionalist perspective is presupposed can we assert that each *individual* use of a sign carries an index of indeterminate otherness. If, on the other hand, we genuinely question this intentionalist perspective, then such an assertion is reduced to a play with the words 'identity' and 'non-identity' which, so to speak, lacks the firm ground of a meaningful use of the word 'meaning'. The point of Wittgenstein's thoughts on the subject was, precisely, that the word 'meaning' points to the practice of a common use of language; what we call a *single* meaning can only be elucidated by recourse to a – real or potential – *plurality* of situations in which a linguistic sign is used. The common practice in question is admittedly only discernible from the performative attitude of participants; the comprehension of meanings, intentions or texts cannot be reconstructed as a knowledge of objective (signitive) facts, nor can the act of 'comprehending' or 'meaning' itself be understood as an objectifiable psychological fact. An objectivist way of looking at things can only lead to a radical hermeneutical scepticism here, which can only result ultimately in the dissolution of the very concept of meaning. There is no answer to the question, 'How do you know what you mean?' as long as we try to answer it from the same objectivist perspective from which it is put.

> The sceptical argument, then, remains unanswered. There can be no such thing as meaning anything by any word. Each new application we make is a leap in the dark; any present intention

could be interpreted so as to accord with anything we may choose to do. So there can be neither accord, nor conflict.[62]

This is how S. Kripke tries to reformulate the *problem* which confronted Wittgenstein. But Wittgenstein's *solution* of the problem, as Kripke shows, does not really consist in answering the sceptical question, but in fending off the objectivistic approach that underlies it. The question can only be answered if we consider what role the ascribing of meanings, intentions or 'understanding' plays in our language. The resolution of the sceptical paradox requires a change of perspective. By reminding us of the grammar of the words 'meaning', 'to mean' and 'to understand', Wittgenstein also makes it clear that from the point of view of participants in the language game, radical hermeneutic scepticism has no basis.[63]

What I want to say is that the word 'meaning' points to the concept of a rule or a *mode* of application. That is why it makes no sense to say that in every 'repetition' of a linguistic sign an indeterminate displacement of meaning takes place; for after all, 'It is not possible that there should have been only one occasion on which someone obeyed a rule.'[64] But for the same reason it is not possible to gain control of the 'anarchy of meaning' by the unmediated reintroduction of an 'interpreting' subject in the way that M. Frank has tried to do as a *counter* to Derrida. Frank's counterthesis to Derrida, namely that 'human beings arrive at the meanings of the signs they use *by* subjecting them to specific interpretations in particular situations (and never on a once-for-all basis)', is not a way out of the position of the hermeneutic sceptic; it looks much rather like a repetition of premises which that scepticism had destroyed. For if we assume that linguistic signs only acquire their specific meaning through an act of interpretation, then we are surreptitiously falling back on a position that makes 'what I mean' the source of meanings. It then appears incomprehensible how what I mean could ever be understood by someone *else*; indeed, it appears incomprehensible how I myself could understand it. The role of the 'interpreting subject' and the openness of linguistic meanings can really only be understood if we conceive the unpredictable change and extension of linguistic sense, as we apply grammatical rules to it, as carrying an index of generality. For that which changes – i.e. linguistic meanings – itself bears such an index of generality. The new application of a word indicates a new *mode* of application.

Linguistic philosophy decentres the subject, but in doing so it provides no legitimation for either hermeneutic objectivism or hermeneutic anarchism. Still less does it justify the irrational consequences that are occasionally drawn by postmodern thinkers. Linguistic philosophy cannot simply be short-circuited with a psychological critique of the subject. To decentre the subject philosophically – as opposed to psychologically – does not offend our narcissism; rather it means the discovery of a common and previously 'disclosed' world within reason and the subject (within all *possible* forms of the subject). But this common, linguistically disclosed world is not made of such stuff as could be explained in terms of the economy of the libido or a will to power. The body, the will to power, desire are *present* in this world – but as something that is linguistically disclosed and always to be linguistically disclosed anew. Violence is also present in this world, but it too is linguistically disclosed, and thus only ever present as something distinguished from its own Other, i.e. from non-violent communication, from dialogue, from the openness of human relations, from voluntary co-operation. In a certain sense we have to explain words, as Wittgenstein said that we should, in terms of their normal use; for then it becomes clear that the philosophy of total unmasking is fed by the same rationalistic metaphysics that it claims to be destroying. If, on the other hand, we bring the distinctions between reality and semblance, between truthfulness and lying, between violence and dialogue, between autonomy and heteronomy back down to earth from heaven, so to speak – and it is only on earth that they can be located – then it would no longer be possible to assert (other than in the sense of a bad metaphysics) that the will to truth is *in itself* a will to power; that dialogue *as such* is symbolic violence; that speech that is orientated towards truth *is* terror; that moral consciousness *as such* is a reflex of internalized violence; or that the autonomous human being *as such* is *either* a fiction *or* a mechanism of auto-suppression *or* a bastard of patriarchy, etc. In other words, the linguistic critique of rationalism and subjectivism does provide an opportunity for thinking in new ways about 'truth', 'justice' or 'self-determination'; but at the same time it will make us suspicious of those who want to give an affirmative twist, in the manner of Nietzsche, to the psychological critique of the subject – by which I mean those propagandists of a new era which shall have cast off the burden of the Platonic heritage, and in which rhetoric shall replace argument, the will to power shall replace the will to truth, the art of words shall replace theory, and the economy of desire shall replace morality. We have quite enough of all *that* to contend with, after all, in the world as it is now.

VI Development (3): Towards a Metacritique of the Critique of Identitary Reason

Linguistic philosophy has decentred the subject and criticized the objectification of linguistic meanings, and by doing so it has also destroyed the premises upon which the philosophy of consciousness was able to interpret the unity of the subject and the 'identificatory' concept as the two poles of a 'reifying' spirit which is instrumental in its very origins. It remains to be shown, however, what consequences this destruction of the *premises* of the philosophy of consciousness has for a critique of identificatory thought itself. For Adorno, as for Nietzsche before him, the *proton pseudos* of discursive reason lay in the generality of concepts, in the fact that they 'identify' things which 'do not go by the same name'. As he says in *Negative Dialectics*, the 'semblance' of identity 'is inherent in thought itself, in its pure form'.[65] The 'pure form' of thought, however, is grounded in the generality of the concept, which 'prearranges' and 'truncates' in the way that Adorno describes.[66] Now, the 'rigidity' of the general concept, as Adorno describes it, itself remains in a certain sense a rationalistic fiction. Wittgenstein pointed out that, as a rule, the grammar of our language shows us that words can be used in many and various ways, without our always being able to hit upon a 'fundamental', 'authentic' or 'primary' meaning of words. Wittgenstein uses the image of 'family resemblance', and also that of the rope that consists of a multiplicity of individual fibres, in order to indicate how the various ways of using a word are interrelated. This multiplicity of ways of using a word reflects that 'openness' of linguistic meanings to which I referred earlier. We might even say that there is a mimetic force at work in the life of linguistic meaning, a force which enables what is non-identical in reality – as Adorno would say – to be reflected as something non-identical in linguistic meanings. Thus – to express the point paradoxically – the ability to 'exclude' what is different depends upon the ability to 'include' it. Adorno himself saw language as possessing such a mimetic force, otherwise he would not have been able to demand of philosophy that it strive 'by means of the concept, to transcend the concept'.[67] *In a certain sense*, this seemingly paradoxical demand is always fulfilled by language – or rather, by those who speak that language. But if this is the case, then the demand for a reflexive, non-reifying, 'inclusive' use of language acquires a less paradoxical and despairing character than it has in Adorno's writings. It comes closer, as it were, to something that we might cautiously circumscribe with words like 'judgement', 'imagination', or even 'reason', without necessarily having to conjure up a utopia of reconciliation as we do so.

This is admittedly only an outline of a metacritique which remains to be filled in. It cannot be our purpose to deny the weight of the *problems* which lay at the base of Adorno's critique of identificatory thought; the point is rather to see these problems correctly. The correct form for a metacritique of Adorno's critique of the concept would be a reformulation of the problems which provided the motive force for Adorno's philosophizing. In what follows, I should like at least to give some indications of how this might be done.

What we need to understand – or rather, the thing whose latent sense we have to decipher – is what Adorno means when he speaks of 'the non-identical' as something which is reduced to a mere example, is 'prearranged', or has its integrity violated by the generality of the concept. As Adorno conceives it, this 'violation' of the 'non-identical' by the concept also constitutes the *untruth* of the conceptual judgement. He takes on board the paradox that what we normally call 'true', namely linguistic propositions, is at the same time supposed to be 'untrue'. But not only does this mean that the *emphatic* concept of truth, which Adorno – by contrast with Nietzsche – brings into play *against* the truth of propositions, can no longer be set in any obvious connection with what we call truth; it also means that we are unable to *say* in what way the general concept does an injustice to the individual particular – unless we wanted to say no more than that because of the general nature of the meanings of words, a linguistic sign does not *itself* express the *specific* circumstances in which the particular sign is used. However, it is only possible to see in this a *falsification* of reality and – as Adorno sees it – an *injustice* towards the particular, if we try to understand the dialectic of the universal and the particular as it goes on *within* the life of linguistic meaning from outside, so to speak, by interpreting it, for example, in the sense of a 'tool theory' of language, as if words really were ideational 'tools' with which we can 'get a grip on' reality, as we read in the *Dialectic of Enlightenment*.[68] If we apply the metaphors of 'prearranging' and 'truncating' to language as a whole, then they reveal an intentionalist prejudgement about language; in fact they reveal, as can easily be seen, a naturalistic variant of the philosophy of the subject-as-constitutive-of-meaning.

It is not the aporetic and paradoxical nature of Adorno's basic idea that makes it appear questionable, but the fact that in terms of linguistic philosophy it contains a residue of naïvety. It is true that Adorno recognized and repeatedly emphasized that philosophy cannot adopt a position outside language from which to formulate a critique of conceptual thought; but the very idea of a critique of *the* identificatory concept presupposes such a position outside language. Adorno's philosophy is a running up against the limits of language – or more precisely, of the language of the *philosophy of the subject*. It expresses the secret of the philosophy of the subject, but without comprehending it. For it was no coincidence that for the philosophy of the subject, from Kant to early Wittgenstein, it was mathematical physics that provided the paradigm of cognition of the real world. There is an internal relationship between theory and technique, between cognition and action, which is inherent in the grammar of physical theories; and it is consistently assumed by the critique of identificatory thought that this relationship is characteristic of general concepts as such, and thus also of discursive reason. This is how it can appear that, because of its 'identificatory' character, thought – and with it the normal use of language – necessarily does the same violence to the social and historical reality of human existence that it does to nature by capturing it in a network of nomological relations, *and* that it does indeed do violence to nature itself. It is this basic constellation of ideas that explains the perspective of reconciliation in Adorno's philosophy, and also the irresolvable aporias of his philosophy. Adorno can only conceive of the better Other of the instrumental spirit as a world beyond discursive reason, and he can only conceive of a non-violent organization of society in terms of nature as a whole achieving a state of redemption.

The 'mindfulness [*Eingedenken*] of nature in the subject', as demanded in the *Dialectic of Enlightenment*,[69] is not enough to demystify the idealistic philosophy of the subject. It is only through the mindfulness of *language* in the subject that we can escape the thrall of the philosophy of the subject; this is what renders visible the communicative praxis which is fundamental to the life of linguistic meaning, whereas the 'representing', 'judging', conceptually 'identifying' and instrumental acting subject only provides a silhouette of that praxis.[70] To say this is to remove the basis for a critique of the 'identificatory' concept. If we want to speak seriously of a connection between the 'truncating' or 'violent' and 'untrue' character of linguistic judgements and their generality, then we can only treat it as a problem *within* language. The capacity to 'prearrange' and 'truncate' would then be attributable not to the general concept as such, but to a specific *usage* of general concepts; and what is 'untrue' in such linguistic usage would have to be understood as untruth *in* the language (and not as untruth *by virtue of* the use of language). It is possible to reformulate (and differentiate) Adorno's philosophy accordingly, by understanding the 'violent' aspect of identificatory thought in the sense of *specific* blockages, pathologies or perversions of linguistic communication or social praxis. Then, and only then, does it become possible to comprehend the sense in which the integrity of something 'non-identical' is *violated* or the specificity of a phenomenon is *obscured* by the general nature of linguistic meanings. Only if we retrieve Adorno's notion of the 'non-identical' from the world beyond language, so to speak, and place it within the horizon of intersubjective linguistic praxis, does it become clear when and in what sense the disproportionality between the general and the particular *can*, in individual instances, signify a 'violation' or 'prearrangement' of the non-identical, and what specific disturbances, blockages or limitations of communication can find expression in such disproportionality. But to the extent that we succeed in *naming* the 'injustice' that is done to the particular in specific instances by the 'reifying' use of linguistic clichés or generalizations, we shall also implicitly have named those resources within language on which we can draw in order to enable the particular to come into its own. For purposes of clarification I should like to cite three examples (or types of example) in which the problem of disproportionality between the general and the particular presents itself in various ways.

1 The experience of speechlessness in the face of one's own experience

The limits to the faculty of speech and communication which we encounter here are certainly connected with the generality and intersubjectivity of linguistic meanings, which on the other hand constitute the precondition for the possibility of linguistic communication (including communication with oneself). We might even speak here of a speechlessness of language itself; Adorno undoubtedly has something similar in mind when he speaks of the disproportionality between intuition and concept. This is also apparent from the immense importance that Adorno attaches to all forms of literary usage and aesthetic objectivation as *correctives* of the discursive use of language. Poetic, literary, rhetorical and 'configurative' uses of language represent productive extensions of the faculty of speech by means of which the ineffable becomes expressible and that which is locked within the muteness of individual experience becomes accessible and communicable. Here we really are dealing with a *paradoxical* aspect of what language accomplishes, for in entering into the arena of public communication, the successful linguistic expression also becomes *more* than an *individual expression*; it opens up a piece of *common* reality. Here too, as in the Wittgensteinian example of the expression of sensations, the 'non-identical' aspect of experience becomes communicable by virtue of becoming intersubjective, and thus *alienated* from its own private nature. 'Running up against the limits of language', in art as in the most trivial manifestations of our productive speech faculty, is the answer to the recurring problem of the speechlessness of language. But in language, which is to say, in the faculty of speech, both things are contained: the possibility of becoming empty of meaning and falling silent, as well as the possibility of renewing and extending meaning. Only if, like Adorno, we conceive the transcendence of speechlessness in messianic terms, as the acquisition of a 'true language' in which 'content itself is revealed',[71] do we have to regard the resources within language, which *recurrently* enable us – with greater or lesser success – to transcend the speechlessnes of language, as hopelessly inadequate. The point at issue is not that our language, *sub specie aeternitatis*, is hopelessly inadequate, but whether this is capable of yielding a correct conception of how our language works in reality and what its possibilities are.

Speechlessness in the face of one's own experience is also speechlessness in the face of reality. To this extent, the productive powers of speech to which I referred also have a significance for the description of reality, for moral discourse or philosophical argument. Adorno, like no other, has drawn attention to the significance which 'expression' and 'presentation' have for philosophy, in other words that there is an 'aesthetic moment' which is 'not accidental to philosophy'.[72] But since Adorno only poses the problems in terms of a polarity between 'subject' and 'object', he cannot convey the various forms in which problems of presentation and problems of truth are interrelated. The next two examples are intended to clarify *differences* of this kind.

2 The 'prearranging' and 'truncating' use of language, and the interconnection between un*truth* and in*justice*

We find a suggestive description of the problem in Thomas Bernhard's story 'Wittgenstein's Nephew':

> The so-called psychiatric consultants came up with one term or another for my friend's illness, without having the courage to admit that there was no correct term for *this* illness, or for any other illness, and that all terms were *necessarily* false, necessarily misleading, since, like all other doctors, they were ultimately trying to make things easier and, in a murderous way, more convenient for themselves *by always applying the wrong term to illnesses.* They were forever using the word *manic*, forever using the word *depressive*, and every time it was wrong. They were forever taking refuge (like all other doctors!) in yet another scientific word for the sake of their own protection and security (not the patient's).[73]

I chose this short extract from Bernhard because its meaning is elusive enough to permit associations in a great variety of directions. We might begin by saying that Bernhard describes a psychiatric practice which is *uncritical* from the cognitive point of view and *inhuman* from the point of view of therapy. Psychiatric technical terms are being used in order to objectivize and classify human beings as cases, and to fit them into the routine of medical treatment. 'They were forever taking refuge . . . in yet another scientific word'. This makes us think of a lack of specialist competence being glossed over with a casual application of diagnostic terms as labels, in order to defend the doctors' own authority perhaps or merely for the sake of their ('murderous') convenience, which will not let the difficulty of individual cases interfere with the smooth-running routine. (Clearly we did not have to invoke instances of bad psychiatry in order to develop this line of thought.) The doctors in our example have made it 'in a murderous way more convenient for themselves'; this means that their incompetence and their convenience have 'murderous' consequences. Instead of protecting the patient, instead of helping him or involving themselves with his case, they are protecting themselves. The terms they apply to illnesses are *false* in the final analysis because they *use* those terms uncritically and for purposes of self-protection. This falseness is part of a false praxis; and the praxis is false because it contradicts the nature of the doctor's task. Within such a false praxis *all* descriptive terms are false because they are *all* falsely used.

Psychiatry and medicine are of course random examples (though presumably not for Bernhard); we might just as easily have taken examples from the areas of justice, bureaucracy, or everyday brutality and stupidity. But let us keep to the example of psychiatry. It is conceivable that the technical jargon of psychiatry could be used *differently*, so that terms like 'manic' or 'depressive' (or indeed better terms) did not represent the *end* of an attempt at classification, but the *beginning* of therapeutic involvement. Whereas in the former case the technical jargon would be used like the terminology for classifying fruit or vegetables which are being sorted for storage purposes, in the latter case they would represent initial suppositions about the character and aetiology of an affliction which serve to guide the imagination of the therapist in a particular direction; and in this case the classification would be placed in the service of a provisional orientation of a therapeutic process, the ultimate *aim* of which is that the patient should master his *concrete* personal history. It is not possible to tell from the words (or sentences) themselves whether they are being used in the one way or the other. But only when they are being used in the second (correct) way do the conditions obtain which make it possible to ask questions about the truth or falsehood of statements and suppositions in the *correct* way, so to speak.

By varying the 'experimental conditions' slightly (albeit in a way that has profound moral implications) we might move from the consideration of people or illnesses to the classification of socio-cultural phenomena such as works of art. There is a way of using categories of form or style which has much in common with the use of technical terminology or clichés in a dismissive, labelling fashion in social life. The concept of sonata form, for instance, can be used to pigeon-hole everything from Haydn to Beethoven and Schubert; but it is equally possible to differentiate the concept historically, along with other categories of music theory, and make productive use of it for purposes of individual analysis – as Adorno demonstrated in incomparable fashion. But instead of following the strands of association that lead from here to questions of social and cultural science, let me return once more to the example of psychiatry. As Bernhard uses the word 'false', it is reminiscent of Adorno's description of 'identificatory thought' as *untrue* to the extent that it *violates* the non-identical. In our example, the non-identical is represented by individual human beings with their personal case histories; and a violation takes place to the extent that they are being denied communicative attention, and that their opportunity of 'regaining' themselves is being truncated. These people are being 'reified', reduced to mere examples, dismissed. This is how the doctors behave in Bernhard's story, and, as Bernhard puts it, so do 'all other doctors'. It is not Bernhard's enraged and unjust generalizations that should interest us here, of course. But the generalizing phrase can be read as an indication that reifying practices in modern society present themselves in the form of *institutions* (and, of course, not only in psychiatry). As institutionalized practices they acquire an opaque potency which, as it were, surpasses questions of moral responsibility. 'All doctors' – this no longer means people behaving falsely as individuals, but members of an institution who are performing their preordained role (Marx would have called them 'character masks'). We might speak – in order not to lose sight of our example – of an institutionalization of false linguistic usage. But in the modern age, institutionalizations of this kind are linked to forms of systematic production of knowledge, i.e. to the institutionalized discourse of the empirical sciences. In order to capture all the connotations of the word 'false' as Bernhard uses it, then, we also have to discuss the sciences which provide the cognitive frame for reifying practices. This leads us back to Adorno. For Adorno, reifying *practices* in modern society are inextricably linked to the reification of people by *science*. A science of humanity is 'reifying' if its methodological ideal is derived from physics; because this means that the same relationship between 'knowledge' and 'technique' is built into its method of inquiry that we find in the logical grammar of the theories of physics. If we imagine – to take a hypothetical example – a science of psychiatry that conceives itself in this way, then we should find the same denial of communication built into the *language* and the *techniques* of psychiatry that Bernhard lays at the door of the doctors. In this case, Bernhard's use of the term 'false' would have to be understood, not in the sense of a false use of psychiatric terminology which was in itself meaningful, but as the description of a scientific language which was false because the reification of the patients was necessarily implied by the rules for its normal use.

What I want to say is this: Bernhard's text prompts us to think of various ways in which language might be used inappropriately, and in which the *untruth* of statements is associated with the *injustice* of actions and attitudes. 'Identificatory thought' is linked here with a *denial* of communication and a *violation* of personal integrity. It would of course not be possible to conceive of such a relationship between 'untruth' and 'injustice' if the respective 'objects' of investigation were not also 'given' to us as potential co-subjects of linguistic communication.[74] In the final analysis we only have access to social and psychological facts through the performative attitude of *participants* in a communicative process. This is not only the source of the limits to a potential objectivation of social and psychological phenomena, it is also the reason why a false use of general concepts (or a use of false general concepts) can present itself on the level of statements as *untruth*, and on the level of actions and attitudes as a *violation* of the 'non-identical'. I am not concerned at this point with the philosophical justification of an alternative to empiricist philosophy of science. All I want to say is that we can only take the view that a critique of 'reifying' linguistic usage, along the lines that I have *indicated* here, compels us to pass beyond the *concept* in its 'normal sense' if, like Adorno, we take the view that the 'physicalism' of a non-communicative objectivation of reality is inherent in the conditions for linguistic representation of reality. But in fact we are not so compelled; we are compelled only to pass beyond a dogmatically constrained interpretation of language or science.

3 The compulsion to systematize and the 'rage' towards all
that is non-identical[75] as blocks to reflection

The principle of contradiction, as we read already in the *Dialectic of Enlightenment*, is 'the system in a nutshell'. The 'semblance of identity' which, according to Adorno, is inherent within conceptual thought, is also the semblance of an order of things that is produced by the compulsion of conceptual thought to systematize. Adorno understands this compulsion to systematize in psychological terms: he sees it as the correlate of the 'ego-principle', of the compulsion to develop a unitary sense of self. It is a compulsion which makes everything non-identical, everything that is incommensurable, everthing that does not fit, appear threatening; rage and fear are the typical forms of reaction to the experience of the non-identical. Defence mechanisms have to be erected against the non-identical; it has to be repressed (as in the process of socialization), declared to be taboo (as in primitive societies),[76] denied (as in all kinds of dogmatism), or even physically eliminated.

The view that the process of rationalization in the modern world is also largely a process of *systematization* is familiar to us from the writings of Max Weber – systematization, moreover, on the level of knowledge as much as of action. Adorno took over this idea of a connection between rationality and system, with its theoretical and practical implications, from Weber, but in a certain sense he inverted the image, emphasizing the manic aspect of the compulsion to systematize. Adorno finds this manic quality not only in the systems of paranoiacs, in ideological 'world-views' or in the bureaucratic passion for order; he also detects a manic or compulsive element even in philosophical systems. Adorno's critique of 'identificatory thought' turns into a critique of totalizing reason, and his own philosophy becomes an attempt to wrestle himself free of the systematizing compulsion of conceptual thought.

It is only within the framework of a one-dimensional subject–object model, however, that it is plausible to make the discursive nature of conceptual thought responsible for the rigidity of the system. As Adorno uses it, the term 'discursive' is conceived monologically: he thinks of justification and argument according to the model of a deductive relationship between statements. That is why he is bound to interpret those idealizations which are fundamental to formal logic – i.e. the idealizing assumption of 'rigid' meanings – as a property peculiar to concepts themselves. He sees the rigidity of the deductive system as something inherent in the general concept as such. But Adorno's *psychological* explanations of the compulsion to systematize are more convincing than his attempts to explain it in terms of the *logic of concepts*. The decentring of the subject by linguistic philosophy obliges us, amongst other things, to the view that the discursive nature of conceptual thought cannot be adequately characterized in terms of a deductive relationship between statements. Argumentation does not only entail a moving back and forth between concept and object, it also entails moving back and forth between one concept of an object and another. Argumentation, which by definition implies a plurality of subjects (even where it takes the form of internalized reflections), not only does not possess the linearity of deductive relationships between statements, it also lacks the stability of 'rigid' meanings. To the extent that points of view, attitudes and linguistic usages collide and are called into question in argument, argument acquires a dimension that makes it 'constitutive of meaning', and it comes to provide a reflexive form for the life of linguistic meaning. What I mean to say is that although an 'identitary' dimension is essential to the nature of argument (as indeed to all speech), we have not understood the specifically reasonable quality of argument if we reduce it to this identitary dimension. This is precisely what has become apparent in recent discussions of scientific theory; even the rationality of scientific progress as epitomized in physics cannot be understood in terms of a formal model of argumentative rationality. To this extent it would be correct to reproach Adorno with having uncritically adopted a rationalistic concept of discursive reason; only because this is so does his critique of *totalizing* reason turn into a critique of *discursive* reason.

It follows from what I have said above that the 'rage at the non-identical' which expresses itself in the 'compulsion to systematize' is not an *expression* of discursive rationality, but that it indicates a *lack* of discursive rationality. This lack of discursive rationality manifests itself as an incapacity for experience and as the blocking of argument. I spoke of a blocking of *reflection* because this expression combines the incapacity for *experience* (in the sense of 'engaging' with the subject in question or with reality) with the incapacity for self-*revision*. The rigid system corresponds to a rigid ego; on this point, I believe, Adorno was correct. But we do not have to go beyond discursive reason in order to conceive of a 'coherence' beyond the compulsion to systematize, or of a form of individuation beyond the compulsory form of a rigid ego-identity, as Adorno tried to do.[77] The normative perspective of an *unforced* unity is much rather inherent in the linguistic foundations of discursive reason.

Adorno's concept of discursive reason is like the image of reason as it was depicted by the Enlightenment after it had gone through a scientistic narrowing of its perspectives – except that Adorno has inverted the image. Whereas the scientistic Enlightenment derived its affirmative image of reason from the paradigm of mathematics and mathematical physics, these provide Adorno with a paradigm of rationality which reifies, *as* discursive rationality. With the decentring of the subject by linguistic philosophy, however, both 'thesis' *and* 'antithesis' equally lose their justification. By the same token this means that formal logic, mathematics and physics are also demythologized (or de-demonized). For their own rationality does not match the image that a scientistic Enlightenment fashioned of it. Mathematics and physics, too, are tied to systems of linguistic signs, the meanings of which can only develop, stabilize and alter within the medium of communicative praxis; they, too, are practices with 'fuzzy edges', as is *shown* in controversies about their foundations. It is true that physics is the prototype of an *objectivizing* way of thinking. By 'constructing' and investigating reality as a network of nomological relationships, it also opens reality up as a field of potential instrumental intervention and technical control. But *as* an objectivizing way of thinking, physics is unable to take account of its non-objectivizing foundations, of its basis in an historical praxis. Just as formal logic abstracts from the life of linguistic meaning, so too does physics abstract from the communicative dimension of human praxis. To a certain extent it *is* knowledge of reality from the point of view of a singular subject, hence its central role in modern philosophy of the subject. But it is not in physics, but in the philosophy of the subject that scientism resides; the critique of identificatory thinking is in a certain sense simply an inversion of scientism. It reproaches the concept for something which metaphysics, in its forgetfulness of language, has turned it into. The fact that for Adorno, as for the early Wittgenstein, what really matters cannot be said (although Adorno also says that philosophy must insist, *contra* Wittgenstein, on 'saying the unsayable'[78]) is connected with the fact that under the premises of a philosophy of the subject the subject, which forms the 'limit' of the physically objectifiable world,[79] cannot also be a part of that world. Thus the attempt to pass beyond the boundaries of the instrumental spirit becomes an aporetic 'striving' of philosophy 'by means of the concept, to transcend the concept'.[80] That which in 'true' reason goes beyond instrumental reason – Adorno calls it 'mimesis' – he can only conceive of as being extraterritorial to the sphere of conceptual thought. When linguistic philosophy decentres the subject, by contrast, it shows that there is a communicative–mimetic dimension *at the heart* of discursive reason – which is always more than just formal logic, instrumental reason, or a compulsion to systematize. This is why it requires only an unleashing of the potential *within* it to restrain the claims of instrumental reason and dispel the semblance of false totalizations.

The linguistic critique of subjectivism makes it possible to differentiate the critique of identitary reason, and thus to relativize it. What is left is the kernel of the critique of identificatory thought, which it is not possible to relativize metacritically, and which concerns the position of philosophy itself. Adorno's characterization of philosophy in terms of a 'striving, by means of the concept, to transcend the concept' remains valid in *one* respect even if Adorno's concept of the 'identificatory' concept has been called into question. The point I mean is one on which Adorno's thinking accords with that of Wittgenstein – of the later Wittgenstein, that is. Here we are no longer dealing with the utopian perspective of a transdiscursive reason, but the 'oblique' nature of philosophical discourse, namely the relationship between 'saying' and 'showing' in philosophy. Philosophy presents that which eludes the medium of linguistic presentation; not because the particular retreats before the generality of the concept, but because the relationship between the particular and the general – the connection between language and world – itself becomes the theme of philosophy. At the same time we are concerned in philosophy with the question of how we are to understand ourselves, *as* speaking beings. Alongside the connection between language and world, the problem of rationality is the most important philosophical topic. The purpose of philosophy, however, is neither to prove the validity of assertions about reality, nor to provide justification for rules of behaviour, but to dispel confusion, to recall what is generally known (Wittgenstein), or to be mindful of what we have forgotten (Adorno). The kind of understanding that philosophy aims for is a matter of 'getting one's bearings' in what we are doing with language and what we are through language. All philosophical descriptions, explanations, arguments and presentations serve this purpose. But these descriptions, explanations, arguments and presentations make use of an objectivizing language which is inadequate to the subject in hand because that is something which cannot be objectivized – any more than can linguistic meanings, which do not just happen to have become the central topic of contemporary philosophy. This should not be taken to mean that philosophical statements are in reality all false or nonsensical; what it means is rather that the correct use of philosophical statements is an oblique one. Philosophical statements have fulfilled their purpose if they have enabled us to see things correctly. They are trying to *show* what they are *saying*. *This* is why, as Adorno says, 'the presentation of philosophy is not an external matter of indifference to it but immanent to its idea;[81] *this* is why philosophy is 'essentially . . . not expoundable',[82] and *this* is why philosophy misconstrues itself if it thinks of itself in terms of a philosophical system (if this means a cognitive system in the literal sense).[83] In philosophy we really do come up against a boundary of the concept, as Adorno said, but only because in doing philosophy we are operating at the frontiers of language; we are neither wholly inside language nor, as we might like to be, outside its boundaries.

I have investigated the critique of 'identitary' and 'totalizing' reason with reference to Adorno because he seems to me to be the most important representative of this line of thinking. It is true that the postmodernist critique of totalizing reason is distinguished from that of Adorno by its unequivocal rejection of a philosophy of reconciliation. But this brings only an apparent gain by comparison with Adorno. In the context of Adorno's writings, the philosophical perspective of reconciliation stands not least for a *defence* of reason against irrationalism, and for the unceasing dialectic effort to render visible the feeble traces of a better reason that are contained within bad reason. As the metacritique of the critique of identificatory thought shows, these traces are clearer, and harder to efface, than Adorno realized. There is no need of messianic hope in order to make them visible. On the other hand, if we merely abjure the messianic hope of the absolute without also reconsidering the absolutist character of the critique of reason, then a critique of totalizing reason can only end in affirmation, regression or cynicism. What the case of Adorno really shows is that the decentring of the subject by linguistic philosophy also necessitates a *relativization* of the critique of reason, for the critique of totalizing reason does not strike at discursive reason as such, but only at the inadequate, bad or perverted *use* of reason. Relativization does not necessarily mean an *attenuation* of the critique; relativization ought rather to mean something like a staking-out of boundaries within which the critique of reason is meaningful without itself turning into metaphysics or cynicism. By staking out the boundaries of a meaningful critique of reason in this way, reason itself, and with it the subject, is being given another chance. It cannot, admittedly, be the sort of chance that was once held out for reason and the subject alike by a rationalistic Enlightenment. What kind of chance would it be? It is with this question in mind that I return to the subject of modernity and postmodernity.

VII Reprise

With the 'death of God' virtually forgotten, the contemporary postmodernist debate frequently proclaims the 'death of modernity' instead.[84] And notwithstanding the variety of interpretations brought to bear on the subject, the death of modernity is invariably conceived as something entirely warranted: it is seen as the termination of a terrible mistake, a collective madness, a relentless compulsion, a deadly illusion. The obituaries for modernity are often full of sarcasm, bitterness and hatred. Never has a project that began with such a proliferation of good intentions – I mean the project of the European Enlightenment – had such obloquy muttered over its grave. Other advocates of postmodernism have painted a more differentiated picture. For them, modernity is not dead, but undergoing a transformation, although it is not yet possible to discern whether its new shape will be a modernity that has acquired a more advanced consciousness of itself, or a society that has regressed culturally and politically as the control of information has become technically more sophisticated.

I pointed out these and similar ambiguities of postmodernism (they are equally ambiguities of contemporary society itself) in my 'Exposition', and in my 'Development' sections I discussed the ambiguities of the critique of rationalism. I should now like to return to the theme of the Exposition and try to separate out a particular aspect of the puzzle of postmodernism, namely the impetus towards a 'self-transcendence of reason' (Castoriadis), which would represent neither a messianic principle of reconciliation nor a cultural and political regression, but a historical project for humanity.

I shall begin once more with a simplified picture of that 'modern' constellation which provides the point of departure for *this* kind of postmodernism. There are two elements in my picture:

1   The project of enlightenment as Kant conceived it was concerned with the emergence of humanity from its 'self-imposed condition of dependency', but by the time that Max Weber was writing, little remained of that project except a continual process of rationalization, bureaucratization, and the relentless encroachment of science into social existence. The capitalist economy, modern bureaucracy, technical progress and finally those ways of 'disciplining' the body which are analysed by Foucault have assumed the proportions of a gargantuan process of destruction – destruction of traditions, destruction of the ecological environment, finally the destruction of 'meaning systems' and of that unitary self which had been the product as well as the driving force of the enlightenment process. The type of reason that we see at work historically in these rationalization processes is firmly

associated with the 'logic of identity', it is a reason which plans, controls, objectifies, systematizes and unifies – in short, it is a 'totalizing' reason. Its representative symbols are mathematical deduction, the basic geometrical forms, the closed system, the general deductive–nomological theory, the machine and the experiment (as technical intervention). In the context of the modernization process, the practice of politics becomes reduced to the technique of retaining power, of manipulation and organization; democracy becomes merely an efficient form of organizing governmental control. Art, finally, becomes absorbed into the culture industry of the capitalist economy, reduced to a pseudo-autonomous pseudo-life.

2   The modern world has repeatedly shown itself capable of mobilizing counter-forces against this form of enlightenment as a rationalizing process. We might include the German Romantics among these counter-forces, but also the early Hegel, Nietzsche, the young Marx, Adorno, the anarchists, and last but not least, a significant proportion of modern art. But on closer inspection it becomes apparent that the 'romantic' counter-forces to modern 'rationalism' remain curiously dependent upon the rationalist myth of modernity, at least in so far as it articulated itself theoretically and politically, as opposed to aesthetically. From the young Hegel to Adorno, the idea of reconciliation remains a utopian counter-image to the reification, fragmentation and alienation of modern society, firmly tied to identitary reason, as much through mere negation as through its anticipation of a perfection of 'meaning' (*Sinn*). In the mature works of Hegel, and in Marx, reason asserts its totalizing impetus once again: the critique of bourgeois society and its 'rationality of understanding' becomes compressed into a dialectic of history, which in Marx's case even embraces the utopian counter-image of the Romantics, 'rationalizing' this in turn, as it were. With this aspiration to totality, the dialectic of history ends by proffering itself as an instrument of legitimation and control in the service of modernizing elite groups. While the totalitarian impulse of this dialectic eases the conscience of state-organized repression (including the Stalinist reign of terror), the anarchist negation of the state, so it might seem, provides a legitimation for *individual* terrorism – which serves to intensify the vicious circle instead of breaking out of it. In this interplay of undialectical affirmations and negations, then, the European Enlightenment appears to have consumed

itself, while the process of industrial modernization has proceeded unabated.

I have left out of my picture those outbursts of sheer
irrationalism which have accompanied the history of European
rationalism from time to time, German fascism being the most
ferocious of them. I have left out the regressive or neo-conservative versions of postmodernism, which could be sketched in
without disturbing the overall picture. The interplay of rationalism and irrationalism, of rationalization and regression, is, as
it were, the exoteric counterpart of that esoteric interplay of
Enlightenment and Romanticism to which I have just referred.
Finally, I have also omitted any reference to that strand of Western
democratic tradition which has enabled political, social and cultural countermovements to seek legitimation and inspiration
within those democratic traditions themselves. And this last
omission represents a point that will be central to my own
interpretation of the 'postmodern impetus'.

Let us return for the moment to the subject of modern art. We
saw how postmodernism has largely remained a form of aesthetic
modernism, or at least that it is firmly anchored in aesthetic
modernism. Modern art appears here as the terrain on which the
form of rationality that is characteristic of the modern world has
long since been challenged – and challenged, so to speak, at the
level of modernity itself. This is the idea that already runs through
Adorno's aesthetics of negativity. It is my belief that we only
need to read Adorno's aesthetics against the grain, as it were, in
order to discover within it elements of a philosophy of postmodernism instead of a philosophy of reconciliation. For Adorno,[85]
modern art signifies the abandonment of that notion of unity
and of a totality of meaning which bourgeois culture at its height
saw embodied in the closed unit of the work of art just as much
as in the unity of the individual self. In Adorno's eyes, aesthetic
enlightenment discloses that there is something forced, unreflected and illusory in the traditional unity of the work of art, as
well as in the bourgeois 'unity of the subject'; for this is a kind
of unity which was only attainable at the price of suppressing
and bracketing out anything that could not be integrated, anything that had been mentally repressed or otherwise excluded
from general consciousness. What that unity represented was the
pseudo-unity of a fictitious totality of meaning which remained
analogous to the conception of a unified, God-created universe.

The open forms of modern art are, according to Adorno, a way in which the emancipated aesthetic consciousness responds to the illusory and forced nature of such traditional totalities of meaning. It is these illusory and forced aspects of traditional concepts of integrated 'meaning' that Adorno has in mind when on the one hand he describes modern art as 'putting the work of art on trial', and when on the other hand he claims for modern art a principle of individuation and the 'progressive articulation of details'. The link between these two ideas is the recognition that for modern art a more flexible and individualized mode of organization becomes necessary in the same degree as it comes to incorporate what had previously been excluded as disparate, alien to the subject, and senseless. The opening-up of the work of art, the dissolution of its boundaries, is seen as closely related to an enhanced capacity for the aesthetic integration of the diffuse and the disparate. In a peculiar way. Adorno's own perspective was always narrowly concentrated on the *producers* of works of art. But if we extend the argument to include the *recipients*, then we could say that the open forms of modern art are not only the aesthetic mirror of a decentred subject and of a world that is out of joint, but that it also represents a new possibility for the perceiving subject to come to terms with its own loss of a centre. That is to say, modern art corresponds to a form of subjectivity which no longer displays that rigid unity of the bourgeois subject, but rather the more flexible unity of an individual self that has learned to communicate 'in a fluid medium'.[86] Modern art registers the advance tremors of both these developments, the shaking of the subject and of those systems of meaning in which it had dwelt, *and also* the possibility of widening the boundaries of the subject, making it possible to come to terms with a decentred universe. We might thus argue that modern art brings to bear an *emancipatory* potential within modernity directed against the excrescences of technical and bureaucratic rationality, and thus against the dominant forms of rationality in modern society. For in modern art we might discern a new type of 'synthesis', of 'unity', in which those non-integrated elements, the diffuse, the disparate and the meaningless become incorporated into a realm of non-violent communication, manifest in the open forms of art as well as in the open structures of a no longer rigid form of individuation and socialization.

As I say, we have to read Adorno against the grain to some

extent in order to find elements of a post-rationalist, 'postmodernist' conception of reason and the subject in his concept of aesthetic modernism. To this end we have to separate his aesthetics from the dialectical philosophy of reconciliation in which it is embedded. But if we do this, then the cultural and systemic processes of differentiation within the modern world (the processes by which economics, politics and the law have become separated out into autonomous institutions, or by which science, art and morality have become distinct validity spheres in the way that Habermas describes) can no longer be viewed as such from the perspective of a unity that can be restored (*qua* 'reconciliation'), and interpreted as symptoms of a reified rationality. We have no option, therefore, but to go along with Lyotard and abandon any hope for a reconciliation of all language games. There seems to be a contradiction between the two conclusions I have drawn from my reading of Adorno. But it is precisely the attempt to resolve this apparent contradiction that seems to me to constitute what I earlier called the 'postmodern impetus', the impetus towards a 'self-transcendence of reason'.

I share with Lyotard the basic premise that in any modern (or postmodern) society we are confronted with an irreducible plurality of interconnected language games. This is true, for example, in the sense of Kant's distinction between theoretical, practical and aesthetic reason (the separate modes of discourse for science, practical morality, and aesthetics). But it is equally true of Wittgenstein's notion of a pluralism of life-forms, of a network of 'local' but interrelated language games, and of a continual process by which new 'linkages' occur, individual systems distinguish themselves or forge connections without the possibility of a comprehensive 'metadiscourse' emerging (whether in the sense of a 'grand theory' or an ultimate justification), and without the opportunity – or even the desirability – of a general consensus. So far, so good. But it is perfectly obvious that this still does not provide an answer to our question about the nature of 'postmodern' reason; at best it provides only a *negative* answer. Lyotard leaves open the question of the possibility of 'justice without consensus': to *whom* does the rule of 'let us play in peace' actually apply, and *who* is going to be bound by that rule? At the end of *The Postmodern Condition*, Lyotard posits an alternative which in certain respects repeats the naïveties of liberal and anarchist traditions, when he says:

> We are finally in a position to understand how the computerization
> of society affects this problematic. It could become the 'dream'
> instrument for controlling and regulating the market system,
> extended to include knowledge itself and governed exclusively by
> the performativity principle. In that case, it would inevitably
> involve the use of terror. But it could also aid groups discussing
> metaprescriptives by supplying them with the information they
> usually lack for making knowledgeable decisions. The line to fol-
> low for computerization to take the second of these two paths is,
> in principle, quite simple: give the public free access to the mem-
> ory and data banks.[87]

This call for public access to the information that is necessary for
open discussion at least represents an important concession to
the democratic universalism of the Enlightenment; and it unex-
pectedly endorses the basic idea of Habermas's theory of communicative rationality. But does this differ in any way from what
Marx meant when he spoke of 'producers in free association'
bringing their metabolic relationship with nature under communal control? It was not this idea I had in mind when I spoke just
now of the naïvety in Lyotard's argument, I meant rather the
assumption that what is involved is in any way simple. It is
characteristic of the anarchist line in postmodern and post-
empiricist thinking that Lyotard really only deals in subordinate
clauses with *the* central problem for the liberation struggles of
subjugated peoples or oppressed minorities, the struggle for a
democratic psychiatry, and ultimately all conflicts and crises in
contemporary industrial society. And the real difficulty here is
that no one can say how and in what form the idea of a universal,
individual and collective self-determination could possibly be
realized for the individuals, groups and nations that inhabit the
world.

What Lyotard has formulated on the level of postmodern *knowledge* is something that we still have to formulate for the purposes
of postmodern *practice*. But what this would mean would be
the translation of the democratic and universalist ideas of the
Enlightenment into a political philosophy in which the pluralism
of 'language games' is converted into a pluralism of institutions,
be they formal or informal, local or central, temporary or permanent. But such a pluralism of institutions embodying the democratic self-organization of societies and groups would not be
possible unless the fundamental mechanism by which action was

co-ordinated were to take the form of communicative action in the sense that Habermas has defined it. In fact it would be impossible if individuals did not have the chance to *acquire the habits* of dealing rationally with conflict situations and to *grow into* the social ambience of individual and collective self-determination.

We have investigated the notion of a pluralism of language games and uncovered within it the problem of the democratic institutions necessary for mediating between individual and collective self-determination. On this basis two things become clear:

1   Firstly it becomes clear that we cannot proceed beyond the democratic universalism of the Enlightenment without first newly appropriating that principle and 'sublating' it. This is the dominant theme of the philosophies of modern society that have been outlined by Habermas on the one hand and Castoriadis on the other. Democratic universalism in its practical political implications cannot be reduced to a 'project' of modernity in the sense of an identitary rationality; to do that would be vulgar Marxism or worse. However, even under the conditions of 'postmodernism' this democratic universalism has to be predicated on the existence of *common elements* which concern this democratic universalism itself – not as an abstract principle, but as an ensemble of shared practices, meanings and basic orientations. It might be better to speak of *second-order* practices, meanings and orientations, because we are dealing here not simply with one or another set of values, one or another life-form, or with types of institutional arrangement. What is at issue is a shared basis of second-order social habits: the habits of rational self-determination, democratic decision-making and the non-violent resolution of conflict. To establish this would amount to a realization of the ideals of 'liberty, equality and fraternity' in the sense that humanity had grown up beyond the stage where it was dogged by the *problems* which lay behind the articulation of those ideals in the first place.
2   Our consideration of the political dimension of a 'pluralist' conception of reason also makes clear that we cannot proceed beyond Marx's problematic either without thinking it through afresh. It is all well and good to interpret the processes of differentiation characteristic of the modern age (the separation out of the economy, the state, the law, administration, science, art, etc.) as

having generated an irresolvable pluralism of interrelated systems, practices, fields of activity and modes of discourse, where there is no possibility of 'sublating' these disparities into a general condition of immediacy and harmony. The problem nevertheless obstinately remains of how the 'life-world', as Habermas puts it, can control the 'system', and this problem seems to me much more complex than Lyotard appears to recognize in the passage quoted above. It is not simply a problem of the general accessibility of information, it is a matter of *both* the interrelationship of technical, systemic, economic processes on the one hand and political processes on the other, *and also* of the organization and self-organization of the political processes as such.

The objection we are bound to make, from our present-day perspective, to the bourgeois notion of democratic universalism is that democracy remains unreal unless it is allowed to permeate the pores of social existence. Against Marx and the anarchists we are bound to say that this does not imply a situation of general harmony and abolition of 'alienation'. And against the rationalists in general we have to say that we cannot expect *either* ultimate justifications *or* final solutions to our problems. But this does not mean that we have to bid farewell to democratic universalism and its associated principle of the autonomous subject, *nor* do we have to abandon Marx's project of an autonomous society, *nor* do we have to jettison the idea of reason itself. What it means is that the moral and political universalism of the Enlightenment, the ideals of individual and collective self-determination, and the ideas of reason and of history all have to be thought through afresh. It is in the attempt to achieve *this* that I would envisage a genuine 'postmodern' impetus to the self-transcendence of reason.

I earlier pointed out the significance of Wittgenstein's views on language for the attempt at a (philosophical) 'defence' of reason and the subject. We might say that the defence consists in the radicalization of scepticism to the point where it can serve as an antidote to the sceptical undermining of reason and the subject – a sceptical return to common sense, as it were. While destroying the ideals of reason, the foundationalism that looks for ultimate justifications, and the utopianism that seeks final solutions, Wittgenstein's philosophy of language at the same time 'localizes' reason within a network of changeable and changing language games which has no beginning and no end, and no possibility of ultimate certainties, but which also has no fixed boundaries and does not block transitions once and for all. To 'localize' reason in this way also amounts to showing that there are in principle *no limits* to rational discourse and that our cognitive faculties (in Kant's sense) are not, as Lyotard has argued against Habermas, 'separated by chasm'.[88] What Habermas had said was this: 'Aesthetic experience not only renews our interpretations of those internal needs which help determine the way we perceive the world; it simultaneously influences our cognitive interpretations of what we perceive and the normative expectations we have of the world, and changes the way that all these factors are related to each other.'[89] What Habermas is saying is that aesthetic experiences, cognitive interpretations and normative expectations are *not independent* of each other, still less are the modes of discourse of aesthetics, practical morality, and the realm of 'facts' separated from each other by a chasm. They are, on the contrary, interrelated in many and various ways – even if the criteria of validity are bound to be different for each of these distinct realms and not susceptible to reduction to a single set of criteria.[90] The goal ahead for us in this area, indeed the only goal we can ever hope to achieve, is not a 'reconciliation of language games', but the mutual 'permeability' of the various modes of discourse, i.e. the sublation of a unitary notion of reason within a plurality of interacting rationalities.[91]

VIII Coda

The dialectic of modernism and postmodernism is something that remains to be written. But more important still, it remains to be worked through in a practical sense. 'The social transformation required by our times,' writes Castoriadis, 'is inseparably bound up with the self-transcending of reason.'[92] Postmodernism, properly understood, would take the form of a project. And in so far as it is something more than just a fashion, a manifestation of regression, or the expression of a new ideology, postmodernism is best understood as a movement engaged in a search, an attempt to register the signs of change and to define the shape of that project more closely.

3

Art and Industrial Production:

The Dialectics of Modernism and Postmodernism*

I

Beauty which, according to Kant, is purposiveness without a purpose, did not originally exist as a phenomenon in its own right, but was simply woven into the purposive constellations of society. Beauty was bound either into functions of the sacred realm – and thus placed in the service of religious purposes – or else into functions of the profane – where it represented a moment of craftsmanship. It was, in the words of Octavio Paz, 'subordinate, in the one case to usefulness and in the other to magic'.[1] The rise of autonomous art is co-terminous with the rise of industrial production: both are due to a process of cultural modernization which has led, in Max Weber's terminology, to the 'disenchantment' of the world, to the rise of the bourgeois class and the establishment of the capitalist mode of production. Art becomes autonomous by detaching itself from religious and cultic purposes; and at the same time, potencies which have lost their religious significance become invested in art itself, living on as the 'aura' of the work of art, to use Benjamin's term. 'The religion of art,' says Octavio Paz, 'was born of the ruins of Christianity.'[2] Conversely, with the progressive 'rationalization' of industrial production, usefulness emancipates itself from

*Speech on the occasion of the seventy-fifth anniversary of the German Werkbund, given in Munich, 10 October 1982.

beauty. Under the conditions of industrial production, that aesthetic surplus which breathed life into the products of craftsmanship appears obsolete, as if any aesthetic surplus inevitably rang
false in an industrially manufactured utility object, or else
degenerated into illusionistic decoration. It is this sort of experience that underlies the functionalist postulates that were
espoused in the early years of this century, not only by represen-
tatives of the Werkbund, but above all by its best-qualified critic,
Adolf Loos. The functionalist creed determines that industrial
products can only be called 'beautiful' if they are constructed in
a manner that accords with both their purpose and the material
out of which they are fashioned. Thus while the aesthetic function
of autonomous art becomes detached from all external purposes,
in the industrial product it seems to merge with the very idea of
purpose. The retreat of beauty in autonomous art from all external
purposes means that works of art attract unto themselves the
cultic aura of religious symbols, that they become constellations
of meaning obeying their own internal dynamics which only
point beyond themselves by virtue of their own complexion,
their own immanent values. The reduction of beauty to purposiveness, on the other hand, means that industrially manufactured
objects become inimical to any dimension of meaning, and
become merely a token of their own function, a means to an end.
From this point of view the products of a craft culture appear,
as Octavio Paz argues, to occupy a medial, a mediating position.
These products have a significance of their own, a life and a
meaning of their own, beyond their immediate utility value; they
have properties which enabled them to become crystallization
points for a concrete space and a concrete time, for the structure
of a habitable location which is, as it were, simultaneously
charged with meaning and with *sensual* force. In the words of
Octavio Paz, 'The beauty of industrial design is of a conceptual
order; if it expresses anything at all, it is the accuracy of a
formula. It is the sign of a function. Its rationality makes it fall
within an either/or dichotomy: either it is good for something
or it isn't. In the second case it goes into the trash bin. The
handmade object does not charm us simply because of its usefulness. It lives in complicity with our senses . . . The pleasure
that works of craftsmanship give us has its source in a double
transgression: against the cult of utility and against the religion
of art.'³

Paz speaks of a transgression where, in the light of what we have said so far, the transgression seems rather to have taken place in the opposite direction: it is a transgression or supersed- ing of the mode of craft production that takes place with the separation out of art and industry. And even if Paz can point to the resurgence of craft production *within* industrial societies – in the nooks and crannies of the capitalist economy, so to speak – that makes no difference to the situation. Nevertheless, when he speaks of a double transgression against the cult of utility and against the religion of art, he is doing more than just conjuring up the past. The craft product serves to illustrate an unresolved problem of industrial society, namely that as art has become autonomous, so the life-world has largely suffered a process of aesthetic deprivation. It was against this aesthetic deprivation of the life-world through industrial production that the Werkbund directed its efforts. The formula of a double transgression against the cult of utility and against the religion of art is a pretty exact description of the programme that the founders of the Werkbund hoped to realize, and to realize moreover under the conditions of an *industrial* mode of production.

II

When it was founded in 1907, the German Werkbund tried to establish itself at the spearhead of industrial development.[4] Its leaders believed that it would be possible in the long term to achieve a kind of convergence between technological and aesthetic modernism. They hoped that it would be possible to reconcile the spheres of art and industry, which had become separated out since the craft mode of production had come to an end, and to reunite the functions of artist, technician and merchant – which had formerly been concentrated in the per- son of the craftsman – into a harmonious unit at a higher level of differentiation. The result would be the release and unfolding of a genuinely modern aesthetic and moral culture.

If one might speak of a central illusion that is fundamental to the original programmes of the Werkbund, then it is that the interests that respectively demanded the humanization of working conditions, the expansion of capitalist markets, and the development of new attitudes to form and material were ultimately all pulling in the same direction, or at least that they could be made to converge.[5] The great achievements of the Werkbund up until the end of the 1920s lie, so to speak, beneath the threshold of that cultural renewal that its founders had anticipated, namely in areas concerned with appropriate ways of dealing with new materials and construction processes arising from more or less clearly defined (and therefore limited) problems. Examples of this are the pioneering factory buildings designed by Behrens and Gropius, the Weissenhof housing estate in Stuttgart, or the design of modern forms for objects of everyday use. On the other hand, not only the two world wars, but also the dynamics of industrial development itself, have made it clear meanwhile that the cultural renewal dreamed of by the artists, architects and social strategists of the Werkbund simply was not part of the logic of that development. By contrast with an important section of the cultural avant-garde of the turn of the century, and well into the 1920s, the cultural avant-garde of today sees technological modernization largely as a synonym for the destruction of tradition and the environment. In proportion as the process of modernization begins to impinge on the deepest layers of inherited life-forms (whether urban or rural), in proportion as it threatens ecological balances and thus the natural basis of human life, so too have the destructive consequences of industrial progress become generally apparent. Today, it would seem more natural for art to forge an alliance with ecology than with industry.

The history of the Werkbund is intimately connected with the functionalist and constructivist impulses of modern architecture and modern industrial design. At the same time the Werkbund can to a large extent be viewed as voicing objections to the trend to barbarism that is inherent in capitalist mass production if it is left to its own devices. These two central motifs complement each other, but a state of tension also exists between them. It was soon recognized by 'modernists' within the Werkbund that functionalist postulates were not a sufficient basis for pursuing an aesthetic and moral renewal of culture in the face of the momentum of capitalist modernization. This is what is meant when Muthesius and others speak of the 'spiritual' dimension of form, as opposed to categories of mere purpose and the possibilities inherent in the materials, as the thing which makes 'beauty' possible in a world of industrial production. The 'spirituality' of form was also intended to characterize the role of the artist in the collaboration between art and industry. It was against such a distribution of functions between art and industry that Adolf Loos objected with polemical vigour as early as 1908, soon after the founding of the Werkbund, arguing that 'to revitalize art by means of utility objects' meant subjecting it to 'the strongest form of debasement that it is possible to contrive'.[6] If we think of the history of industrial design, then this objection appears in retrospect to be far from unjustified. But if, on the other hand, we think of the genuine social problems which prompted the establishment of the Werkbund and kept it alive subsequently, then we can see that Loos's radical functionalism did not contain the key to their solution either. What, then, are the actual limits of functionalism, of which the term 'spirituality' of form gives only a rough indication?

I should like to use the concept of functionalism here in a wider sense, so that it encompasses not only the postulate that 'form follows function', but also the demand for a construction that is transparent as well as being in keeping with the materials used. The earliest meaning of functionalism was certainly that of a critique of ideology. With reference to industrial kitsch, or the eclecticism and historicism of architecture at the turn of the century, the postulates of functionalism signified a moral and aesthetic purification comparable with the language criticism of Karl Kraus or the early Wittgenstein. Just as the early Wittgenstein insisted that 'What we cannot speak about we must pass over in silence,' so might we also summarize the postulates of functionalism in the demand that 'What has no meaning (function) should not become manifest (as if it had a meaning, that is)'. And just as the ascetic view of language in early Wittgenstein leads to an extreme concentration of the aesthetic quality of his prose, so might it also be said of the best examples of the new architecture that the clarity of functionalist language has led in such works to an extreme aesthetic concentration which is derived from the merging of construction, purpose and expression. But just as we find already in Logical Positivism that, compared with the philosophy of the young Wittgenstein, the impulse to purify language becomes transformed into a hypostatization of scientific and technological rationality, so too does the critique of ornamentation become transformed in vulgar functionalism into a hypostatization of the internal logic of technological development. This meant, amongst other things, a drastic reduction in the grasp of fundamental functional relationships themselves. Light, air, the needs of hygiene and the demands of transportation – nobody would dispute the importance of all of these, particularly when they constituted vastly unsatisfied needs; but it can scarcely be said that they yield a concept of what the functional relations in European urban culture once represented, or a concept of what a modern city could be once it has asserted the humane potential of technology against its potential for destruction. By analogy with Marx's critique of mechanistic materialism, we might speak of a 'mechanistic functionalism', to which we might oppose a 'historical functionalism', i.e. one that reflects history and incorporates it within its programme.

Elements of a mechanistic functionalism, of a technocratic simplification, can also be found in great modernist architects, even in the utopian schemes of Le Corbusier. But in his best constructions, Le Corbusier in particular represents the *other* side of modern architecture, its aesthetic potential. Even Le Corbusier's 'human delights' – *air, son, lumière* – can scarcely be adequately understood as physiological needs in the sense of vulgar functionalism, as Julius Posener has emphasized. What appears to be meant is rather the kind of delights that the architecture of Greek antiquity was able to derive from an as yet mythical landscape. In this great architect who, as Julius Posener says, 'seized Europe from behind',[7] the radically modern and the archaic converge. Liberated architecture appears, not least, as a release of impulses and experiences that had been lost to view as the world had become disenchanted, as a conjoining of origins and utopia. Le Corbusier's best buildings are like eloquent objects – this is where they transcend any vulgar functionalism; and it is as if dead materials were being reawakened in them – this is where they show the real potential of constructivism.

By contrast with this, the kind of functionalism that has become historically predominant is afflicted with formal and mechanistic simplifications of the sort that suited the technocratic spirit of the times. In particular it is afflicted with a lack of adequate reflexion of the functional and purposive relations which would have provided the *goals* for functional production and construction. This is precisely what made it possible for vulgar functionalism to be absorbed totally into the service of a modernization process that was determined by the interests of

capital investment and the imperatives of bureaucratic planning. Only in the 1960s, when the last – or nearly the last –
ornamental façades of the Wilhelmine era threatened to fall
victim to the post-war vogue for modernization in Germany
did a broad public awareness develop that these elaborate
Wilhelmine façades, which were anathema to the functionalists,
conserved more of the urbanity and humanity of European urban
culture than did the functionalist deserts of modernized urban
areas. It may well be that, as W. J. Siedler stresses in his 1964
publication *Die gemordete Stadt* (The Murdered City),[8] the over-
elaborate and eclectic façades of the 1880s and 1890s concealed
architecture that was disproportionate and poor in quality. But
what was laid bare as these ornamental façades were removed
was not only the disproportionality of the architecture beneath,
but also that of the dialectic peculiar to the functionalist movement. For a functionalism which uncritically accepts a definition
of functions and priorities that is laid down for it can ultimately
only mean sanctioning a devastation of our cities that takes place
in the name of returns on investment, transport planning, and
administrative imperatives. Even if the ornamental façades of the
turn of the century were dishonest and ideological in character,
they nevertheless carried a memory of urban life-forms and a
promise of their continuation, whereas the simple destruction of
what has come to be seen as an ornamental superstructure only
serves, here as elsewhere, to reveal the barrenness of the 'base'
that lies beneath it, while also threatening to wipe out those
memory traces which alone could help to kindle the impulse for
change. The functionalistic modernization of West German cities
since the war has an aspect of self-mutilation about it – as if its
purpose were to hasten the transformation of humanity into a
breed of merely functioning creatures that lacked any sense of
history. This move away from the city – in its traditional sense
– and towards ahistorical settlements for modern nomads reaches
its culmination in the sunny, grassy dormitory towns of the post-
war period, specially designed for families and road traffic. Of
course, no one could deny the enormous progress that urban
modernization has *also* brought in terms of general comfort; to
that extent we should beware of romanticizing the old working-
class tenements. But what was largely lost in the process of this
modernization was the city as a public space where a multiplicity
of functions and forms of communication interacted, or – in

the words of Jane Jacobs – the city in the sense of 'organized complexity'.[9] In short, what we have lost is the city as it had developed in European history as a place of civic freedom, as well as a focus of cultural activity.

III

In a speech which Theodor W. Adorno made to the Werkbund in 1965, he once more defended the functionalist and constructivist impulses of modern architecture against the vulgar functionalist manner in which they had been put into practice. As he says there, 'We should expect architecture to achieve a higher quality in proportion as it mediates between the two extremes of formal construction and function.'[10] Adorno is thinking of a mutual penetration of materials, forms and purposes in such a way that none of these moments can be regarded as the ultimately decisive one, or as some absolute 'primal phenomenon' (Urphänomen). Materials and forms, too, are not ahistorical in nature; history has left its traces in them, a spirit is 'stored' in them. 'Artistic imagination awakens this stored spirit by becoming aware of the problem. The steps in the imaginative process, which are always small ones, respond to the question which the materials and forms pose in their mute language of things. This is how the separate moments become interwoven, and purpose and immanent formal principle along with them.'[11] It is only in this mediation between materials, forms and purposes that Adorno sees the deeper justification of the functionalist impulse, and also the aspect of functionalism that points beyond the criterion of mere technical adequacy to purpose. 'The sense of space,' he says, 'is intertwined with the sense of purpose; where it attains abiding value in architecture as something that transcends mere adequacy to purpose, it also resides in the purposes themselves. It is surely a criterion of great architecture that it achieves such a synthesis. The question that great architecture asks is how a particular purpose can become space, in what material and in what forms; all moments are reciprocally related to each other. Architectonic imagination is thus the ability to articulate space through the purposes served, enabling those purposes to become space; it means erecting forms according to those purposes.'[12] Adorno is trying to use the language of functionalism in order to capture something that goes beyond mere functionalism – at least in the sense in which it is ordinarily understood. Adorno attempts to decode the expression, the meaning, the 'language' of architectural configurations – i.e. those aspects for which Muthesius or Le Corbusier would have used the code term 'spirit' – as something *immanent* to the postulates of functionality and of remaining in keeping with the materials. For Adorno, then, architecture would be truly functional if it achieved an articulation of concrete spaces in which human beings were able to recover their subjectivity in an objectified form, and which also provided a spatial structure charged with meaning, upon which their subjective impulses could become refracted and enhanced. Spaces that can be inhabited and brought to life, then; spatial objectivations of communicative relations and potential meaning.

There is an element inherent in Adorno's interpretation of functionalism – and in practice also in the works of Le Corbusier – which points beyond functionalism to that aesthetic dimension or 'language' of architecture of which the proponents of so-called postmodern architecture have emphatically reminded us, and which they have opposed to the merely formal or functional aesthetic dimension.[13] Amongst them, Charles Jencks in particular has celebrated the rediscovery of the language of architecture as the true discovery of postmodern architecture.[14] In Jencks's case the metaphor of 'language' serves as the key to a critique of functionalism and constructivism. Since the postmodernists, in contrast to Adorno, see in functionalism primarily what has grown out of it historically, namely the vulgar functionalism of the 'international style', the rediscovery of the language of architecture means for them essentially a rejection of the 'rationalism' of modernism.

From the point of view of language, it is true that a great deal of what has been built in the era of modern architecture appears utterly impoverished, a mere cipher of the technical process itself. Jencks criticizes the 'univalency', the one-dimensionality, the ahistoricity and the rationalism of the sign-system of modern architecture – against which he sets the polyvalency, the semiotic complexity, the contextuality and the stylistic pluralism and eclecticism of postmodern architecture. The rehabilitation of eclecticism is justified for Jencks by one simple consideration: the stylistic homogeneity of an architecture that embodies 'meanings' can only exist in societies with a generally accepted 'system of signification', i.e. in traditional societies. Since no such system of signification any longer exists in industrial societies, architecture today can only draw on the semantic potentials of the past in an ad hoc fashion, with a sense of historical distance or in a spirit of ironic refraction, while on the other hand precisely this semantic potential is freely available to it in all its diversity, not excluding exotic and archaic forms of expression.

If this were all, then the programme of postmodern architecture would contain an admission that it is incapable of achieving a language of its own. It would be making a virtue of necessity in using its own lack of a language to justify playing an arbitrary or frivolous game with the languages of the past. And this, it seems to me, is indeed one, i.e. the truly postmodern aspect of postmodern architecture. Its other, productive aspect points rather to a transcendence of modern architecture *under its own momentum*, in the sense that it has freed itself of the simplifi-cations and limitations of a technical rationalism. The most inter-esting aspect of Jencks's thinking for me is the point where he constructs a connection between the development of the language dimension of architecture on the one hand, and new, partici-patory forms of town planning on the other. For it is at this point that something which Adorno only hints at becomes clear, namely that the metaphor of the 'language' of architecture points to the actual language of those who are affected by the architec-ture. Unlike musical composition, which was the model that Adorno had in mind, architecture must combine the mutual interpenetration of materials, forms and purposes with the com-municative clarification of those purposes if 'meaning' or 'expression' are not to become arbitrary in nature. Buildings, after all, do not exist as works of art sufficient unto themselves. I find Jencks's remarks very helpful, therefore, in clarifying the concept of an architecture which neither succumbs entirely to functional relations nor indulges in idiosyncratic aesthetic ges-tures. It is the concept of an architecture which would be bound into constellations of 'communicative rationality' (to use a phrase of Habermas's[15]) in a sense that lies beyond mere technical, economic and bureaucratic rationality, but also beyond the mere wantonness of aesthetic gestures. Participatory forms of town-planning and urban 'restoration' would be *one* aspect of such an architecture; another would be what the Dutch call 'polyvalent space', i.e. the conception of a space which is open to individual variation and interpretation of basic patterns of a collective character, in other words the conception of spaces which can be individually *interpreted* (Hertzberger). Van Eyck, in this connection, has coined a nice phrase: he speaks of 'labyrinthine clarity'.[16] The concept of a labyrinth stands for all that appears dysfunctional, unforeseen, unplanned and superfluous from the point of view of technocratic planning. It also stands for the round-about nature, the ambiguity and complexity of structures and relations, as they might arise from the unregulated experience and personal activity of a *multiplicity* of subjects; and from *their* point of view, things that seem confused to an observer obsessed with technocratic ideals can appear clear and transparent. Again, a parallel to linguistic philosophy suggests itself: Wittgenstein's critique of the 'preconceived idea of crystalline purity' in linguistic philosophy corresponds to postmodern architecture's critique of the ideals of geometric clarity and functional unequivocality. Wittgenstein's demand that 'the axis of reference of our examination must be rotated, but about the fixed point of our real need',[17] is a demand that we consider the structures of everyday language from the point of view of the person *using* them, for then what appears confused from the point of view of a constructive semantics might present itself instead as clear and ordered. The concept of 'labyrinthine clarity', when understood in this way, could be treated as a category of 'communicative rationality'. When compared with technocratic notions of rationality, both can be attributed to a 'rotation' of perspective around the fixed point of the needs of concrete, historical subjects.

Both communication *and* rationality are conceived simultaneously, however, in the concept of communicative rationality. The concept stands not only for the complex structures of everyday communication, but equally for the normative core of an emancipated consciousness. It carries within it the idea of an 'open society' in the modern sense, i.e. a post-traditional democracy that has a universalist claim. The concept of communicative rationality therefore signifies conditions under which it is no longer possible for universally binding systems of signification (in Jencks's sense) to exist *legitimately* except on the meta-level of universalistic fundamental values. It is no longer possible to advance a system of objectively binding meanings against the false uniformity of technically impoverished sign-systems – unless it be at the price of a violent curtailment of communication.

All that we can set against it is a *pluralism* of values, meanings and life-forms resulting from the liberation of communicative potentials. And the freedom to have recourse to traditions and the semantic potentials of the past, each of us in our own way, is part of this pluralism of values and life-forms. This is presumably what Jencks has in mind when he speaks of a new and more authentic eclecticism in postmodern architecture by comparison with the eclecticism of the nineteenth century.[18] He is thinking of a productive use of the new degrees of freedom which modern consciousness has acquired in its relationship to tradition, of the possibility of kindling new life in the fossilized language of the past and converting its inscriptions into readable texts by working them into new configurations. If we choose to call this eclecticism, then it is an eclecticism of the *creative present*, a power to select and bring relics of the past to life. It is not the eclecticism of an indiscriminate playing with styles which vainly seeks footholds in the past because it is incapable of coping with the present. Jencks's idea of an 'authentic' eclecticism, too, should thus be understood in connection with his demand that 'the whole system of architectural production' should be changed,[19] a demand which aims at enabling the utility value of architecture to be determined once more by those who are affected by it.

The repudiation of a one-sidedly technocratic modernism by postmodern architecture clearly does not *have* to be understood as a rejection of modernity or of the tradition of the Enlightenment; it can also be understood as an immanent critique of a modernism that has fallen away from its own concept. The rediscovery of the language dimension of architecture, the contextualism, models of participatory planning, the emphasis on the 'fabric' of cities instead of monolithic structures that have no context, even the historicism and eclecticism if we understand them as a rediscovery both of the historical and social dimension of architecture and of cultural tradition as a reservoir of semantic potentials – in short, much of what distinguishes so-called postmodern architecture from the technocratic utopian features of classical modernism, can be understood as the progress of architectonic consciousness and as a corrective *within* the modern tradition. But on the other hand, eclecticism and historicism also carry the potential meaning of a *rejection* of the constitutive features of modernity, namely enlightenment, universalism and rationality. To this extent, postmodern architecture participates in an ambiguity which is characteristic of many trends which are referred to nowadays as postmodern, whether we think of alternative social movements or of 'postmodern' theories of science and culture – from the epistemological anarchism of Paul Feyerabend to French post-structuralism. It is the ambiguity of movements, of political and theoretical impulses, which are on the one hand directed towards the defence of communicative structures, semantic potentials, ecological balances or possibilities of unregulated self-expression on the part of subjects, as opposed to a technocratically perverted modernity, and thus towards the defence of conditions which have to be preserved if the modern world is not to bury its particular potential for humanity beneath itself; while on the other hand these movements and impulses, with their rejection of technocratic modernity, often enough proclaim a retreat from the modern world altogether. Where this happens, the critique of technocratic rationalism turns into irrationalism, contextualism becomes particularism, the cult of local tradition becomes mere fashion (or worse, it becomes a regression), and the rediscovery of the symbolic function of architecture becomes an ideological or authoritarian gesture. Jencks, this much appears to me beyond doubt, is at bottom one of those proponents of postmodern architecture and town-planning whom we should think of as radical moderns; the clearest indicator of this is his emphasis on the connection between urban life-form and democracy. In a certain sense, Jencks constructs his 'postmodern' critique of modern architecture from the perspective of a democratically conceived form of town-planning. To that extent his critique of modern architecture is, contrary to his intentions, not a critique of enlightenment, but part of a 'critique of instrumental reason'.

IV

The example of developments in architecture does not permit us to draw direct conclusions about possibilities for a new mediation between art and industrial production in other areas. There is a special sense in which individuality and 'language' represent possibilities for architectural structures; architecture is a sphere that is open in the direction of visual art. Because they lack individuality, industrial mass products also lack an important

condition that makes language possible: they are unable to indi-
vidualize the purposes that they embody, and this places limits
on the possibilities for *expression* based on the mediation between
materials, forms and purposes. It is frequently the case that
industrial products are signs only in the sense of signifying a
function, as Octavio Paz says, or perhaps also as status symbols,
as symbols of technical progress or as projected symbols of a
realm of infantile imagery. That is to say that industrial mass
products, unless they have an ornamental or symbolic significance laid upon them from without, are incapable of expressing
any constellation of *meanings* by virtue of their own composition;
they *embody* a constellation of *functions*, but they do not express
it.

 This does not mean, of course, that industrial products are
necessarily expressionless. Expression is a phenomenon of interference, as Adorno put it,[20] and can scarcely be separated from
beauty. It is perfectly possible for industrial products to be
beautiful, i.e. when a perfect construction and an evident function
are made *visibly* apparent. The distinction between visible and
invisible constructions is in some respects more important than
the distinction between houses and machines. The fact that the
iron constructions of the nineteenth century often appear beautiful today is not merely nostalgia, not merely a romantic glorifi-
cation of the 'ruins' that remain from a past industrial age; rather
it results from the fact that their construction is *visible*. In the
case of steam engines and even bicycles, too, the moment of
expression depends on the visibility of the construction. Where
the combination of perfect construction and evident function
results in expression – even where what is accomplished is
simply a correspondence to the gestural–motoric space of the
human body – then objects acquire a significance of their own:
as functionally beautiful objects they are also more than just
means to an end, they come to objectify also a purposiveness
without purpose. Of course, this form of beauty is rapidly disap-
pearing in an age of electronic technology, the products of which
are monstrous, express nothing, or are visible only as smooth
surfaces which hide something that cannot be sensually apprehended, just as everyday objects hide the processes at work within
the nucleus of the atom. The objects that can still be beautiful
today by virtue of their excellent construction are those utility
objects that remain closely related to the human body, the eye

or the hand: tools, furniture, lamps. But even this beauty of perfectly constructed objects is different from the 'eloquent' beauty of perfectly constructed buildings; indeed, the difference is greater in proportion as the function of the objects can be described in a technically more precise, and thus in a more general way. To this extent, Loos is still right.

The lessons that can be drawn from the example of architecture are to be found on another plane. They concern the functional *relations* and the *life-forms* that are embodied in industrial products. For the products of industry come together in configurations, in functional networks, which *determine* the course followed by life and work, which *reproduce* social hierarchies or forms of communication, or *embody* social priorities. These configurations are comparable with architectural structures in that they restrict or expand the possibilities for life to articulate itself, blunting sensibilities or stimulating them, blocking autonomous activity or encouraging it. They form the boundary lines, the openings, the utensils, or even the prison walls of the human life-world in general. Taking up Ivan Illich's concept of 'tools for conviviality', we might distinguish a technology that is orientated towards human needs, human autonomy and communicative rationality from one that is orientated towards investment return, bureaucratic control or political manipulation. *This* distinction, and not the one between industrial kitsch and functional design, is what marks the boundary line today between aesthetic and moral culture on the one hand and barbarism on the other.

What we are becoming aware of here, by comparison with the turn of the century when the Werkbund was founded, is a profound shift in the nature of the problem – if not an objective shift, then at least a shift in social consciousness, which finds expression in the retreat of problems of 'production aesthetics', as I should like to call them, behind problems of 'utility aesthetics' (*Gebrauchsästhetik*). Behind the functionalist and constructivst impulses of modern design and modern architecture lay the conviction that it was necessary to find technically impeccable, materially appropriate and aesthetically agreeable solutions to match *predetermined* purposes: this is precisely the problem of finding forms appropriate to the times. But even if we understand the problem in Adorno's terms as a mutual interpenetration of materials, purposes and formal construction, there nevertheless remains the question of how to clarify those purposes themselves adequately – and Adorno would have been the last to deny this. Although it is possible for the purposes to become concretized and materialized in the way that materials, forms and purposes are mediated with each other, this does not really lead to their clarification. On the other hand, the connection between the beauty and the purposiveness of utility objects can only be established as real and understandable when the purposes themselves are evident and identifiable as the purposes of the subjects concerned. Where these purposes and the functional relationships that serve them are not clarified, then, it is not possible for a world of utility objects to be 'beautiful' even in the functionalist sense of the word. I believe that this is one of the reasons why so much of modern architecture, even if it appears successful in terms of its immanent criteria, nevertheless tends towards the sterile beauty of 'decorative formalism' (A. Schwab),[21] or what Bloch called the 'kitsch of light',[22] or else becomes a 'polished death' that is 'administered like the gleam of morning'.[23] There is, says Bloch, 'no third element between plush and steel chair, between post offices in Renaissance style and egg-boxes' which 'seizes the imagination any more'.[24] Such a third element could only come from a change of 'life-style', i.e. from a clarification and change of functional relations *out of which* and *for which* objects are produced. I should like to use the term 'utility aesthetics' in cases where the aesthetic quality of the life-world is dependent upon the functional relations that are embodied in utility objects being openly apparent. My thesis is that the problems of 'the appropriate form for the times' are today above all problems of utility aesthetics, and that the model of an interplay between art and industry no longer yields an adequate idea for dealing with these problems.

There has probably always been something naïve about the notion that the weak forces of aesthetic enlightenment were capable of humanizing and domesticating the inherent dynamism of industrial progress, even if what was envisaged included the aim of enlightening a broad public about the aesthetics of materials and production processes. But it has only been since the mid-Sixties, roughly speaking, that it has become more generally recognized that functional relationships have concretized themselves and acquired autonomy in the world of industrially manufactured products, often without it being possible to set them in a recognizable connection with what the living subjects in that world would be able to acknowledge as the functional relations of their own lives. Wherever questions about the fashioning of utility objects are of more than mere private or ephemeral interest today, where the questions concerned are not merely those of a new 'style' or a new fashion, it is the question of purposes and functional relations itself that enters public consciousness. This is as true of questions of town-planning, urban renewal or urban conservation as it is of questions about sewage disposal or land-scape protection, about building hospitals, roads and nuclear power stations, or indeed about alternative technologies. In all these areas, questions of design have acquired an inescapable social, political or ecological dimension in addition to their tech-nical and aesthetic components. What is missing from the old Werkbund formula of splitting the functions of the traditional craftsman into those of the technician, the salesman and the artist is not only the dimension of capital and labour, but also the *social* components of design (Burckhardt),[25] namely the role of the craftsman as the representative of a collective life-form, which he articulated in his products. Where the collective life-forms are destabilized, however, where they become problematized and their very substance is threatened, so that they become depen-dent upon democratic processes of clarification, then it becomes openly *apparent* that the question of functional relations extends into the aesthetic problems of design.

This means, amongst other things, that the aesthetic imagin-ation faces a new challenge. As Adorno says, purposes are not 'primal phenomena' (*Urphänomene*), any more than materials and forms are; which is to say that where we are not simply dealing with purposes which can be precisely circumscribed in technical terms (and this is the case with architecture), then the articulation of the purposes themselves is once again dependent upon the possibilities, the concretizations, and the 'language' that accrue from the materials and the formal construction. In the traditional relationship between architect and builder, it is the former who confers a precise shape and articulation upon the purposes of the building. In a similar way, it would be possible today for the constructive and aesthetic imagination of artists to intervene experimentally and in an 'articulating' function in the process by which purposes are clarified in communicative terms. And unless the aesthetic imagination is allowed to contribute to the *clarifi-cation* of purposes in this way – and not merely to their *realization*

– then relations between people are likely to forfeit a crucial dimension of their language, and their purposes will become 'speechless'.

The double transgression that Octavio Paz saw in the craft mode of production – passing beyond the cult of utility and beyond the religion of art – cannot be carried into the heartland of industrial production by means of a direct reunion of art and industry as it was envisaged by the founders of the Werkbund. But it might well be conceivable that industrial production could be *made to abide* by purposes established through a process of communicative clarification, and that art and aesthetic imagination could become *implicated* in the communicative clarification of mutual purposes. It would then perhaps be possible for art and industry to come together as moments of an industrial culture through the mediation of a third element, i.e. in the medium of enlightened democratic praxis.

4

Ethics
and
Dialogue:

Elements of Moral Judgement in Kant and Discourse Ethics

Introduction

The scepticism of moral philosophy on the one hand and revolutionary humanism on the other are natural offspring of enlightenment. This is already true to some extent of the Enlightenment period in ancient Greece, and it is much more obviously true of the modern European Enlightenment. In both instances, Enlightenment means the discovery that seemingly guaranteed norms of correct living, the 'justification' for which lay in the order of things, the will of God, or the authority of tradition, have no conceivable foundation other than in the will of men. I imagine that this discovery must have induced a sense of vertigo in those who first made it, a sense of vertigo in which a wide variety of factors may well have been present. They would have felt that their existence was being shaken to its foundations. They would have glimpsed a freedom which was either chilling or exhilarating. Or they may have discovered that the social order in which they lived was founded on coercion, suppression and illusion. And according to the viewpoint or the social position of those who were infected with this enlightened consciousness, one or another of these factors will have dominated. Philosophical scepticism, conservative cynicism, and revolutionary humanitarian pathos are all equally possible as reactions to the discovery of this Enlightenment.

Cynicism (the 'black' version of scepticism) is a psychological and moral problem rather than an epistemological one, and will therefore not be dealt with here.[1] Scepticism and revolutionary (or at least universalistic) humanism on the other hand are, from an epistemological point of view, alternative responses to the discovery of the Enlightenment. Scepticism disputes the possibility of a new foundation for morality, whereas revolutionary humanism sees such a possibility in the united will of rational beings. For the time being I do not wish to elaborate on this distinction, although we shall return to the subject of philosophical scepticism later. What interests me in the first instance is the fate – the philosophical fate – of revolutionary humanism. Not that I want to retell the whole story, rather I wish to examine revolutionary humanism in two of its most advanced versions with a view to drawing conclusions about its possible (philosophical) fate. By 'advanced' I mean advanced for their times. And the epithet 'revolutionary' is intended to indicate a *philosophical connection* between the humanism we are discussing here and the revolutions of modern times; it does not say anything about the subject of investigation itself. What we are discussing is not the theory of revolution, but (universalistic) ethics.

The two positions I wish to investigate are the formal ethics of Kant and the discourse ethics developed by Habermas and Apel. These are both forms of a universalistic ethics of reason or, as Habermas would say, of 'cognitivistic' ethics. Both positions are characterized by the pursuit of a *formal* principle as a basis for ethics, which by virtue of its formal character is also a universalistic principle. Moral validity is here grounded in a rational *procedure* which, because it *on the one hand* characterizes some such thing as a core of rationality universally shared by rational beings, *on the other hand* relates to all rational beings as in a fundamental sense free and equal individuals. The question of universal validity is inextricably linked with the universalistic character of the moral principle itself: on this point Habermas and Apel are in fundamental agreement with Kant and, at least as far as the concept of legal 'legitimacy' is concerned, with the revolutionary doctrine of natural law. It is precisely in this sense that the authors we are dealing with belong in the camp of Enlightenment humanism.

In what follows I shall not be giving an exhaustive account of the positions in moral philosophy adopted by Kant, Apel or Habermas. The purpose of my analyses and interpretations is more limited than this. My interest in Kant's ethics is rather of a heuristic nature. My selective interpretation of Kant is intended to bring out the strengths and weaknesses of his ethics in such a way as to make clear both the motives behind the development of a 'communicative' or 'discourse' ethics and also those aspects of such a theory which stand in need of demonstration. I am clear from the outset that Kant's ethics cannot be defended in their entirety, and that is why I have sought to bring out their *strengths* in particular. Some readers might object that I have behaved rather like a temple-robber on occasions, rescuing those items which particularly appeal to me. But in dealing with discourse ethics, on the other hand, I have treated with all seriousness its claim to have developed a system which solves Kant's problems by means of a universal or transcendental pragmatics and thus 'sublates' Kant's form of ethical universalism in a dialogic form of universalism. I do not believe that discourse ethics has yet achieved this ambition, and that is why I proceed more rigorously towards it than I do towards Kant's ethics. I use the latter, so to speak, as a yardstick which may itself have become questionable, but which can nevertheless perform useful service when it comes to judging the potential for problem-solving of theories which themselves claim to have 'sublated' Kant's ethics.

In criticizing Kant, discourse ethics has concentrated on three weak points in his ethics. Firstly it has criticized the formally *monologic* character of Kant's moral principle which, contrary to Kant's own opinion, leaves unanswered the question of the possibility of *intersubjectively valid* moral judgements. Secondly it has criticized the *rigorism* of Kant's ethics with its singularly formalistic hypostatization of the concept of law. And thirdly it has criticized Kant's attempts at a philosophical justification or *grounding* of his moral principle. Discourse ethics attempts to overcome these three weaknesses of Kant's ethics by 'sublating' Kant's formally *monologic* universalism within a formally *dialogic* universalism. It does this firstly by reformulating the moral principle in such a way that what is demanded of morally valid maxims is not that *I*, but that *we* can will them to have the validity of universal laws. Secondly it formulates the moral principle in such a way as to permit the question of right action to be understood as a question of rational interaction between individuals, all of whom possess their particular needs and vulnerabilities: this is how it excludes the fixed attitudes of ethical rigorism.

Thirdly and finally, discourse ethics claims, with its reformulation of the moral principle, to have made it possible to achieve a new form of fundamental grounding: Apel and Habermas have tried to show that the moral principle is founded on universal structures of argumentation. Now my own objection to discourse ethics in its current form is, in a word, that it has remained *too Kantian* on the one hand, while departing *too far from Kant* on the other. Discourse ethics has remained too close to Kant in two respects, namely its dependence on assumptions of consensus theory and its programme of an ultimate or fundamental grounding (*Letztbegründung*). On the face of it, of course, these two aspects of discourse ethics have little to do with Kant. But as I shall try to show, in terms of the kind of problem they present us with, the construction of concepts describing ideal conditions in consensus theory and the attempt to derive a universalistic ethics, as it were, directly from universal structures of reason, without the mediating instance of a *history* of moral consciousness, are both Kantian. To be sure, I am not saying that it is possible for us today to retrace the path that leads from Kant to Hegel. Although Hegel was the first to show, with the utmost clarity, how Kant's moral philosophy leads to dead ends, any attempt to avoid these dead ends – while not ignoring Hegel's *criticisms* – should steer well clear of Hegel's *system*. In place of an interpretation of a universalist ethics of dialogue in terms of consensus theory (which echoes Kant's notion of a 'kingdom of ends') I propose a *fallibilistic* interpretation; in the place of a strong and one-dimensional claim of justification I propose one that is weak as well as multi-dimensional. Once moral consciousness has become universalistic in character, it really does not need to live in anticipation of a state of reconciliation (however this might be formally described), nor does it need the assurance of an ultimate philosophical grounding. I believe rather that as long as universalistic ethics clings to these two absolute notions it remains just as vulnerable to the objections of Hegel as it does to those of the sceptics. With my criticism that discourse ethics remains too close to Kant, then, I am proceeding on the assumption that ethics needs to advance beyond the false antithesis of absolutism and relativism, which is to say that morality and reason do not stand or fall with the absolutism of ultimate agreements or fundamental groundings.

When I say that discourse ethics is *not Kantian enough* I mean that if fails to come up to what Kant had already achieved in terms of differentiation. I am thinking in particular of differentiation between problems of morality and problems of law. There can be no doubt that it was Kant's intention to link law and morality together, but at least he distinguished analytically (and with good reason in my view) between problems concerning the *legitimacy* of norms and the problem of morally right action. I am not concerned with the details of Kant's construction of the connection between law and morality (which are often enough problematic in themselves), but rather with the manner in which Kant, through his formulation of the moral principle, distinguishes between questions of morally right action and question concerning the justice of norms. Discourse ethics has not yet matched the degree of differentiation that Kant achieved in this respect; and this is so for reasons connected with its consensus-theoretical premises. Both the fact that discourse ethics remains too close to Kant *and* the relative loss of differentiation it shows by comparison with Kant are, then, connected with the problematic assumptions of a consensus theory of truth.

The basic intuitions of discourse ethics, which I wish to defend, also concern its position towards Kant. I consider the criticism of the formalistic – monologic rigorism of Kant's ethics, as well as the attempt to go beyond this rigid formalism by a dialogic expansion of ethics, to be entirely justified. Finally, like Apel and Habermas, I perceive a connection between the transition from a formalistic to a dialogic ethics on the one hand, and the transition from a philosophy of consciousness to a philosophy of language on the other. To be sure, I believe that we need to determine anew those points in Kant's ethics which may be considered as points of departure for a dialogically conceived ethical universalism. This is what I propose to do in the first part of my essay. Part 2 contains a critique of discourse ethics and its consensus-theoretical premises. In part 3 I wish to show how the basic intuitions of discourse ethics can be reformulated in terms of the 'quasi-Kantian' perspective developed in part 1.

One final prefatory comment on the problem of scepticism in moral philosophy. I believe that there is just as good a case for taking it seriously as there is for not taking it seriously. It should not be taken seriously as a *moral* attitude, but it should be taken seriously as a way of questioning rationalist and foundationalist claims to knowledge. By this I mean that I believe that rationalism can absorb scepticism and convert it into a catalyst of the enlightenment process. A rationalism enlightened by sceptism would be neither rationalistic nor sceptical, but it might perhaps be reasonable. I believe, then, that our best prospect for continuing the tradition of the Enlightenment, and of revolutionary humanism, is to bid farewell to certain ideals of reason. This does not mean bidding farewell to reason itself; rather it means bidding farewell to a false conception that reason has of itself.

The critique of Apel and Habermas in part 2 of this essay should also be seen to some extent as self-criticism on the part of the author, although I have not taken the trouble to indicate precisely where this is the case. It will be apparent to the reader, however, that while criticizing Apel and Habermas on particular issues I am also indebted to them both for ideas which have had a decisive and lasting impact on my own thinking.

I A Kantian Exposition

I

In various places, and most recently in his essay 'Diskursethik – Notizen zu einem Begründungsprogramm'[2] (henceforward cited as DE), Jürgen Habermas has drawn an analogy between the universalization principle in ethics and the so-called induction principle of empirical science. For reasons which should become clear later, I consider this analogy to be problematic, although the force of it immediately becomes apparent if we understand it in a weaker sense as has variously been put forward by M. G. Singer[3] and R. M. Hare[4], namely as a 'generalization principle' which is constitutive of both causal and moral judgements.

This generalization principle expresses the respective general character of causal and normative judgements, and of the corresponding relationships between sufficient reasons and consequences – a character which is part of the logical grammar of the words which we use to formulate causal and normative judgements. For causal explanations, for example, the following rule applies: if a because (causal) b, then – other things being equal – a must always follow b. The identification of a causal relationship means, by implication at least, the identification of a causal *regularity*. But this, I would argue, is the essence of what has been called the 'induction principle'. Something analogous to what applies in the case of the causal 'because' also applies for the normative 'because': if someone ought to (must, may) do a because conditions b obtain, then – other things being equal – everyone ought to (should, might) do a when conditions b obtain. The conjunction 'because', whether used in its causal or its normative sense, carries an index of generality; it possesses the generality of those linguistic expressions which it conjoins – always with the proviso, of course, of other things being equal. 'Moral judgements are thus analogous to causal judgements and "because" statements generally in possessing this character of implicit generality.'[5] We might speak of an 'equality principle' instead of a generalization principle, since the generalization principle demands the equal treatment of equal cases. In the case of both causal and normative 'because', an unequal treatment of prima facie equal cases requires an explanation (or justification) showing that the cases that have thus been treated differently are in some relevant respect, whether causal or normative, not in fact equal. Presumably the generalization or equality principle has a more general significance comparable in some ways to the logical principle of contradiction, but what interests us here is only the significance it acquires in the context of the logical grammar of causal and normative 'because' statements.

The normative equality principle already betokens an elementary concept of 'justice', which means nothing other than the equal treatment of equal cases, and which incorporates a notion of impartiality implying above all the impartial application of established norms. This is the sense in which we call an umpire 'impartial'. In an analogous sense we call a teacher fair when he has no 'favourites', or a judge just when the judgements he pronounces are not 'arbitrary'. The equality principle is admittedly not limited to the application of established norms, but also implies a sense for the precedents which may be created by individual actions and judgements. Just as the causal interpretation of singular events contains an indeterminate indication of a causal regularity, so too does the normatively conceived precedent contain an implicit norm. Both causal and normative precedents contain an implicit rule concerning an equal treatment of equal cases; they limit the freedom for the causal or normative interpretation of *future* cases.

In its normative sense, the generalization principle is really expressing nothing other than the connection between expressions like 'should', 'must' or 'may' and the concept of a norm. For this reason, of course, the elementary concept of justice which we have just been considering becomes largely inapplicable as soon as we raise the question of how the norms are *grounded* by which standards for the equal treatment of equal cases are defined in the first place, which is to say as soon as the 'justice' of these norms themselves is called into question. After all, the equality principle only concerns the general character of relationships between grounds and consequences; it therefore provides a criterion for the *appropriateness* of causal explanations or normative justifications only in the sense of a principle of *consistency*. When we seek a justification for norms, on the other hand, we are concerned amongst other things with the question of *which* standards for the equal treatment of equal cases are the *right* ones. This is the question which Aristotle discusses in his *Politics*, posing it in the form of asking whether property-owners, freemen or the virtuous should respectively be treated as 'equals' when it comes to the apportionment of the rights and duties of a citizen. The idea that human beings *qua* human beings should be regarded as equals in the matter of fundamental rights is a universalistic principle which only surfaces in *modern* conceptions of morality and justice. We might concede that it is the only principle which could reasonably win the approval of all human beings (without whose acceptance normative principles cannot 'live'), now that traditional justifications of the inequality of mankind have lost their credibility and authority. Thus, as soon as we consider whether it is even possible in principle to justify norms if they can no longer be attributed to a transcendental authority – to justify them, moreover, in the eyes of those who are expected to acknowledge their validity – the logical grammar of basic normative terminology almost inevitably assumes a universalistic significance: we cannot rationally apply these terms in anything other than a universalistic sense. This is how the impression arises that the normative generalization principle and the universalization principle are *one and the same thing*. In my view, however, we should first distinguish between the two layers of meaning, one of which concerns the general character of normative judgements, while the other relates to the universalistic conditions for the possible intersubjective *validity* of norms. The fact that in Habermas's interpretation of the universalization principle the two layers of meaning coincide is already connected with his consensus notion of practical truth. In other words, it is connected with the fact that for him the *meaning* of normative validity claims coincides with the universalistic *conditions* of their possible intersubjective recognition. In what follows I shall first discuss the basic meaning of the generalization principle, and then proceed to an interpretation of Kant's moral principle as a generalization principle of the second order.

II

Like Singer and Hare I proceed on the understanding that the generalization principle we have been considering is in itself an essential aspect of what Kant formulates as the categorical imperative. But I should immediately add that, for one thing, the 'fact of reason' as Kant understands it is not reducible to this generalization principle, and that secondly it is not possible to derive a universalistic moral principle from this generalization principle even with the help of a supplementary premise (such as Singer's 'principle of consequences').[6] We might clarify the sense in which the generalization principle is an essential aspect of Kant's moral principle in the following way: the categorical imperative requires that I should only act according to maxims which I can will to have the validity of a universal law. But *as a rule*, what I can will as a universal law will in fact be determined by my own, pre-existing normative convictions, especially by the socially determined normative expectations I have of *others*. In so far as this is the case, what the categorical imperative is ultimately saying is this: 'Do what you think *one* must do,' or even 'Don't do what you think *one* must not do.' In other words, 'Make no exceptions for yourself where normative matters are concerned,' or simply 'Do what you ought to do.' It will not be superfluous here, I think, to point out that the categorical imperative, even in this more or less basic interpretation of it, already presents a demand which is *by no means trivial*, namely that I should act in accordance with previously acknowledged normative obligations, and that I should do so *here and now and without self-deception*. Kant is entirely correct to describe *this* postulate as something simple and readily apparent to all, but which is nevertheless difficult to fulfil. The requirement to act in accordance with my own normative convictions does not mean, after all, that I stop and work out a suitable justification for each of my actions in turn; nor does it mean that I should act in accordance with what I can *present* as my normative conviction *in each instance*. What it requires incorporates a demand which really is difficult to fulfil, namely that I should not deceive myself as to what I would really expect of *others* in the event that they should find themselves in my situation.

To be sure, the categorical imperative, as has already been emphasized, is not reducible to this basic meaning. The categorical imperative is intended to explain the very possibility of that categorical 'ought' or 'must' which is always implied within any 'normative conviction', and to explain it moreover as the possibility of an 'ought' or 'must' which can be *rationally understood*. It is in this way alone that the categorical imperative can become a universalistic moral principle; the generalization principle as such may be a valid principle for all 'rational beings', but it is not a principle which necessarily distinguishes universalistic norms from others.

We may call the categorical imperative a generalization principle of the second order; only at this point does the notion of a universalization principle become relevant. This universalization principle is no longer something which can be understood as a simple analogue of the induction principle. For here we are no longer concerned only with the general character which belongs to the logical grammar of 'ought' or 'must' statements, but also with the common will of rational beings (and therefore also with the intersubjective *validity* of moral judgements). The categorical imperative is a principle which not only has validity *for* all rational beings, but also refers *to* all rational beings (as is most clearly shown by the so-called 'ends formula').

In what follows I should like to reconstruct the meaning of the categorical imperative to the extent that is necessary in order to show clearly both the motives for moving to a dialogic ethics and also the burden of proof which arises for such an ethics. In my reconstruction I shall proceed selectively; of the various possible interpretations of the categorical imperative I shall adopt the one which appears to me to carry the most substance. The most appropriate of Kant's texts on which to base this interpretation is the *Groundwork of the Metaphysic of Morals*.

My starting-point is the following formulation of Kant's: 'We must be able to *will* that a maxim of our action should become a universal law – this is the general canon for all moral judgement of action.'[7] The requirement that I should only act in accordance with maxims which I can will to be valid as universal laws is identical in meaning with the requirement that I should only act in accordance with maxims of which I can will that all others should act (e.g. towards me) in accordance with them. Now for Kant it goes without saying that if *I* am unable to will that a maxim should be valid as a universal law, then any rational being will be similarly unable to do so: the test of whether a maxim can be generalized is also a test of whether it can command general approval. Maxims which cannot be generalized are therefore those which I would not, in Gert's phrase, be able to 'publicly advocate'.[8] This holds in a double sense, moreover: for one thing I should not be able to will that others should adopt such maxims, and secondly I should not be able to expect that the others could approve of such maxims as a universal rule (and of my following such maxims in particular). The maxims which cannot be generalized are therefore the ones upon which rational beings would not be able to agree as rules for common practice.[9] There is, of course, a problem involved in Kant's assumption that when it comes to the generalization of maxims *my* 'being able to will' or 'not being able to will' must necessarily coincide with that of all other rational beings. And it is precisely this problem which has given rise to the attempt to expand Kant's ethics into a dialogic ethics. But I should like to pass this problem over for the moment and say something more about the connection between the categorical imperative, moral norms, and moral judgements.

We might say that the real point of the categorical imperative is that it enables the categorical 'ought' or 'must' or 'may' of moral norms (i.e. of 'categorical imperatives' in the plural) and of moral judgements to be seen as rationally understandable derivatives of the categorical 'ought' of a single meta-principle. The only thing which then remains to be explained is this categorical 'ought' itself. As long as we assume that Kant suceeded in elucidating this fundamental categorical 'ought', then it is also possible, with recourse to his arguments, to elucidate the 'ought' or 'must' or 'may' of our ordinary moral judgements and norms. In contrast to some of Kant's assertions, but in agreement with Ebbinghaus[10] and Singer,[11] I argue from the premise that the obligation implied by the categorical imperative is 'transferred' to substantive moral norms and judgements primarily by way of a *prohibition* of actions (or maxims) which are not capable of being generalized.[12] Let us take as an example the maxim that if need be I shall get myself out of difficulties by making an insincere promise.[13] Like Kant, I assume that *we* – as rational beings – cannot will that such a practice should become universal. Now the categorical imperative evidently says that under these circumstances I (like X or Z) *may not* act according to the maxim 'if need be make an insincere promise'. In the concrete situation we are imagining this means that if p signifies the act of making an insincere promise and not-p signifies not making such a promise, then I *may not* do p, or I *ought to* (should) do not-p. The 'ought' in 'I (or one) ought to do p' would thus result from the fact that I *cannot* will of a particular maxim that it should have the validity of a universal law. The 'must' or 'ought' of our ordinary moral convictions could be 'derived' from the categorical imperative only *via negationis*, as it were.

According to the interpretation I am offering here, on the other hand, the generalizability of maxims would merely mean that it is morally *permitted* to act in a corresponding way. Now it is impossible to overlook some formulations of Kant's in which he says that maxims which can be generalized *are* eo ipso practical laws.[14] In order to resolve this contradiction we must clarify the concept of 'generalizability', which is to say the meaning of the expression 'being able to will that a maxim should be valid as a universal law'. Now it is no accident, as we shall shortly see, that Kant himself uses examples of a *negative* nature. He demonstrates, for example, that I *cannot* (reasonably) will of certain maxims that they should be valid as universal laws, either because I cannot even conceive of them as universal laws, or else because my will would then be 'in conflict with itself'[15] (for instance if I simultaneously *wanted* other people to help me and *did not want* them to help me). At this point it is important to remember that the categorical imperative, in so far as it contains a 'procedure of examination', does not relate to random propositions, but to maxims which someone – the performer of an act – 'has'. This is what gives rise to a characteristic asymmetry: someone who might, for sake of argument, have the maxim not to tell the truth if to do so would result in his own disadvantage can readily comprehend that he cannot will that this maxim should be valid as a universal law. But someone who has the maxim to tell the truth on all occasions even if this results in his own disadvantage *does* eo ipso will that this maxim should be valid as a universal law (and by the same token he also *can* so will it). But this is something which we cannot straightforwardly assert about the person with the bad maxim. (In what sense could we possibly say of him that he 'can will' the maxim of truthfulness to be a universal law? For his own part, he wants to follow a different rule, and where others are concerned, perhaps it is good enough for him if they are just truthful towards *him*.) Let us take as another example someone whose maxim is never to show weakness however difficult that might be. *If* this is his maxim, then he will also be able (and perhaps even want) to will it as a universal law. But the same is true of a person whose maxim is to show weakness in preference to always playing the strong man. From these few examples we can already see that the answer to the question whether someone is able to will a particular maxim to be a universal law depends on what maxims he does in fact have. Thus the question of whether someone is able to will a maxim to be a universal law cannot decide the issue of whether this maxim is a 'practical law'. But if I assert that I *cannot* will my maxim to be a universal law, then it necessarily follows from this that to act in accordance with this maxim would be morally reprehensible (because I am making an 'exception' for myself): I 'must' not act in accordance with this maxim. Now if I were to adopt the maxim *not* to do what is prohibited by a maxim of the 'non-generalizable' type, then we could call this new maxim the 'negation' of the original one. (In this sense, the maxim 'I shall always tell the truth even if it is to my disadvantage to do so' is the negation of 'I shall not tell the truth if it is to my disadvantage to do so'.) If this new maxim really is the maxim by which *I* act, then I am also willing it to have the validity of a universal law. But in this instance the fact that I can will my maxim to be a universal law has a special significance by virtue of the logical process out of which my 'being able to will' has arisen, namely the fact that my maxim is the negation of a non-generalizable maxim. A maxim which can be generalized in *this* sense expresses a moral obligation, at least for *myself*.

What I would propose, therefore, is that we distinguish between a 'weak' and a 'strong' notion of the generalizability of maxims. The *weak* notion of generalizability is adequate for the purposes of eliminating maxims of the non-generalizable type, but it is not adequate to support the thesis that generalizable maxims are practical laws (i.e. moral norms). For this purpose, a *strong* notion of generalizability is necessary, bearing in mind that the generalizability of maxims in this strong sense has to be understood in terms of a negatory relationship between these maxims and the non-generalizability of the maxims which they negate. Note, however, that *this* negatory relationship with non-generalizable maxims must be distinguished from the negatory relationship which *every* generalizable maxim (in the weak sense) has with its 'negation'. If my maxim is never to show weakness even in the utmost extremity, and if I will this maxim to be a universal law, then this means, of course, that I *cannot* will the maxim to show weakness rather than always playing the strong man to be a universal law. But in *this* case, my 'not being able to will' is dependent upon the fact that an opposing maxim is already *my* maxim (so that the 'not being able to will' is here secondary to the 'being able to will'). The 'not being able to will' in the case of a maxim which is *mine* is quite different, for the non-generalizability of such a maxim is independent of other maxims which I might have in addition.

Thus it is only possible to assert that generalizable maxims are eo ipso practical laws if we limit our understanding of 'generalizable' to those maxims whose negation is non-generalizable, even assuming that such maxims were *mine*. This is what provides the philosophical justification for the emphasis on negation when putting the question about the generalizability of maxims. The problem of the intersubjective *validity* of moral norms, however, cannot be definitively solved even in this way. It is far from clear (contrary to what Kant believed) that the moral obligations which I acknowledge must necessarily be acknowledged by every other rational being (and vice versa). This is a problem to which I shall return. For the purposes of the deliberations which follow, meanwhile, I shall assume for simplicity's sake that the moral norms distinguished by the categorical imperative do have intersubjective validity.

III

Next I should like to discuss Kant's thesis that the norms distinguished by the categorical imperative are *universally* valid,
that is, they are binding 'practical laws' which admit of no
exceptions. It is possible – using Kant's own arguments against
him – to justify this thesis if it is formulated with sufficient
caution. Let us take for example the maxim, 'If it suits my
purposes I shall tell an untruth,' which we may safely assume to
be non-generalizable. When we say that the categorical imperative forbids us *once and for all* to act in accordance with this
maxim, we mean that a categorical prohibition is placed on the
telling of any lie that might be justified (or motivated) by this
maxim; and this prohibition applies in the sense of strict universality (in the sense of Kant's *'universalitas'*).[16] As a moral norm
this might be formulated as follows; 'One may not lie' or 'Thou
shalt not lie'. But we must not overlook the fact (even if Kant
himself overlooked it) that the universal validity (*universalitas*) of
this norm results from the non-generalizability of *a particular
type* of maxim (or from the inadmissibility of *a particular type* of
reason for acting). The strict prohibition applies to a class of
reasons for acting; it *cannot* apply as a strict prohibition to the
corresponding *actions* (in this case, lying). Kant's polemic against
the possibility of exceptions is quite correct if it is applied to the
right sort of exceptions. The norm 'Thou shalt not lie', if understood in the sense we have outlined above, admits of no exception
whatsoever. But this is not to deny the possible existence of
reasons for acting which do constitute *generalizable* exceptions
by virtue of the fact that they can be 'publicly advocated' or, to
keep closer to the terms of our own argument, that the maxims
to which they correspond can be generalized. It appears that
Kant has confused two distinct categories of 'exception'; provided
that we ourselves avoid this confusion, we shall have no difficulty
in viewing derived moral norms as universally valid in the strict
sense *while also* admitting the possibility of exceptions.
   The distinction we are dealing with here is, incidentally, not
identical with the distinction between 'egoistic' and 'altruistic'
motives. I may not lie, *regardless of whether* the advantage I hope
to attain thereby is for myself or my child or my friend. What is
prohibited by the norm we are discussing is the telling of a lie

for *private* ends (whether these are egoistic or altruistic in nature). Saving an innocent person from the Gestapo, for example, would not be a private end in this sense, but rather one which could be justified by means of a *different* moral norm, namely that we may not deny help to innocent victims of persecution. The transgression against a moral norm ('Thou shalt not lie') could be defended in this case with reasons which can be 'publicly advocated' (even if under the implied circumstances I should not be able, in a phrase of Kant's, to 'openly express' them). In other words we might say that the corresponding maxim, 'I shall try to save innocent victims of persecution, and if need be I shall tell a lie in order to do so,' is generalizable. A difficulty arises at this point, however, which Kant was excused by his rigoristic interpretation of moral norms from having to answer. It is this: whereas it is self-evident that the maxim we considered earlier, 'If need be (i.e. if is suits my purposes) I shall tell an untruth,' *cannot* be generalized, the generalizability of the maxim we have now arrived at is, on closer inspection, by no means self-evident. This maxim is too *vague* to permit a clear decision. The difficulty we have might be summed up as follows: I am only able to will *this* maxim to be a universal law if I can be certain that all mankind possesses sufficient judgement and good will to decide correctly when the 'needs' of the situation really justify a lie. If I could be certain of *this*, however, there would no longer be any need for our maxim, because then there would be no persecution of innocents. We must therefore acknowledge that Kant is being consistent when he rejects such maxims as an unsuitable basis for law-making in any conceivable kingdom of ends. In order to justify any exception to the rule 'Thou shalt not lie', we should clearly have to discuss the particular circumstances of a concrete situation. The reasons which I could 'publicly advocate' in justification of this exception might in principle be capable of expression in the form of a generalizable maxim, but in the process we are confronted with the dilemma that the more *precisely* I describe the type of situation involved, the *smaller* the *field of application* for such a maxim becomes, and that the more *general* I make my description, the more *indeterminate* it becomes. What this means is that the justifiable exceptions to moral norms are not subject to rules in the same sense as the actions which those norms prohibit (or command), and that is why the *faculty of judgement* plays a much more fundamental part in the application of moral norms than Kant wished to admit. This is also why, in matters of moral controversy, it is not as a rule the basic moral norms that are at issue, but the descriptions of situations or of types of situation. As soon as we have agreed upon these descriptions (and thus on the 'facts' in the broadest sense of the word), the moral controversies as a rule resolve themselves; in this sense we might say that moral demands reside in the concrete circumstances of action.

I should like to conclude my analysis of the example we have been looking at by modifying my assumptions about the moral problems it presents us with in one further important respect. This modification amounts to 'dissecting' the problem into two component parts. If we look at the question in terms of moral *norms* rather than maxims for action, then the problem consists precisely in a conflict between two norms, the first of which requires that I assist persecuted innocents, while the second requires that I should not lie. Now if I consider the way in which these two norms are related in a negatory fashion to non-generalizable maxims for action, then it immediately becomes clear that our hypothetical situation represents a case of the *direct* application of the *first* norm, but only the *indirect* application of the *second* norm. In other words, the command to lend assistance results from the non-generalizability of the maxim 'I shall only assist persecuted innocents if it is not to my disadvantage to do so'; in this instance the *aim* of my action (to assist persecuted innocents) is positively *commanded*. The prohibition against lying, on the other hand, results from the non-generalizability of a maxim which – under the conditions we are assuming – is not even at issue in the situation we have described, namely the maxim 'I shall tell falsehoods if it appears advantageous to me to do so'. This is just another way of saying that what is at issue here is not lying as a means of achieving a 'private end', but as a means of realizing an end which is morally *commanded*. Thus if we take account of the inherent relationship of each of these norms to non-generalizable maxims, and if we also take account of the specific nature of the situation in which the action takes place, our conflicting norms are revealed to be different in kind. For cases of this sort we should therefore be able to agree with Kant's thesis that there is in reality no conflict between different kinds of moral duty, even if this thesis now acquires a somewhat un-Kantian twist.

My second description of our exemplary situation shows up an aspect of that situation which in my first characterization – with the help of a quasi-generalizable maxim for action – remained obscured. Conversely it is also true to say that the second description obscures an aspect which the first had highlighted, namely the problems concerning the application or 'concretization' of moral norms. We only have to modify the extreme case suggested by our example very slightly in order to see that a lie can by no means always be a legitimate means of assisting persecuted innocents. This means, however, that in spite of the general nature of the argument we have just developed in order to resolve the apparent conflict between norms, the solution we have proposed can only be valid in extreme cases. The full implications of this aspect of the problem become clear if we try to subsume the exception to the command to be truthful under a generalizable maxim, i.e. if we try to formulate a kind of law of permission. As we have seen above, it is not possible, strictly speaking, to formulate generalizable maxims of this kind because they would have to contain some indexical element. A 'law of permission' could therefore only take the form 'In situations such as *this* it is permitted to lie'. The general validity of exceptions, unlike the general validity of moral commands themselves, can ultimately only be demonstrated in the sense of a justification of particular actions in concrete situations. This is where 'situationist' or 'existentialist' ethics contain an element of truth. We cannot but marvel at the immense astuteness of Kant who, because he had made no provision for such a 'situationist' element (implying the exercise of judgement) in his ethics, adhered with the utmost consistency to the only possible alternative, namely a rigoristic ethic of duty.

Let me now return to the thesis that 'derived' moral norms – as strictly general norms which nevertheless admit of possible exceptions – arise by a process of negation from non-generalizable maxims. This thesis does not imply that, when considered in the light of the categorical imperative, all basic moral norms take the form of prohibitions – along the lines of 'Thou shalt not lie', or 'Thou shalt not kill', or even *'Neminem laede'*.[17] It is much rather the case that even norms like 'Help the needy (as far as you are able)' – which, according to Kant, correspond to ethical duties that are 'of broad obligation'[18] – can, in the same way as moral norms of prohibition, stand in a negatory relationship to non-generalizable maxims such as, for instance, 'I shall help nobody if it is of no advantage to me to do so'. The difference between these 'positive' moral norms, which come close to what Gert calls 'moral ideals',[19] and moral norms of prohibition is that the latter prohibit actions, while the former prohibit the *omission* of actions (or *attempts* to act). But whereas the prohibition of an action means the same as a command *not* to perform *this* action, the prohibition of 'remaining inactive' (in particular situations) does not as a rule mean the same as a command to perform *a particular* action. Broadly binding ethical duties leave, as Kant remarks, 'a latitude within which we may do more or less without being able to assign definite limits to it'.[20] We might say that positive norms command us to act in a particular way (making the happiness of others my aim, to put it in Kantian terms), but they do not command us to perform a particular act.

Excursus   R. M. Hare has tried to solve the problem of exceptions to moral 'prima facie principles'[21] in a somewhat different way from the one I have proposed here. Hare distinguishes between two levels of moral thinking, which he calls the 'intuitive' and the 'critical'.[22] On the intuitive level of moral thought we are concerned with prima facie principles which are both *general* and more or less *unspecific*, i.e. they admit of exceptions. It is only in situations of moral conflict that we are forced to switch to the *critical* level of moral thought, which implies the formulation of critical moral principles which can be of 'unlimited specificity'.[23] For Hare, prima facie principles are merely a means of disencumbering ourselves of complexities, so to speak (or of developing moral 'habits'), in the moral practice of everyday life. If we had the intellectual capacity of an archangel we would be able to exercise critical moral judgement on all occasions and thus allow our actions to be determined by moral principles which consistently did justice to the particularity of the situations we found ourselves in.[24]

Hare's 'critical moral principles' are prima facie principles which have been modified by exception clauses in some such manner as this: 'One ought never to do an act which is G, except that one may when it is necessary in order to avoid an act which is F, and the act is also H; but if the act is not H, one may not.'[25] (This example of course provides only the starting-point for the critical specification of a prima facie principle.) The reason why this method of solving the problem of 'exceptions' seems to me cock-eyed is that we do indeed require the notion of an archangel (or a god) in order to combine the universality of principles with the particularity of situations in the manner which Hare is describing; which is to say that we need the image of an infinite intelligence which would be capable of 'sublating' the particular completely within the universal. Only if we presuppose such an infinite intelligence as the ultimate goal of our finite mental efforts can we attempt to solve the problem of moral exceptions or conflicts (i.e. moral *problem* situations) with reference to the unlimited specifiability of moral norms. In using this image, Hare is importing a figure of thought which is in a certain sense legitimate in the field of the natural sciences (i.e. the idea that there are no limits to the possibility of specifying causal laws) into the realm of practical, historical phenomena. If for no other reason, this importation should be disqualified on the grounds that in the field of history (to which all action belongs) the notion of an 'ultimate' language, of an 'exhaustive' description, does not even make sense as a regulative idea.

There is a way of formulating the objection to Hare's notion of the unlimited specifiability of moral principles which is both more specific and more precise. We have seen that, proceeding on Kantian premises, it is possible to distinguish clearly between maxims which are (in the strong sense) generalizable and from which it is possible to derive universally valid moral norms, and 'quasi-generalizable' maxims for which the equivalent moral norms would have to take the form of 'laws of permission'. We have also seen that, because of their imprecise nature, it is not in fact possible to formulate such laws of permission as laws in the Kantian sense. This is because they cover an indeterminate number of cases in which what they seem to permit would be morally prohibited. In Hare's example of a norm that is specifiable (within limits), quoted above, the first 'except' clause represents a law of permission of the kind we mean, whereas the second 'except' clause signifies a limitation of the permission. Now Hare, too, argues from the premise that as creatures of finite intelligence we must get by with *finite* specifications of moral principles. But if the critical moral principles upon which we base our judgements include among their components 'laws of permission' which, because of the limited specification of our principles, can, as it were, only be furnished with a basic minimum of necessary qualifications, then these moral principles are themselves, almost *of necessity* and certainly *predictably, false.*

Let us consider for example the following principle: 'It is forbidden to kill people except when it is necessary in order to perform an act of mercy towards a terminally ill patient who asks you to release them from their sufferings.' In advocating such a principle we have particular situations in mind in which it may be defensible, and perhaps even commendable to act in such a way. But it is obvious that not only could such a principle, if it were to become enshrined in law, be subject to infinite abuse (this is the *exoteric* side of the problem), but also that in this general form it is probably morally wrong, even presupposing that it were applied in a spirit of *good will.* In the vagueness of the formulation (*when* is an action *necessary as an act of mercy?*) there also lurk a thousand counter-arguments which might occur to us in concrete situations (and even at our desks), and I mean counter-arguments against the principle itself in its general formulation. In concrete situations, however, we have to assume responsibility and act as best we can. Now if we were to reconstruct the logic of moral judgements or justifications as Hare understands it, our moral justifications in problem situations would be necessarily false because they were based on false principles. But in reality, the fact that in concrete situations we have principles (albeit not yet sufficiently specified ones) by no means prevents us from having reasons for doing the right thing *in* these situations. Whether the reasons we have are watertight depends, it seems, more on our apprehension of (these) situations than on the availability of generally valid principles. Or to put it another way, even if reasons and descriptions of situations always have something general about them, in the cases which we are considering here the justifications which we are able to formulate invariably include an indexical element, and that (if anything) is what decides whether they are watertight. Our apprehension of the situation always exceeds what is made explicit in our descriptions and justifications; that is why even our (critical) principles, *if* we formulate them, contain an implicit reference to paradigmatic situations with which we have to be familiar in order to *apply* these principles. The principles *themselves* contain an indexical element; otherwise they would not be able to play any part in moral thinking without having been adequately 'specified' in advance. The same is not true, however, of prima facie principles if we understand them as moral norms whose universal validity resides in the negatory relationship in which they stand to non-generalizable maxims.

It is my view, then, that whatever else we might think of Kant's ethics, they do allow us to formulate a categorical distinction between moral norms and 'laws of permission' which shows up something of the 'fine structure' of moral judgements and justifications, a fine structure which is, moreover, lost to view if in the formulation of 'critical' moral principles we interpolate moral commands or prohibitions on the one hand and 'laws of permission' on the other, in the way that Hare does. It was for this reason, and because of the rationalistic implications of his approach (as described above), that I called Hare's solution to the problem of moral exceptions 'cock-eyed'.

Now although these ideas of Hare's which we have criticized belong to the same rationalist tradition as Kant's philosophy, it appears that Kant, in contrast to Hare, has retained an element of Aristotelian caution when transferring the concept of law into the realm of moral philosophy. It is precisely for this reason that he would have been bound to find it impossible to mediate between general principle and particular situation in the manner in which Hare attempts it. Kant's philosophical rigorism in moral questions is the rationalistic conclusion he had drawn from this very difficulty; this conclusion was the price he paid in order to be able to define moral action generally in terms of moral laws. On the other hand we saw that it is perfectly possible to preserve the *'universalitas'* of fundamental moral norms (i.e. the 'prima facie principles' in Hare's sense) if we relate them in a negatory fashion to non-generalizable *maxims* for action. The problem of 'exceptions' then appears in a different light, namely as one that can ultimately only be solved in concrete situations, and then by means of *reasons*, not by means of an unlimited specification of *principles*.

I do not want to exaggerate the differences I have with Hare. In a certain sense it is possible to see Hare's distinction between 'intuitive' and 'critical' moral principles as a translation of my own proposed solution to the problem of 'exceptions' (working with a Kantian perspective) into a different philosophical language; the structural homologies are plain to see. Looked at like this, Hare is closer to an Aristotelian tradition than Kant. But when Hare talks of 'principles' where strictly speaking it is no longer possible to formulate them, I consider this to be, to say the least, misleading. Even if the reasons which we might adduce for moral judgements in concrete situations always carry an index of generality, in cases of moral conflict they nevertheless remain 'linked' to the situations in question in such a way that they can at best be converted into ad hoc principles, i.e. into rules, the correct application of which is tied to a capacity for judgement which can in turn only be formed through a process of (moral) familiarization with corresponding exemplary situations. This is not true of those moral principles which 'correspond' to non-generalizable maxims; here we really are dealing – in the sense which I have explained above – with *universal* principles. I therefore believe that my own proposed solution to the problem of moral exceptions – at least within a Kantian perspective which, in a broader sense, Hare also shares – is more convincing than Hare's solution.

IV

Kant evidently never conceived the individual will that is capable of willing a maxim to be a universal law as anything other than the expression of a will that is *common to all mankind* as rational beings. The 'cognitivism' of Kant's ethics, i.e. the claim of moral judgements to universal (in the sense of *intersubjective*) validity, stands and falls with this presupposition (leaving aside for the present the problem of 'fundamental' grounding). The problematic nature of this presupposition is plain to see: the expression 'capable of willing' contains an irreducibly 'empirical' element, and we must therefore reckon with the possibility that different people are capable of willing *different* ways of acting as universal ones. I have shown above that this problem can be alleviated *to a certain degree* if we keep the concept of *non*-generalizability to the forefront of our minds whenever we consider the concept of a generalizable maxim (in the strong sense). For when the matter is defined in terms of 'not being able to will', then the individual exercising moral judgement is placed in a privileged position: if *I cannot* will something to be the case, then *we cannot* will it.

This is not to say, however, that the intersubjective validity of moral judgements is thus secured, for what we can or cannot will as general ways of acting is indubitably decided from case to case by the matrix of concepts through which we interpret social reality and our own needs. Let us consider, for instance, the authoritarian maxim of not beating about the bush but immediately taking stern measures when confronted with insubordination (of pupils, subjects, persons under my command). Whether or not I judge this maxim to be generalizable depends on whether I, as an authoritarian teacher or officer, interpret social reality with the help of a matrix of concepts in which obedience and insubordination represent, as it were, the positive and negative poles of an ordered existence, or whether, as a democrat, I interpret them with the help of concepts related to a normative scale that runs from self-determination at the one extreme to dependency at the other. A moral principle like the categorical imperative can never operate in a 'vacuum' where norms are concerned. But if this is so, then following the categorical imperative in concrete situations does not *by itself* guarantee the intersubjective validity of corresponding moral judgements. And it is initially *quite impossible* to see how the categorical imperative could help us to secure a moral consensus. And if we also bear in mind the problems surrounding the question of 'exceptions', or rather of the situational aspect of moral judgements, which we saw earlier, then we are confronted with a tangle of difficulties which Kant was only able to hide beneath his 'formalistic' interpretation of the categorical imperative. This formalistic interpretation comes to the fore in the *Critique of Practical Reason* where, at decisive points of the argument, what can be 'willed' is revealingly replaced with what can 'hold good', the criterion for which is what can be 'conceived'.[26] The following passage is typical:

> Therefore, either a rational being cannot conceive his subjective practical principles, that is, his maxims, as being at the same time universal laws, or he must suppose that their mere form, by which they are fitted for universal legislation, is alone what makes them practical laws.[27]

By making the 'form' of maxims as 'laws' the criterion for morally correct action, Kant – seemingly – preserves the objectivity of morals. But if we follow this thought to its logical conclusion we find that the fruitful ambiguity of Kant's moral philosophy has been abandoned in favour of a formalistic ethic of duty which can scarcely be of serious interest to us today.

My own view – which is surely compatible with nearly all contemporary philosophies of morals which take Kant as their starting point – is rather that the productive element in Kant's formulation of the moral principle in the *Groundwork* resides precisely in the reference it makes to the empirical will of the person performing the act, even if it conceives the object of that will to be general ways of acting rather than individual goals. We might say that *if* there is anything correct in Kant's reconstruction of our moral intuitions, then it must be the way that the rationality of moral judgements is anchored in a particular relationship between what is (empirically) 'willed' and what 'ought' to be the case. A large part of contemporary moral philosophy can be understood as the attempt to emphasize this basic Kantian intuition over against the decline of Kant's ethics into formalism; indeed, this is the common ground between rule-utilitarianism and communicative ethics. And if we take seriously the problem that lies behind Kant's construction of a connection between rationality and the will of beings who have the capacity to act, then crudely speaking there appear to be three possible alternative solutions for an ethics based on Kant.

The *first* of these alternatives consists in conceding that different rational beings might be able to will quite different ways of acting as universal ones. In this case we are denying the necessary condition that the rational will of all beings capable of action should coincide; the moral universe disintegrates – potentially – into a plurality of moral worlds, as is the case at least in the earlier work of Hare.[28] Hare incidentally eliminates the 'problem of fundamental grounding' by deriving the universalism of ethics directly from the logical grammar of basic moral terminology ('ought', 'must' etc.). He anchors ethics, so to speak, in a fact of *our* (modern) reason.

The *second* alternative consists in the attempt to establish a minimal ethics, the contents of which more or less correspond to moral norms which we also encounter in Kant if we consider examples of non-generalizable maxims. The negatory relationship between moral norms and non-generalizable maxims reappears in this second variant on 'Kantian' ethics, but in an altered form: moral norms are in the first instance prohibitions on ways of acting on which rational beings would not be able to agree as admissible ones. The word 'rational' should here be understood in a *weak* sense: the 'rational' will is a self-interested one which takes account of the consequences of alternative possibilities for regulating action – just as in the corresponding points of Kant's argument. I believe that the theory of B. Gert,[29] some thoughts of G. H. von Wright,[30] and to a certain extent also the theories of Singer and Rawls[31] belong to this second alternative. Since in this second alternative the moral 'ought' is reconstructed from its basic contents it is true in a sense that the unity of the moral universe remains intact, but here it is the concept of moral obligation that presents a problem instead. Once the rational sense of the moral 'ought' has been called into question, it is no longer possible to resort to a Kantian coup in oder to justify the demand that – here and now – I *ought* to act according to generalizable maxims or, in Gert's terms, according to reasons which can be 'publicly advocated' – in other words, that I should act *morally*.[32] The reconstruction of intersubjectively valid moral contents in Kant's sense has the (paradoxical) consequence that the immediate identity of the *rational* will with the *moral* will breaks down.[33] It can only be restored – not by means of an ultimate grounding, but in weaker forms – if the categorical 'ought' is linked once more with an (empirical) 'willing'. The second alternative thus reveals the deficit in Kant's ethics regarding *a philosophical grounding*; the more convincing it becomes as a reconstruction of basic ideas in Kant's ethics, the more clearly it reveals that the unconditional moral 'ought' of the categorical imperative can scarcely be an 'ought' of pure practical reason.

The *third* and last alternative consists in the expansion of Kant's moral principle into an ethics of discourse as has been proposed not only by Apel and Habermas, but in a different form also by the 'constructivists' of Erlangen and Constance.[34] Much as in the case of the alternative we have just been looking at, valid moral norms are here equated with those rules upon which we should be able to agree in a rational dialogue. The decisive point in which this alternative *differs* from the previous one is that it abandons the claim to a philosophical grounding of substantive moral norms and replaces it with a principle of dialogic agreement which *takes the place* of Kant's moral principle. By taking this approach, it also becomes possible once more to tackle the problem of fundamental grounding. At least Apel and Habermas have tried to show that a principle of uncoerced dialogue for settling normative validity claims is 'built into' the conditions for communicative action as a constitutive principle, which must therefore always have been acknowledged, implicitly at least, by beings that have the capacity for speech and action. Of the three alternatives for developing an ethics based on Kant, or on 'Kantian' precepts, which we have outlined here, only the third represents a serious attempt to rehabilitate an emphatic concept of practical reason in Kant's sense of the term, that is to defend *both* the possibility of justifying moral norms *and also* the rational sense of an unconditional moral 'ought'. I shall examine the difficulties which arise from this third alternative at a later stage.

V

The selective reading of Kant's moral principle which I have been propounding so far corresponds structurally more or less to the *second* of the three alternatives outlined above. Accordingly I have so far omitted any discussion of whether it is possible to provide a philosophical grounding for the categorical imperative, which also means that I have not addressed the question of the rational sense of the moral 'ought' in the light of the categorical imperative. I find myself in agreement with other critics of Kant when I say that Kant himself gave no satisfactory answer to this question. But as we have seen, this is not the only weakness in Kant's moral philosophy. If I have so far emphasized it *strengths*, then I did so because on the one hand I wanted to show that Kant's reconstruction of moral judgement can be made entirely plausible for a *limited* but *fundamental* class of moral problems, and also because, by emphasizing the strengths, I wanted to throw the *weaknesses* of Kant's argument into sharper focus. In this way I hope both to have established a certain standard by which we can measure the achievement of an ethics that attempts to go beyond Kant, and also to have characterized the problem areas in which it is possible to discern the motives for the development of a dialogic ethics. For the problem areas of Kant's ethics, as characterized above, prompt the thought that we might situate the formal principle of ethics that Kant was looking for one step lower, as it were, and try to identify it in the connection between (intersubjective) *validity* and (rational) *grounding*. This is what Apel and Habermas try to do, replacing Kantian formalism with a 'procedural' formalism. The intention is that the formulation of a moral principle in procedural terms should not only open the way for philosophical investigation of those problem areas which remain as blank spots on the map of Kant's ethics, but that it should at the same time also enable us to solve the problem of 'fundamental grounding' without relapsing into metaphysics. These two basic intentions of dialogic ethics are interconnected in a systematic way, as we shall see later. But in order to clarify these intentions a little further, and in the process to show exactly what claims are being made by discourse ethics and the points that remain for it to demonstrate, I should first like to pursue the question of whether it is not possible to find in Kant's own writings points from which to develop a dialogic expansion of ethics.

John R. Silber has attempted to show that the formalism of Kant's ethics must *in itself* be understood as a 'procedural' formalism.[35] What he means by this is not the 'procedure' of a real dialogue, however, but the procedure of forming a moral judgement. Silber tries to explain the 'procedural formalism' of Kant's ethics by interpreting the categorical imperative in the light of what Kant calls 'maxims of common human understanding'.[36] In our context it is the second of these maxims ('Think from the standpoint of everyone else') that is especially important. In the light of this maxim, says Silber, the moral examination of a maxim for action requires a hypothetical shift of perspective, since it is only by thinking from the standpoint of others, and particularly of those who would be affected by our actions, that we can arrive at a considered judgement as to whether – as rational beings – we can reasonably will a maxim to be a universal law. 'In order to respect the humanity of all rational beings the moral agent must put himself into the place and point of view of others. In this way he will understand the values and needs of other beings and by moving out beyond himself will limit his tendency to concentrate upon the fulfilment of his own needs to the neglect of the needs and legitimate desires of others.'[37]

Silber's interpretation of the categorical imperative in the light of Kant's maxim from the *Critique of Judgement* might seem to suggest that Kant's ethics contains the inherent possibility of a link to a dialogic ethics. For if I am only able to give an adequate answer to the question whether I can (reasonably) will a maxim to be a universal law if I also let the others speak in my own mind, as it were, and give due weight to the perspective – the values and needs – of the others (and this can only mean others *as they really exist*) in my own considerations, then it seems to me that two things follow from this:

1 that a hypothetical element is inherent in moral judgements (it is possible for me to be *mistaken* in my assessment of the standpoint of others), and
2 that it is in the nature of moral thinking that it points to real dialogue (since I should only be able to test my apprehension of the standpoint of others by means of real communication).

In other words, if 'thinking from the standpoint of everyone else' presupposes, in the case of moral thinking, an apprehension of the standpoint of others, then the idea of moral insight guided by the categorical imperative represents a *problem* which I can only ever solve in a hypothetical and provisional sense. The question of the generalizability of maxims then becomes a question of whether *we* are able to will a maxim as a universal law; and this is a question which it is *ultimately* only possible to answer by means of real communication among those concerned.

It is true that Silber himself has not completed this step that leads from a 'procedural' to a dialogic ethics. What Silber is trying to show with his repudiation of 'formalistic' interpretations of Kant's ethics is precisely that a 'monologic' application of the categorical imperative in the examination of maxims is perfectly adequate, as Kant believed, for producing agreement between individual and general will. Looked at in this way, Silber's reference to the maxims of common human understanding should be understood as an attempt to show that the categorical imperative represents the precise *specification* of those maxims by which reason constitutes itself *as practical*. It is in this precise sense that Silber says, 'The moral law is itself to be understood as a principle which specifies the procedure of judgement in the act of moral schematism.'[38] But what Silber leaves unclear is the question of how a 'monologic' application of the categorical imperative can be reconciled with the requirement that we must give the perspective of others – their needs and values – due weight in our moral thinking, for *this* requirement seems to point to the necessity for a transition from solitary reflection to a real dialogue.

Silber admittedly concedes the *fallibility* of moral judgements. In this connection he points to the demand, which Kant cites with approval, that we must 'work out our own salvation with fear and trembling'.[39] But what is actually implied there is the infinite potential for self-delusion, in the sense that we can never be entirely certain that our *basic way of thinking* is morally good. On the other hand, the question of correctly apprehending the needs and values of others, in the way that Silber presents it, is not in the first instance at all concerned with the problem of moral self-delusion, but much rather with the problem of the appropriate apprehension of situations, including the precise manner in which those affected by a particular action are involved in the situation. As far as this problem is concerned, Silber's demand that in making a moral judgement we must put ourselves in everyone else's position appears less as a proposal for *solving* the problem than as a – somewhat misleading – reformulation of the problem itself. But then if Silber were correct with his thesis that the procedural formalism of Kant's moral principle at least *aims at* a solution of precisely this problem, we should also have to concede that it is in the nature of the categorical imperative to require a transition to *real* dialogue, for only in the medium of real communication and discourse would it be possible to clarify whether I have put myself in the position of others *in the correct manner*. Silber's thoughts would then have to be understood as pointing to an inherent 'dialogicity' in Kant's moral principle. The question is, can we concede that Kant's ethics – implicitly – contain such a dialogic principle without simultaneously calling into question Kant's own grounding of his ethics in a 'monologic' moral principle?

For the purposes of answering this question, I should like to distinguish between a 'dialogic ethics' and an 'ethics of dialogue'. By 'dialogic ethics' I mean an ethics in which the dialogue principle *is substituted for* the moral principle; by 'ethics of dialogue' I mean an ethics in which the dialogue principle occupies a central position among the *derived* moral principles. My thesis is that it is not possible to move to a dialogic ethics while remaining true to Kant's thinking, but that it may very well be possible to expand Kant's ethics into an ethics of dialogue. It is precisely such as expansion of Kant's ethics, which we might call 'dialogic' in a narrow sense, that is suggested by Silber's reflections. It would be an expansion of Kant's ethics which acknowledged the existence of a plurality of needs and values, as well as the necessity of mediating between these transsubjectively, and took account of them as *problems* which Kant had neglected. The decisive thought is this one: in so far as it is *possible* for individuals to resolve differences in the way they understand themselves and the situations they find themselves in by means of dialogue, and in so far as it is *possible* for them to achieve a mutual understanding about their respective needs and values, then the Kantian ethic also *demands* that this should be done. For a maxim of refusing to enter into dialogue in situations where incompatible claims, needs or interpretations collide with each other is not (in the Kantian sense) generalizable. A dialogue principle that is derived in this fashion will not, however, be primarily concerned with the question of the generalizability of maxims, but above all with the question of an adequate apprehension of situations and the way individuals see themselves. It will be particularly effective in cases where a correct understanding of the needs and values of others is required. What we are dealing with here is, as it were, the 'communicative substructure' of Kant's ethics, i.e. that dimension of practical reason that has to do with problems concerning the 'commonality' of our world and the adequacy of our understanding of situations and of ourselves. This dimension of the way we form moral judgements is largely excluded from Kant's argument. Silber's reflections at least point towards it, even though he fails to clarify how this dimension of moral judgement could be deployed in the context of a Kantian perspective. Silber fails to recognize that Kant himself systematically trivialized this problem.

The trivialization can be seen at work, for example, in the case of the non-generalizable maxims we referred to earlier. It would certainly be possible to say that the act of asserting that these maxims are non-generalizable also presupposes a kind of hypothetical shift of perspective, in the sense that it must *in principle* be possible for me to put myself in the place of a helpless person in order for me to arrive at the judgement that I cannot will the maxim of refusing help as a universal law. This is a matter of anthropological common factors of a fundamental kind, which were so self-evident to Kant that he would have envisaged the shift of perspective called for by Silber as having already been effected in the very act of somebody in a particular situation recognizing the predicament of somebody else *as* that of someone in need of help. Kant thus presupposes that the shift of perspective which is necessary in each instance has already been effected *before* the question of the generalizability of maxims for action presents itself. And in the context of the 'elementary instruction' in morals to which his ethics is ideally 'suited', this makes good sense. Things are very different in the non-elementary domain of moral reasoning, where we are concerned with an adequate apprehension of complex situations or the historically variable ways in which people see themselves and the world in which they live. At this non-elementary level of morality, not only the *knowledge*, but also the adequate *apprehension* of the needs and values of others becomes a *problem*, and with it my own understanding of myself and the world. Together, moreover, these things constitute a problem which has to be solved before there can be any possibility of forming a correct moral judgement.

Silber tries to interpret Kant's moral principle in such a way that it incorporates *this* dimension of the formation of moral judgements. In the nature of Kant's ethics, there is certainly some justification for 'opening the subject up' in this way. But Silber obscures the difficulties that lie in the way of such an 'opening up' of ethics from a Kantian point of view. That is why it also remains unclear at which point the *problem* of a hypothetical shift of perspective presents itself within the framework of a Kantian ethics.

Neither Silber's reflections nor the thoughts we have developed from them have so far enabled us to escape from the magic circle of a 'monologic' moral principle. But at least it has become clearer that the 'problem areas' of Kant's ethics, to which we referred earlier, also represent a dialogic dimension of morals which Silber's reflections have at least pointed us towards. For the moment, however, our attempt to develop Silber's interpretation of the categorical imperative and find a basis in Kant himself for a dialogic ethics has led us back towards the *second* of the three alternative ways of reconstructing Kant's universalism which we outlined earlier.

In the sections that follow I should like to discuss the third alternative – the one that makes the stronger claim – in the form in which it has been elaborated by Habermas and Apel. This is the alternative in which a dialogue principle *is substituted for* the moral principle.

II A Critique of Discourse Ethics

VI

In this part of my essay I shall concern myself primarily with that form of discourse ethics which has been developed by Habermas. Only when I come to discuss the way in which discourse ethics is based on premises drawn from consensus theory, and also when I discuss the problems of fundamental grounding, shall I deal explicitly with Apel's version of discourse ethics (and with W. Kuhlmann's more closely argued presentation of the question of fundamental grounding). This manner of proceeding obviously imposes its own limitations; I consider it to be justified nevertheless, because my purpose is the *exemplary* clarification of certain matters of principle with reference to a conveniently concise and particularly rich text. I believe that my objections to Habermas's formulations of discourse ethics apply equally to Apel's more recent reflections on the subject[40], but this is not the place for me to demonstrate the point.

Habermas has compared the historical (phylogenetic) transition to a universalistic moral consciousness with the (ontogenetic) emergence of a post-conventional moral consciousness in adolescents. In either case, the emergence of a post-conventional moral consciousness is a response to the fact that previously unquestioned norms come to be seen as questionable and *in need of* justification. Where this happens, argument itself – as the 'reflexive' form of communicative action'[41] – becomes the only possible authority for redeeming normative validity-claims. The transition to a post-conventional moral consciousness also means the transition to a new way of *understanding* normative validity-claims, in which the intersubjective validity of such claims is understood as the expression of a potential accord among those affected by a given norm, freely achieved by means of argument. A procedural criterion – the redeeming of normative validity-claims by means of argument – is substituted for material criteria such as are characteristic of the conventional form of moral consciousness. The following quotation from Habermas describes the ontogenetic development of a post-conventional moral consciousness in a suggestive manner:

If we imagine for the sake of argument the phase of adolescence
as concentrated into a single moment of time in which, for the
first time, our adolescent adopts a hypothetical attitude towards
the normative contexts of his life-world which enables him to see
through everything unmercifully, then this illustrates the *nature
of the problem* which every individual must come to terms with
on passing from the conventional to the post-conventional plane
of moral judgement. The social world of legitimately regulated
interpersonal relations to which he has been naively accustomed
and which he has accepted in an unproblematical fashion is sud-
denly deracinated, stripped of its natural validity.

If our adolescent is neither able nor willing to return to the
traditionalism and unquestioned identity which characterized the
world from which he has come, then he must reconstruct the
ordered normative relationships which have disintegrated under
this penetrating hypothetical gaze from first principles – on pain
of total disorientation. Out of the ruins of devalued traditions,
which have been revealed as conventional and in need of justification, a new edifice must be constructed that is capable of with-
standing the sober critical gaze of one who will henceforth be
unable to do other than distinguish between socially accepted
norms and valid ones, between norms that are acknowledged as
a matter of fact and norms that actually *deserve* to be so acknowledged. Initially it is with reference to principles that the new
edifice can be planned and valid norms can be generated; but
ultimately there remains only a procedure for the rationally motivated choice between principles which have in turn come to be
recognized as standing in need of justification. When measured
against the moral actions of everyday life, the change of attitude
which discourse ethics demands with respect to the procedure it
singles out (i.e. the transition to argument) retains something
unnatural; it signifies a break with the naivety of spontaneously
held validity-claims upon whose intersubjective recognition the
communicative practice of everyday life depends. This unnatu-
ralness is like an echo of that developmental catastrophe which
the devaluation of the world of tradition signifies historically –
and which is what prompts us to attempt a reconstruction on a
higher plane.[42]

Thus, for Habermas, the transition to a post-conventional moral
consciousness is equivalent to the discovery that there exists no
possible basis for normative (or cognitive) validity beyond the
medium of rational argument. Post-conventional moral consciousness is the result of a reflexive insight into the conditions

for the possibility of normative validity. This thesis marks the starting point for Habermas's reformulation of Kant's moral principle, i.e. for his reformulation of the universalization principle in the terms of discourse ethics.

This reformulation of the universalization principle (U) runs as follows:

> Thus every valid norm must satisfy the condition that the consequences and side-effects which result (foreseeably) from its *general* observance with respect to the interest of *every* individual can be accepted (and preferred to the effect of known alternative possibilites for regulating action) by *all* those affected. (DE 75f)

Habermas also calls the universalization principle a 'rule for argument'. As a rule for argument, principle (U) determines the *aim* of arguments in the context of moral disputes; we might say that it determines the sense of the validity of the moral 'ought'. Now Habermas maintains that this rule for argument cannot be applied in a 'monologic' fashion, but that in the meaning of the term it requires a transition to *real* discourse.

> The given formulation of the generalization principle does indeed aim at a co-operative execution of the argument in question. On the one hand, it is only by the immediate participation of everyone affected that it is possible to prevent the interests of individuals from being distorted in the interpretation by the perspectives of others. In this pragmatic sense, each individual is himself the ultimate authority for judging what really is in his own interests. On the other hand, however, the description of his own interests that each individual acknowledges to be accurate must remain amenable to the criticism of others. Needs are interpreted in the light of cultural values; and since these are always elements of an intersubjectively shared heritage, the revision of values by which needs are interpreted cannot be something which the individual determines in a monologic fashion. (DE 77f)

In this passage Habermas characterizes fairly precisely the blind spots of Kant's ethics to which Hegel – arguing from different premises, it is true – had also drawn attention. Much as Habermas's elucidation is intuitively persuasive, however, the reformulation of the universalization principle itself is nonetheless problematic. This is what I wish to demonstrate below. I shall begin with Habermas's reformulation of principle (U), and then go on to discuss the premise for this reformulation, the consensus theory of truth.

At first glance it appears to be a particular strength of principle (U) that it links questions of morally right action directly to questions of whether norms are just or not. In this way, justice and morality are related to each other from the outset through a concept of what is normatively right that is fundamental to both. This strength of principle (U) is revealed on closer inspection, however, to be a weakness. For principle (U) succeeds in binding justice to morality only at the price of assimilating moral problems conceptually to legal ones. In principle (U), a universalistic moral principle is inscrutably 'shuffled in' with a principle of democratic legitimacy in such a way that it ultimately fails to convince *either* as a moral principle *or* as a legitimation principle. I should like to elucidate this thesis in four stages.

(1) If we try to read principle (U) as a legitimation (or justice) principle, as the formulation of it encourages us to do, then the following difficulty emerges: principle (U) leaves open the quesion of what it means to say that someone (I) 'could accept without coercion' the consequences that the general observance of a norm would have for each individual; consequently it also leaves open the question of what it means to say that a norm is acceptable to *all* in this sense. It is apparent from many of Habermas's formulations that he understands the notion of 'being able to accept without coercion' in the sense of an *impartial* formation of judgement; and this would imply that a norm is valid if and when all those affected can persuade themselves that the general observance of this norm is 'equally in the interests of all those affected' – as Habermas indeed puts it at another point (cf. DE 76). *This*, then, would be what arguments *aim at* if principle (U) were 'applied' as a rule for argument. In an argument about norms, each individual would try to show everyone else that a particular norm is equally in the interests of all. This being so, principle (U) could be reformulated (and abbreviated) as follows:

> (U_1) A norm is valid precisely when the general observance of it by all those affected could be judged to be equally in the interest of all those affected.

According to Habermas, then, we can only discover *whether* this is the case by means of real discourse.

Let us ask next what is meant by the term 'valid' as it is used in principle (U). There are two possible answers to this question. We might try firstly to continue to read principle (U) as a principle concerning the justice of norms. The answer to our question would then emerge from a remark which Habermas makes in connection with his derivation of the universalization principle, where he writes that 'the sense we associate with justified norms is that these regulate social matters in the common interests of those who may be affected' (cf. DE 103). It would seem an obvious step to interpret 'justified' here as identical in meaning with 'valid'; but if precisely those norms are 'valid' of which it can be shown that they regulate social matters in the common interests of those who may be affected, and if we then apply the criterion for the validity of norms as formulated by principle (U), then we are likely to arrive at the following, quasi-circular reformulation of principle (U):

> (U_2) A norm is equally in the interests of all those affected precisely when it can be accepted without coercion by all those affected *as being* equally in the interests of all those affected.

I spoke of a *quasi-circular* (and not simply of a circular) formulation of a principle of justice here because in (U_2) we have to distinguish between different levels on which the expression 'equally in the interests of all those affected' is used. On one level it is presupposed that those affected know the goal their argument must aim for in order to show that a norm is justified; on another level (U_2) is saying that only an uncoerced consensus of all those affected can show *whether* a norm really is 'equally in the interests of all affected'. (U_2) does not provide a plausible interpretation of (U), however, because it in fact contains nothing more than the application of a general consensus theory of truth to the specific case of the concept of justice. To this extent (U_2) is not a specific principle of *justice* at all.

Even setting aside the problems of a consensus theory of truth, to which I shall return, our attempt to interpret principle (U) has so far ended in a cul-de-sac. Evidently our first answer to the question of the sense of 'valid' in principle (U) was incorrect. But then Habermas himself suggests another answer, which leads to an interpretation of principle (U) as a *moral* principle.

(2) The error in our reflections so far lies in the fact that we have
been reading the expressions 'norm' and 'observance of a norm',
as they occur in principle (U), naively, so to speak. This stands
in contradiction to Habermas's own elucidation of the 'grammar'
of normative validity-claims. Moreover, Habermas interprets
moral 'ought' or 'must' as a 'higher degree' predicate comparable
to the predicate 'true' (cf. DE 63). In this case the 'deep grammar'
of the statement

> 'In the given circumstances one ought to lie'

would have to be rendered as

> 'It is right (commanded) to lie in the given circumstances',

where 'is right' should be understood as the normative equivalent, so to speak, of the expression 'is true'. This is how Habermas
arrives at a structural parallel between

> 'It is true (the case) that p'

and

> 'It is right (commanded) that a.' (DE 63)

In this sense, normative rightness can be understood as a validity-claim analogous to truth. This interpretation of the sense
of 'ought' statements would open the possibility of understanding the word 'valid' as it occurs in principle (U) as identical in
meaning with the truth-analogous predicate 'right'. We should
then have to read principle (U) in the following way:

> (U_3) In situations S, it is (morally) correct (commanded) to do a if
> such a way of acting could be conceived as universal and could
> be accepted without coercion by all (those affected) as being equ-
> ally in the interests of all after taking into consideration its foresee-
> able consequences for each individual.

A further possible reading would be this:

> (U_4) In situations S, it is (morally) right (commanded) to do a if
> all individuals can will (without coercion) that a corresponding

way of acting – taking into account the foreseeable consequences
for each individual – become universal.

In this way the apparent norm predicate 'valid' ('justified') would
be replaced with the normative predicate 'right'. Translated into
ordinary parlance, (U_3) and (U_4) would thus read:

> 'One must do a in situations S if . . . etc.'

Alternatively we could revert without fear of further misunderstanding, to the formulation contained in (U):

> 'Every valid norm must satisfy the condition that . . .'

Principle (U) has emerged as a genuine moral principle. But how
do things stand with the parallelization of 'It is true that p' and
'It is right (commanded) that a' which Habermas presupposes?
In the first case we have a valid equivalence of the kind:

> 'It is true that p precisely when p'

whereas in the second case the equivalence could only take the
form:

> 'It is right (commanded) that a precisely when X',

where X stands for the criterion of validity formulated by principle (U). But this means that the *formal* elucidation of the predicate 'true' in the one case would stand against a *material* elucidation of the predicate 'right' in the other. In other words, the
term 'true' would denote that which can justifiably be maintained, without a *criterion* for truth being yielded in the process;
but the term 'right' would denote that which can justifiably be
demanded in the sense of a quite specific *criterion* of rightness. The
sense of the validity of (moral) 'ought' would thus be determined a
priori by a *criterion* of the validity of moral 'ought'.

There is an obvious basis for comparison with Kant here. Kant,
too, had in a certain sense determined the rational *sense* of the
validity of moral (categorical) 'ought' by means of a *criterion* of
the validity of moral 'ought' (the categorical imperative). According to Kant, as rational beings we have always already recognized
such a categorical 'ought' as justified; to act in contradiction of

it would mean acting in contradiction of the conditions for the possibility of our self-respect *as* rational beings. In this sense, the unconditional moral 'ought' as it is expressed through the categorical imperative represents for Kant a 'fact of reason'. In a similar way, Habermas's elucidation of the *sense* of moral validity by means of a *criterion* of moral validity should be understood as pointing to a universal structure of linguistically mediated intersubjectivity; what is expressed in the unconditional character of moral 'ought' is the fact that our possible identity as creatures capable of speech is tied to such a structure of intersubjectivity. I shall return to this idea later. But first I should like to consider the question whether principle (U) is satisfactory when understood as a moral principle – i.e. in the sense of versions (U$_3$) or (U$_4$).

(3) Let us recall that principle (U) should be understood as a reformulation of the categorical imperative in the terms of discourse ethics. In this sense Habermas quotes McCarthy with approval:

> Rather than ascribing as valid to all others any maxim that I can will to be a universal law, I must submit my maxim to all others for purposes of discursively testing its claim to universality. The emphasis is shifted from what each can will without contradiction to be a general law, to what all can will in agreement to be a universal norm. (cf. DE 77)[43]

Thus whereas Kant says that 'we [and therefore *I* – A. W.] must be able to *will* that a maxim of our action should become a universal law – this is the general canon for all moral judgement of action',[44] principle (U) is intended to shift the emphasis from '*I* must be able to will' to '*we* must be able to will'. And the corollary of this would be that we can only find out through real discourse whether *we* are able to will that a maxim should hold as a universal law. Now when Kant speaks of the universalization of maxims he is not at all concerned with the question of the justice of norms. What Kant is postulating is much rather a requirement that I consider whether I would want to live in a world where, as if by a law of nature, everybody acted (and in particular, acted towards me) in the manner suggested by my maxim, and thus whether I could will that the way of acting expressed by my maxim should become universal. When I use the term 'way of acting' here and in what follows, it should be understood in the sense of a 'way of acting in a kind of situation'. I have various reasons for preferring the term 'way of acting' (when understood in this way) to 'maxim'; the crucial reason here is that I wish to avoid any suggestion that we are already discussing *norms* at this stage of the argument, and thus that we might be *presupposing* precisely that moral 'ought' whose sense and possibility Kant is trying to *explain*. (In other words we must conceive of maxims, in so far as they represent 'subjective' principles of action, as being formulated without a moral 'ought'.) Now I have already established (section II above) that Kant's criterion for morally right action only makes sense if we understand it in a *negatory* sense. Contrary to what Kant himself supposed, those ways of acting that I am able to will as universal cannot themselves be the ones that I morally ought to follow; it is rather the categorical imperative itself that says what I 'ought to' or 'must' do, namely that I *must not* perform an act p in a situation S if I am unable to will such a way of acting as a universal one. Thus, if I am unable to will that everyone should lie to me if it is to their advantage to do so, then I may not lie simply because it is to *my* advantage to do so. Now from this it would be possible to derive a moral *norm* to the effect that 'one must not lie' – but with norms like this we should always have at the same time to keep in mind those descriptions of situations from which the non-generalizability of a way of acting becomes apparent.

If we understand the categorical imperative in this way, the 'monologic' character of Kant's moral principle is not such a serious problem as it appears to Apel and Habermas. For if *I* am unable to will that a way of acting should become a universal rule, then *we* cannot will it either (otherwise *I* should be able to do so as well). We might equally express the point like this: in moral judgement I am above all confronted with myself. But the question I always have to answer at that point is clearly of a different kind from the question of whether a social norm is just of not.

The objection is nevertheless valid that Kant was mistaken in assuming that a *serious* moral judgement was eo ipso also *intersubjectively valid*, and thus that *my* 'being able to will' or 'not being able to will' must necessarily coincide with that of all other rational beings. Kant was only able to make this assumption because he immediately went on to develop the fruitful idea of the *Groundwork* in a formalistic manner. But if a monologic application of the categorical imperative does not guarantee the intersubjective validity of moral judgements, then it does indeed seem an obvious step to formulate Kant's *assumption* in the form of a *postulation* of the sort, 'Act in such a way that your way of acting could be willed by *all* as a universal one.' This is how we should also have to understand the reformulation of the categorical imperative by McCarthy which Habermas quotes.

   Now principle (U) seems at first glance to be saying the same thing: a way of acting is right if, when understood as a universal one, it would be acceptable to all (those whom it would affect). (U_4) is the version which most nearly corresponds to this reading. We should have to understand the word 'right', however, as it occurs in (U_4), in the sense of 'morally permitted' instead of 'morally commanded'. For if my comments on Kant were correct, it makes no sense to assume that the ways of acting that we are able to will as universal ones are also the ones that are morally *commanded*. There is no need for us to pursue that particular dispute further, however, since the reading of principle (U) that we now have at least comes very close to a reformulation of the categorical imperative such as this:

   'Act only according to maxims of which *we* are able to will that they should hold as universal laws.'

I believe that (U_4) is the reading of principle (U) which is least encumbered with premises rooted in consensus theory. It is therefore to this reading that I shall return later on.

(4) It is not (U_4), however, but much rather (U_3), that corresponds to Habermas's idea that in an argument about moral norms each individual should impartially assess a norm with a view to deciding whether the observance of that norm is equally in the interest of all. Let us therefore return to (U) as read in the light of (U_3). If we understand (U) as an elucidation of our provisional conception of moral validity, then this means that our moral convictions and our moral judgements must contain implicit judgements to the effect that the consequences and side-effects that the universal observance of a norm would have for each individual could be accepted without coercion by all. But this, it

seems to me, would make it impossible for us ever to arrive at fully justified moral judgements. Let us take as an example norms like '*Neminem laede*' or 'Thou shalt not lie'. Whereas a simple reflection in the spirit of the categorical imperative yields the result that I cannot will that in the world in which I am living people tell untruths or do injury to each other when it pleases them, a corresponding reflection in the spirit of principle (U) presents us with enormous problems. For the sake of simplicity I shall argue from the premise that, given ideal conditions for discourse, all human beings would agree that the *universal* observance of both the above norms would be equally in the interests of all if *ideal* conditions for achieving agreement could be assumed. But of course this still says very little about how we should act in *real* conditions of communication, i.e. in historical reality as it actually exists. If we try to apply principle (U) as a principle for judging action in *non*-ideal conditions, however, the following difficulties result:

(a) Let us first try to clarify what the consequences and side-effects for each individual would be if the norm 'Thou shalt not lie' were observed *universally*, which, if the words 'norm' and 'universal' have any meaning here, can only mean *without exception*. Kant was able to prohibit lying *universally*, i.e. without exception, because he did not concern himself with the consequences. But if we do concern ourselves with the consequences, and if we assume that for the rest the world remains as it is, then we must suppose that the consequences of universal truthfulness would be harsher for the victims than for their persecutors. To this extent the norm 'Thou shalt not lie' – things being as they are – could not possibly be a valid one. In order to find out what is the right way of acting under the *given circumstances*, we should clearly have to formulate more complicated norms with qualifications and exception clauses, much along the lines that Hare has postulated (although in his conception of it this would be a never-ending task).[45] But this increases enormously the difficulty of the task of determining the consequences and side-effects of a *universal* observance of norms for *each* individual and, beyond that, of finding out whether *all* would be able to accept without coercion these consequences and side-effects, as they would arise for each individual. Even real discourse cannot ultimately help us here. For as long as we have to conduct our discourse under conditions in which the victims have to protect themselves from their persecutors by telling lies, it is not possible to imagine any uncoerced consensus existing. Conversely, if it were possible in fact to achieve a general consensus, then the conditions that made exceptions and qualifications necessary would immediately fall away. In any case, it evidently makes no sense to assume that, under non-ideal conditions for reaching agreement, we should be able to solve our real moral problems by trying to achieve *real* consensuses. Where the possibility for reaching agreement ends, the only course that remains open to us is to consider what rational and competent people *would* say, or what those affected by our actions would say *if* they were sufficiently rational, possessed of good will, and competent to judge. And in *this* sense it is of course true that every moral judgement anticipates a possible rational consensus. But if, in the course of every moral reflection (which must ultimately always be monologic in nature), we had to reach a decision on the question whether the consequences and side-effects arising for each individual from the universal observance of a norm – and this would require in turn the *formulation* of a universal norm – could be accepted without coercion by all, then we should never to able to arrive at a fully justified moral judgement.

(b) Another kind of difficulty arises if we consider norms such as '*Neminem laede*' of which it may be assumed that it must be possible to achieve an uncoerced consensus to the effect that the universal observance of such norms is equally in the interests of all, and is so, moreover, precisely if we argue *on the basis* of the non-ideal conditions in which we live. It is meaningful in this instance to assume the possibility of achieving such a consensus because the *universal* observance of a norm such as '*Neminem laede*' would enable us to discount those conditions under which exceptions and qualifications are in fact necessary (e.g. in cases of legitimate self-defence, punishment etc.). But this is precisely why principle (U) produces false results here, namely ones which offend against our intuitive moral judgements. For the – hypothetical – assumption of a universal observance of the norm means in this case that questions of moral rightness are answered with reference to *ideal* and not *real* conditions for action. (U) would thus require us to act in the way that, as far as we are able to judge on the basis of our hypothetical assumption, we really would act if the conditions for acting and achieving agreement were ideal. We might be surprised at this point to find a problem reappearing that also plays a central part in Kant's ethics: Kant's 'practical laws' are in essence norms of action for the members of a potential kingdom of ends. Kant was at least consistent and categorically disputed the possibility of *exceptions* (to the prohibition of lying, for example). But precisely *this* position is not available to discourse ethics; it would contradict the very foundations of its argument.

There is a possibility for escaping the difficulties outlined here, and that is, as it were, to 'de-dramatize' the concept of a norm. We might understand the word 'norm' in the sense of Hare's 'prima facie norms', for example. Principle (U) would then only be concerned with the grounding of *those* norms for which it ought to be possible to achieve an uncoerced consensus to the effect that the universal observance of it *would* be equally in the interests of all under *ideal* conditions of action and communication. Everything else would be a problem of the correct *application* of such norms to a non-ideal reality. But quite apart from the problems which reside in the idealized concepts themselves that we are here presupposing as having been adopted (I shall return to his question in my next section), it seems clear to me that the possibility we are considering is no way out in reality. To give only my decisive reason for saying this, principle (U) would lose its point if the application of it were limited to that area of basic moral judgements for which Kant gives us more or less adequate guidance. After all, principle (U) is *intended* precisely as a principle for judging *such* norms as Kant cannot accommodate *because* he is understanding morally valid norms as norms of action for the members of a kingdom of ends. But if this is correct, then the distinction between problems of the *grounding* of norms and problems of the *application* of norms loses its significance here.

The problems and uncertainties we have encountered in our discussion of principle (U) can, I believe, be attributed to *two* problematic assumptions that Habermas makes. The first (a) is that questions of morally correct action can be treated in a similar way to questions of the justice of norms, and the second (b) concerns the way that discourse ethics is rooted in consensus theory.

(a) Habermas's formulation of the moral principle assumes that in our moral thinking we address the same question as in a discussion about the justice of social norms which we are in a position to introduce or refrain from introducing, to set aside or preserve. In a discussion *such as this* it really is a matter of deciding whether all those affected by a norm ought, as impartial judges, to be able to accept the consequences which would arise for each individual from the universal observance of that norm, and thus whether the introduction or preservation of a norm is 'equally in the interests of all'. A paradigm case of such an *introduction* of a norm would be the unanimous resolution of a body of people to deal with matters of common interest according to a particular set of rules. We can see in a case like this that while the hypothetical assumption of a universal observance of the norm does play a part in assessing the *justice* of the norm in question, another step has to be added beyond the assessment of the justice of the norm – and in this case it is a formal *resolution* – in order to constitute a corresponding *obligation* to act. This obligation, resulting from a common resolution, can be understood as a *moral* obligation; but it clearly cannot be grounded in the same way as the assessment of the justice of a norm which can *in principle* be introduced or set aside by means of a formal resolution.

Kant was well aware of the distinction we are making here, and it is therefore possible to elucidate it with reference to the different approach to the question of an uncoerced consensus of rational beings that is respectively implied in the formulation of the moral principle by Habermas and Kant. As we have already established, the content of a fully grounded consensus in the sense implied by principle (U) would be the judgement that the universal observance of a certain norm is equally in the interests of all (those affected). By contrast, however, the content of a 'Kantian' consensus in the case of moral norms would be that *we* (as rational beings) are unable to *will* that a certain way of acting should become universal. Here I am agreeing with Habermas that Kant's 'I' is to be replaced with a 'we', regardless of the problems that may result. On this assumption, the rational consensus that we would expect to find in a moral judgement from a Kantian point of view would take the form of saying, 'Neither I nor any one of "us" can rationally will that *this* way of acting should become universal.' The word 'rationally' here governs the 'being able to will'; whether we are *in fact* able to will something depends on our interpretations, convictions, and our understanding of ourselves, and *these* things can be more or less 'rational', i.e. appropriate, justified, correct or even truthful. 'Rationally', then, means something like 'if we see ourselves and the world and the situations of others correctly'. In this sense, it is possible to conceive of the argumentative or indeed communicative resolution of disputes, or of learning processes in the medium of argument, without difficulty. But if we understand the discursive dimension of morals in *this* way, then we can get by without a consensus theory of truth; we can construct instead, as I shall show below, a *fallibilistic* interpretation of the rational consensuses we might expect to find in moral judgements. If on the other hand we understand the content of the rational consensus which we 'anticipated' in moral judgements to be the common assessment of the justice of a norm, then it is difficult to see how such an idea could be worked out other than in terms of a consensus theory. This brings me to the second of Habermas's problematic assumptions, as mentioned above.

(b) Since I shall be dealing fully with the consensus theory of truth in my next section, all I should like to do here is point once again to the problems that arise as a consequence of Habermas's commitment to consensus theory. I pointed earlier to the paradoxes that result from the opposition of *ideal* and *real* conditions for communication and discourse, which is effectively built into principle (U). This opposition is a direct expression of premises drawn from consensus theory. My critique of consensus theory will therefore also entail a critique of the idealizations upon which it is based. What we have seen so far is that these idealizations of consensus theory also lead to *internal* difficulties in discourse ethics, difficulties which constitute an affinity with Kant that was certainly *never intended* by discourse ethics. It remains to be shown, however, that it really is the premises of consensus theory themselves that lie at the root of the difficulties of discourse ethics, and no mere contingencies of Habermas's formulation of principle (U).

VII

The fundamental thesis of the consensus or discourse theory of truth in Habermas's version of it is that the validity-claims which can be called 'true' or 'valid' are precisely those upon which it would be possible to achieve a discursive consensus under the conditions of an ideal speech situation. In Habermas's view, the structures of an ideal speech situation (which he also claims is actually *assumed* in any serious argument) are characterized by an even distribution of chances to perform a variety of speech acts, as well as by a tolerance towards any change in the level of discourse.[46] The fundamental thesis of consensus theory thus defines the 'rationality' of consensuses in terms of the formal structural features of an ideal speech situation, and it also defines 'truth' as the content of a rational consensus. By contrast, I should like to show (1) that the rationality of consensuses cannot be characterized in formal terms, (2) that the rationality and the truth of consensuses need not coincide, (3) that the rational consensus therefore cannot be a *criterion* of truth, and finally (4) that if consensus theory is interpreted as not providing a criterion of truth it is rendered, if not vacuous, then at least unsuitable for supporting a universalization principle within discourse ethics.

(1) My thesis is that our assessment of consensuses as rational is dependent upon our assessment of whether our (own or common) reasons are appropriate. This dependence is a *logical* (conceptual) one: the concept of a consensus achieved on the basis of reasons presupposes the concept of a personal conviction achieved on the basis of reasons. It must, of course, be conceded that we cannot consider a consensus rational if we have reason to suppose that some of the participants only appear to agree, or that they do so out of fear or because of some psychological block. To this extent, Habermas's criterion would be correct in a weaker sense: the concept of a rational consensus necessarily implies that it rests on good *reasons* and not on fear etc. But the same is already true of the convictions of individuals: the rationality of these may be judged by whether of not they rest on good reasons.

Now in a trivial sense it is certainly the case that we should consider a conviction that is arrived at in common to be true, and we should hold this opinion on the strength of the reasons or arguments which we have all found convincing. And in so far as we have really become convinced of something in common, we are able to speak of a *rational* consensus. Thus it can appear as if a *rational* consensus is necessarily also a 'true' one. But this is only the way it looks from the point of view of those who are actually involved in the situation: if *I* have reasons for agreeing, then this *means* precisely that I consider a validity-claim to be *true*. But the truth does not *follow* here from the rationality of the consensus, it follows from the appropriateness of the reasons which I can advance for a validity-claim, and I need to have convinced myself that these reasons are in fact appropriate *before* I can speak of the rationality of the consensus. Now in principle it is always possible for such reasons to turn out *after the event* to be insufficient. But if that happens it cannot possibly be identical in meaning with the discovery that an earlier consensus was not *rational* in the sense that the conditions of symmetry and free opportunity which characterize an ideal speech situation were not realized on that occasion. If it is supposed to be possible to characterize these conditions in formal terms, then it is precisely *not* the case that we may allow our assessment of whether such conditions obtain to depend on which reasons we consider appropriate in the given situation. Otherwise the significance of consensus theory as providing a criterion would evaporate. But quite apart from this, there are strong reasons for not equating the rationality with the truth of consensuses. Why should the consensus among leading physicists of the nineteenth century about the truth of Newton's theories not have been *rational* (in the sense of the conditions of an ideal speech situation)? The answer cannot be that physics has advanced since their day.

(2) The truth of consensuses cannot follow from their rationality any more than their *untruth* can automatically follow from their lack of rationality (unless we revert to a tautological explanation of concepts). It is only from the point of view of those involved in the situation that consensual rationality appears to be identical with truth. But this cannot mean that the rationality of the consensus is an additional *reason* for it being true. To say this would be just as false as if I were to advance the fact that my conviction is well founded as an *additional* reason for its truth alongside the reasons that I have for holding it. The fact that I hold something to be true with good reason cannot be an

additional reason for the truth of the thing I hold to be true, at least not *for me;* and by the same token, the fact that *we* hold something to be true with good reason cannot represent *for us* an additional reason for the truth of the thing we hold to be true. In other words, the fact that a consensus exists, even if it were arrived at under ideal conditions, cannot be a *reason* for the truth of the thing that is held to be true. We are then thrown back, however, upon the reasons or criteria for truth which are always available to us if we understand the meaning of validity-claims. We should only be able to deduce the truth of consensuses from their rationality *if* we were to include among the conditions for an ideal speech situation the requirement that all participants have an adequate *capacity for judgement.* But then it would no longer be possible, for one thing, to characterize the conditions for an ideal speech situation in *formal* terms, and for another thing, the consensus theory of truth would effectively be reduced to the thesis that true validity-claims are precisely those upon which an uncoerced consensus can be achieved among those who are sufficiently capable of judgement. But this thesis would be void of any substantial content. Consensus theory as a substantial theory of truth stands and falls with a *formal* characterization of the rationality of consensuses; but precisely this formal condition of rationality renders it false. If, on the other hand, we take the step that suggests itself in the light of what we have seen here, and try to understand the concept of rationality in nonformal terms, then consensus theory stands revealed as empty of content.

(3) More recently, Habermas has distanced himself from the interpretation of consensus theory as providing a *criterion.*[47] Moreover he concedes that in a certain sense we must always know in advance what constitutes good reasons in order to be able to argue at all. But whether such 'good' reasons are ultimately *sufficiently* good reasons, he now says, is something which only 'shows' itself under the conditions of an ideal speech situation.[48] In the light of this new turn in Habermas's thought, I should like to clarify once again the real point of consensus theory as I understand it. If Habermas says that only a consensus achieved under the conditions of an ideal speech situation can 'show' whether our arguments really are sufficiently good arguments, then what he is describing is a specific reassuring function of

consensuses. By achieving a consensus we reassure ourselves collectively that we (each of 'us') really do see things from a public, a general point of view, i.e. that our judgement is not distorted by idiosyncrasies, psychological blocks, emotions, wishful thinking, impaired faculties etc., *and* that our convictions or reasons would stand the test of a renewed discourse among persons of adequate good will and competence to judge. A consensus reassures us that we have not left the territory of a common world or a common language, or that if we did (as in some sense happens again and again in science and philosophy), then we have done so for reasons which make a new and better commonality possible. Now it is possible to interpret this internal relationship between the validity of truth-claims and the commonality of a world in a variety of ways; consensus theory is the attempt to understand it in a *non-relativistic* way. In order to clarify the point I should like to distinguish between two forms of commonality or mutual accord in the medium of language. The first form is the kind of commonality which we must always *presuppose* in language. As far as this sort of commonality goes, we can say, as Wittgenstein does, that what is 'right' or 'wrong' in our use of words or in our judgements is ultimately determined by intersubjective practice. Agreement among adult speakers of a language is thus in a certain sense the criterion of whether a word is being used rightly or wrongly, or whether an assertion is true. As Wittgenstein says, 'If language is to be a means of communication there must be agreement not only in definitions but also (queer as this may sound) in judgements.'[49] But what is implied here is not a matter of consensuses achieved by means of argument, but a mutual accord inherent *in* the language which makes arguments possible in the first place. It happens from time to time, of course, that such a 'natural' accord *in* the language is challenged with good reason; science, for example, might be understood in certain respects as a continual process of language *criticism* taking place in the medium of argument. The thought therefore suggests itself that 'natural' accords *in* the language might in principle be replaced by an accord achieved by means of discourse *upon* the appropriateness of basic concepts and rules of language, in short, of our interpretation of the world through the medium of language. In his essay 'Wahrheitstheorien', Habermas has in fact envisaged such a discursive form of linguistic change and language criticism as something that is possible and in a certain sense necessary. As Habermas puts it, we can only speak of true utterances in the full sense where the language in which we formulate such utterances is itself 'appropriate'[50]; but we should only be able to speak of an 'appropriate' language where the development of that language had itself taken place within the medium of argument, which is to say, where the rational consensus about validity-claims contains within it a rational consensus about the appropriateness of the language.[51] In this way, the *prior* accord *in* the language which Wittgenstein analyses would, as it were, be drawn into (and transformed through) the discursive revision of our convictions. It is only on the basis of such an assumption that the point of consensus theory becomes entirely clear. For if we concede that, at an initial stage, the accord among speakers of a language is a kind of provisional ultimate standard of the truth or falsehood of utterances, *and* if we concede that a discursive revision of such an accord is in principle possible, then we can easily go on to say that, if not a factual consensus, then at least a rational consensus (i.e. one achieved by means of discourse) is an *ultimate* authority by which we reassure ourselves of the truth of our validity-claims. At the same time it becomes clear why the rationality of such a consensus may only be characterized in formal terms. There appear to be only two possibilities: *either* we say that each language, each life-form contains within itself its own standards of 'true' and 'false', with the implication that it is no longer possible to put meaningful questions about the truth or falsehood of these standards (this is the answer given by Peter Winch on the level of cultural comparisons, and by Thomas Kuhn on the level of comparative theory); *or* we resist this deeply disturbing relativistic thesis and hold fast to the unconditional nature of validity-claims, and thus to the possibility of a standard which transcends each particular language and each particular life-form. A counter-thesis to the relativistic position would thus be that it is not the *factual* agreement of the speakers of a language that provides the ultimate standards of truth and falsehood, but only that agreement which can be interpreted as a rational consensus. And here it must be apparent that what is meant by 'rational' cannot be explained by the substantive standards of rationality of *one* particular culture; rather it must be defined by purely formal characteristics. It is therefore entirely consistent with the anti-relativistic approach of the consensus theory of truth when it makes the structural characteristics of an ideal speech situation the defining feature of rationality.

(4) Now, what I have said earlier about the function of rational consensuses in providing criteria applies equally to that 'showing' or reassuring function which Habermas has recently emphasized. For the fact that we can reassure ourselves that our reasons really are good reasons by achieving a consensus through discourse does not alter the fact that each consensus is only provisional. But if it does not necessarily follow from the fact that reasons show themselves within the context of a finite rational consensus to be sufficiently good reasons that they will prove themselves *in the long term* to be sufficiently good reasons, then the undisputed reassuring function of consensuses is not adequate to sustain the heavy burden of a consensus *theory* of truth.

An obvious way out of this difficulty is to transfer the function of consensuses as providing criteria or reassurance to an *infinite* rational consensus.[52] An infinite rational consensus would be one for which it would *never* be possible to present reasons which cast doubt upon it. In this case, therefore, we can discount the problem that results from the fact that every *finite* rational consensus is only provisional and therefore incapable of providing proof positive of 'truth'. As I have shown above, this problem can only be circumvented in Habermas's version of consensus theory by including among the structural characteristics of an ideal speech situation a sufficient competence to judge on the part of all participants. But then it would no longer be possible to characterize ideal speech situations by means of purely formal descriptions of their structure; this is precisely what is necessary, however, if the notion of a 'consensus under the conditions of an ideal speech situation' is to be the substantial explicator for the concept of 'truth'. If, on the other hand, we conceive the consensus notion of truth in terms of an *infinite* consensus, this problem falls away, for the idea of an *infinite* rational consensus contains within itself not only the assumption of rationality, but also the assumption that no new arguments will arise (and of course that none will be suppressed).

Now, an infinite rational consensus is not only incapable of providing criteria, but cannot strictly speaking fulfil a reassuring function either. For it is not an 'object of possible experience', but an idea that points beyond the boundaries of possible experience. This brings consequential changes for the possible *meaning* of a consensus theory of truth: if the guarantee of truth does not reside in *every* rational consensus, but only in an *infinite* rational consensus, then the theory loses that explicative substance that Habermas would like to give it. This can be seen from Habermas's most recent exposition of the basic idea of consensus theory.[53] 'The core of the discourse theory of truth,' Habermas now says, 'can be formulated by means of three basic concepts':

> *conditions of validity* (which are fulfilled when an utterance holds good), *validity-claims* (which speakers raise with their utterances, for their validity), and *redemption* of a validity-claim (in the framework of a discourse which is sufficiently close to the conditions of an ideal speech situation for the consensus aimed at by the participants to be brought about solely through the force of the better argument, and in this sense to be 'rationally motivated').[54]

The crucial point of consensus theory now consists in elucidating what is meant by 'fulfilling conditions of validity' with the help of the other two basic concepts:

> An utterance is valid when its conditions of validity are fulfilled. . . the fulfilment or non-fulfilment of conditions of validity can only be ascertained by means of the argumentative redemption of the corresponding validity-claims. The discourse theory of truth, then, explains what it means to redeem a validity-claim by an analysis of the general pragmatic preconditions for the attainment of a rationally motivated consensus. This theory of truth provides only an explication of meaning, it does not provide a criterion; in the end, however, it undermines the clear distinction between meaning and criterion.[55]

If we understand the 'redemption' of validity-claims here to mean the achievement of a consensus by means of argument under the conditions of an ideal speech situation, then the objections to consensus theory expounded above remain in force. If, on the other hand, we transfer the function of guaranteeing truth to an infinite rational consensus, then it is strictly speaking no longer possible to speak of a *redemption* of validity-claims; and as a result, the explicative connection between the three basic concepts that Habermas constructs would disintegrate. But this difficulty cannot be circumvented by, as it were, merging the particular (empirical) consensus with the infinite consensus. If we say that a rational consensus – *qua* rational consensus – is by definition capable of infinite repetition, then in reality we are making the consensus under the conditions of an ideal speech situation, and not the infinite consensus, the guarantor of truth, and all the objections which I have made against *this* version of consensus theory remain in force. This means that the possibility of an infinite consensus cannot follow simply from the fact that a consensus has been achieved under the (formally characterized) conditions of an ideal speech situation – this was precisely the point of my objections. To assume the possibility of an infinite consensus means something more in reality – or something other – than to assume the rationality of a particular consensus in the sense of the formal characterization of an ideal speech situation. This 'something more' is connected with the fact that, to repeat the point, the *concept* of a consensus achieved with arguments cannot meaningfully be equated with the *concept* of a consensus against which it is not going to be possible to bring forward any apposite arguments at any time in the future. Otherwise we should have to include the condition that all *possible* arguments have been taken into consideration among the conditions of rationality for *finite* consensuses. But this is impossible, unless we were to make the possibility of an infinite consensus the *criterion* that decides whether the conditions of rationality for finite consensuses are fulfilled. But in this case it would no longer be possible to characterize these conditions formally, i.e. in terms of the *procedure* of argument and the *structural characteristics* of an ideal speech situation.

As we can now see, it would be possible to distinguish between a stronger and a weaker version of the consensus theory of truth. The weaker version is the one which sees the guarantee of truth as residing in an infinite rational consensus. It is impossible to resolve all the differences between the two versions of consensus theory because it is impossible to derive from the formal characterization of ideal conditions for discourse any guarantee that a consensus attained under such conditions will stand the test of an *infinite* discursive examination. But might it not be the case that, via the weaker version of consensus theory which, as we have said, can no longer be understood to provide criteria, we could justify the strong background assumptions which underlie the attempt by discourse ethics to reformulate the universalization principle? This is the question I wish to pursue in my next section.

VIII

I have so far refrained from expressly linking the two versions of consensus theory which we have differentiated above with the names of Habermas and Apel. The reasons for this are firstly that both authors have to a certain extent identified themselves with *both* versions of consensus theory, and secondly that Apel's version of consensus theory goes beyond what I have here called the 'weaker' version in one essential respect. This weaker version of consensus theory might be understood as the elucidation of the internal connection between the idea of truth and the idea of a possible universal, rationally grounded accord. These two ideas, we might say, *mutually* elucidate each other: the idea of truth necessarily implies that it will not be possible at any time in the future to advance apposite arguments against what we now see to be true, and this in turn implies that it will not in future be possible to find good arguments with which to call into question the way we talk about the world and formulate our problems. On the other hand it is difficult to see in what sense an *infinite* grounded consensus might not also be called *true*; at any rate we could argue that this would only be conceivable if we were to introduce the problematic notion of a truth that could not be recognized or could not be expressed in language.

Now Apel's version of consensus theory differs from this 'weaker' version in that he elucidates the idea of an infinite (grounded) consensus with reference to the idea of an unlimited *ideal communication community*, which fulfils much the same function within Apel's theory as the idea of an ideal speech situation does within that of Habermas; that is, it represents both a constitutive necessary *assumption* for the situations in which arguments take place, and also a future-orientated ideal or regulative idea. In either case, the idealizing assumption (or anticipation) simultaneously characterizes the conditions which guarantee the rationality of possible consensuses. We have already established, however, *firstly* that the fact that conditions for discourse are ideal can give no guarantee of the truth of consensuses as long as these consensuses are particular (i.e. finite and empirical), and *secondly* that *in actual fact* we must always judge the rationality of consensuses according to the reasons upon which they are founded. From all this it may be seen that the idealization implied in the notion of an ideal communication community gets us nowhere: it contributes nothing to our understanding of what a rationally grounded consensus – or even an infinite grounded consensus – is. On the other hand the notion of an ideal communication community does intimate the possibility of a future location for final and absolute truth, it intimates the idea of an ultimate language in which not only will science have reached its final end, but humanity too would have become fully transparent to itself. To be sure, these are only regulative ideas for Apel; but as regulative ideas, they constitute for him ideal ultimate goals which humanity has the task of realizing, and which it is within humanity's grasp to realize, if perhaps only in the sense of an infinite approximation.[56] What started as presuppositions about speaking and arguing have become ideals of reality which we, as speakers and arguers, are inescapably committed to realizing: here we have arrived at the heart of discourse ethics.

That there is something wrong with this construction has so far only been apparent from the curious redundancy of idealizing concepts when it comes to the problem of truth. Now, I believe that it is perfectly possible to concede that these idealizing concepts are *rooted in* unavoidable idealizing presuppositions about speaking and arguing, as Apel and Habermas state; but I suspect that their way of assimilating and interpreting such idealizing presuppositions is misleading. It is easy to concede that the anticipation of an infinite consensus – like the assumption of an 'ideal speech situation' – comes into play in any consensus achieved by discursive means. But it seems to me that unavoidable assumptions of this kind are hypostatized by the consensus theory of truth in much the same way that formal semantics hypostatizes the equally unavoidable assumption that our words and sentences have a definitive intersubjective meaning. In my view, such unavoidable assumptions about speaking and arguing are vested with a quasi-transcendental, dialectical semblance (*Schein*): in adopting them, we *forget* that linguistic meanings and insights which are capable of linguistic formulation are essentially historical in character, as we can assure ourselves *reflexively*. Only in cases where hermeneutic problems and problems of linguistic expression become marginal – as in mathematical physics, for example – can we understand the unavoidable assumptions about speaking and arguing in a more or less *realistic* sense, as Apel and Habermas do, for it is only in such cases that the idea of an 'ultimate' language, as it is contained within the idea of an infinite consensus in an ideal communication community, makes sense, at least as a *regulative* idea.[57] It is no mere chance that Peirce, whose thinking has inspired Apel's version of consensus theory in particular, developed ideas of this kind in connection with advances in the field of physical inquiry especially. The interpretation of scientific progress as a process of continuous language criticism governed by the regulative idea of an ultimate, 'correct' language (or an infinite consensus) is part and parcel of the pragmatic reformulation of transcendental philosophy which Peirce initiated. But it seems to me that a pragmatically revised transcendental philosophy which tries to 'generalize' Peirce's regulative principle of an infinite consensus within the 'community of investigators' into the idea of an ideal communication community, as Apel does, must ultimately remain trapped within an objectivistic notion of knowledge and experience; and it does so because it fails to see through the dialectical semblance (*Schein*) in which idealizing assumptions about linguistic communication are veiled. The deception arises, not from the fact that such assumptions invariably turn out to be false (whenever our utterances turn out to be incomprehensible, or the situations in which communication takes place turn out to be distorted), but from the fact that these assumptions present themselves to us as ideals to be pursued in human communication and praxis, and thus conceal the historical and imperfectible nature of linguistic meaning. Even after its transformation at the hands of language pragmatists, transcendental philosophy has not severed its contacts with the scientistic tradition of the European Enlightenment, which found its classical expression, after all, in the transcendental philosophy of Kant. Even in its pragmatic form, transcendental philosophy remains, as it were, locked into figures of thought which may not have been derived from the way physical science has progressed, but which are certainly to some extent tailored to the course of such progress. This is admittedly a strong thesis, which I should like to elucidate with reference to an earlier text by Apel, his important essay on 'Scientism or Transcendental Hermeneutics?'[58]

In this essay Apel tries to show that Peirce's interpretation of truth as the 'ultimate opinion' of an 'indefinite community of investigators'[59]can be generalized so as to serve as the *'regulative principle of an ulimited community of interpretation which realizes itself in the long run both theoretically and practically'*.[60] Apel had interpreted Peirce's notion of the consensus within an unlimited community of investigators as the 'highest point' of a pragmatically revised transcendental philosophy, corresponding more or less to the transcendental 'consciousness as such' as the highest point of Kant's transcendental philosophy.[61] The universal realism of Peirce, which is grounded in semiotics and 'dynamized' by the logic of investigation, does not seek the guarantee for the objectivity of knowledge in a categorial synthetic a priori grounded in the transcendental I, but in the logic of a process of inquiry which, through the inventive and self-correcting interaction of abduction, induction and deduction, must in due course eliminate all that is false. What is *true* are those convictions which establish themselves intersubjectively *in the long run*, through this self-correcting process, as tenable; and *reality* is the correlate of such true convictions.

> The real . . . is that which, sooner or later, information and reasoning would finally result in, and which is therefore independent of the vagaries of me and you. Thus, the very origin of the conception of reality shows that this conception essentially involves the notion of a *Community*, without definite limits, and capable of a definite increase of knowledge.[62]

It is with reference to this early formulation of Peirce's that Apel summarizes the essence of Peirce's transformation of transcendental logic:

> In other words, the 'highest point' of Peirce's transformation of Kant's transcendental logic is the 'ultimate opinion' of the 'indefinite community of investigators'. At this point one may find a convergence of the semiotical postulate of the transindividual *unity of interpretation* and of the postulate of the logic of inquiry concerning the *validation* of experience *in the long run*. The quasi-transcendental subject of this unity is the *indefinite community of experimentation* which is identical with the *indefinite community of interpretation*.[63]

What replaces the grounding of synthetic a priori principles in the dynamized version of transcendental philosophy is the demonstration of the necessary validity of synthetic *modes of inference*, namely abduction and induction, *in the long run*.

> In a way he has put Kant's *regulative principles* of experience in the place of Kant's *constitutive principles* of experience, on the assumption that the regulative principles in the long run turn out to be constitutive. Thus by shifting the necessary and universal validity of scientific propositions to the end of the (indefinite) process of inquiry it is possible for Peirce to escape Hume's scepticism without insisting with Kant on the necessity and universality of propositions which for the moment are accepted by experts.[64]

In his essay 'Scientism or Transcendental Hermeneutics', Apel attempts to go beyond the scientistic limitations, as he sees them[65], of Peirce's line of inquiry in developing this future-orientated notion of truth. He would like to see the idea of a consensus within an unlimited community of investigators expanded into the idea of 'an absolute truth of understanding in an unlimited community of interpretation and interaction'.[66] Apel develops this idea initially with reference to the neo-idealistic reinterpretation of Peirce's semiotics by J. Royce, then tries to break free from the idealistic frame of reference and construct a defence against objections from the point of view of hermeneutic philosophy. Against Gadamer, Apel asserts that the regulative idea of an *absolute* truth is fundamental to the activity of understanding meaning, too, and thus to the interpretation of texts, utterances, actions or life-forms.[67] Now this notion of an absolute truth in the context of interpretation is not something that can be explained in cognitivistic terms as the ultimate theoretical conviction of a community of investigators subjecting itself to the methodical discipline of the logical principles of inquiry; rather it is necessary to take account of the moment of *application* in the act of understanding, as described in hermeneutics, and in the last analysis this means taking account of the structure of understanding as something upon which any attempt at a scientific reduction of understanding to a phenomenon within the world of objectifiable facts must founder. It is precisely the point of Apel's pragmatic transformation of transcendental philosophy that it presents the understanding of meaning as a *complementary phenomenon* to the 'scientific knowledge of objective facts'.[68] If, then, we are to transfer Peirce's future-orientated concept of truth to the activity of understanding meaning, this is only possible if we replace the regulative idea of an infinite theoretical consensus with the regulative idea of an *ideal communication community*, i.e. with an 'unlimited community of interpretation and interaction' which simultaneously represents an ideal ultimate goal of understanding, the realization of which would be identical in meaning with the 'abolition of all obstacles to communication'.[69] In the notion of an ideal communication community, theoretical and practical reason converge in the ultimate goal of an ideal situation for communication. The 'absolute truth' of interpretations is only conceivable in connection with the *practical* achievement of such an ideal situation for communication; the practical moment, the moment of application in the act of understanding, necessitates that we relate the truth of interpretation to a living context which has become fully transparent and contains no element of coercion.

It is difficult to resist the fascination of this thought, which occurs in similar form in Habermas: this is where the pragmatic reinterpretation of transcendental philosophy becomes indistinguishable from the pragmatic reinterpretation of Adorno's philosophy of reconciliation. But is the idealization contained in the notion of an ideal communication community a *meaningful* one? Apel formulates the crucial objection himself, albeit in an indirect fashion, when he points to the fact that the infinite consensus of the community of investigators of which Peirce speaks *presupposes* a neutralization of the problem of communication: the 'ultimate' language of physics, the correlate of *ultimate opinion*, is only conceivable as a language which has emancipated itself from the conditions of a hermeneutic mediation of meaning. Peirce's maxim for the clarification of meaning is conceived for precisely this limiting case; it represents the attempt,

> to relate all meaning to operations and correlated experiences which every isolated human subject can have at any time, independently of his historical interaction with others, and which – to this extent – are a *priori* intersubjective, and this means they are also objective. One can detect here the basic desire of every progressive empirical analytical science to make the hermeneutic aids of intersubjective communication superfluous for the future by means of a definitive mode of agreement about meaning, and thereby to establish once and for all the preconditions for the possibility and validity of logically and empirically testable theories.

In parenthesis one might add that the ideal of this definitive meta-scientific agreement would be the abrupt replacement of historically constituted everyday language – including the experimentally proven language of science that developed from the latter – by a universal calculus language, which would be both guaranteed to be non-contradictory and experimentally and pragmatically capable of application. This was the original dream of logical empiricism.[70]

Apel here expresses the point very clearly that there is an *internal* connection in Peirce's thinking between the idea of a 'potential unlimited progress'[71]of science governed by the regulative idea of an ultimate consensus among the community of investigators – an ultimate language of physics – and the conception of the community of investigators as a kind of 'singular in the plural'. *Ultimate opinion* will be formulated in a language which will no longer present any problems of clarification of meaning, any problems of communication, *for the precise reason that* all meaning it expresses is related to operations and experiences 'which every isolated human subject can have at any time, independently of his historical interaction with others'. It is only for this reason that the indefinite community of investigators can assume the role of transcendental subject; the progress of science can be understood as the *process of becoming* of this transcendental subject.

What I mean to say is this: Peirce's philosophy can be seen as a transformation of transcendental philosophy precisely because at the 'highest point' of this philosophy reason would have emancipated itself from its dependence on (ordinary) language, and therefore from that condition of 'linguisticality' which transcendental hermeneutics had always insisted upon *against* Kant. To put it in terms that are less open to misunderstanding, at the highest point of this philosophy the language of science would have attained that post-hermeneutic state which was, in Apel's words, 'the original dream of logical empiricism'. The idealization that is at work here concerns not the (pragmatic) structures of communication, but the (ahistorical) intersubjectivity of linguistic meanings. The crucial problem therefore lies in the inconspicuous shift from the idea of an infinite consensus of investigators to the idea of an ideal communication community as the location of an absolute truth of *interpretation*. Are we to think here, too, of an 'ultimate' language in which the truth content of all philosophical texts would have become available as a perfectly transparent one? This would represent the idea of ideal communication in the sense of a *state of perfect understanding and agreement* – a state of communication in which humanity would be finally relieved of the trouble of forever having to acquire philosophical or practical truths anew. Or should we think of ideal *conditions* for communication, conditions in which communication and self-expression might still be necessary, but were able to proceed, as it were, without friction? This would represent the idea of ideal communication in the sense of *being willing and able to reach understanding and agreement time and again*, and in so far as the connotation of an infinite consensus is indeed to be preserved, it would also represent the idea of a rational consensus that was forever *renewing* itself. I maintain that the two interpretations we have distinguished here necessarily intersect in Apel's concept of the ideal communication community, so that what is *intended* as a situation of ideal communication stands revealed as a situation that lies beyond the necessity (and beyond the problems) of linguistic communication. This would mean, however, that, within the notion of the ideal communication community, the constitutive plurality of sign-users would be suspended in favour of the singularity of a transcendental subject which has now also attained an understanding of itself in practical, hermeneutic terms – a subject which, having undergone a process of becoming, is now, as it were, *in the truth*.

To clarify my thesis, I should like to try to express more precisely what is meant by 'unlimited mutual understanding' or 'ideal communication'. Apel also speaks of the 'abolition of all obstacles to communication'.[72] We might start by trying to understand the ideality of communication situations in the sense of Habermas's conditions for an ideal speech situation, an approach which Apel himself occasionally seems to encourage. But we have already seen that the concept of an ideal speech situation, as we have so far understood it, is not adequate to encompass that convergence between successful communication and intersubjective validity which Apel envisages under the notion of an ideal communication community. If the ideal communication community really is intended as a location of absolute truth – albeit merely an anticipated one – then this is only possible if the assumptions that every speaker makes in the act of speaking about the comprehensibility of validity-claims and their capacity to produce a consensus are constantly *fulfilled* within that communication community. As far as comprehension is concerned, this statement follows directly from the ideality of communication situations as such, and as far as the capacity of validity-claims to produce a consensus is concerned, it follows from the fact that in the limiting case of ideal communication it would no longer be possible for the 'anticipation of perfection' in the act of interpreting texts and utterances to founder on the factual limitations of non-ideal conditions for communication. This is something which Apel indirectly makes clear when he attributes the failure to anticipate the truth 'in the sense of a potential *consensus omnium*'[73] when interpreting texts to the non-ideality of factual conditions for communication[74]: hermeneutically speaking, what is untrue is that which cannot be understood.

As Apel says elsewhere:

> in a normative sense, the ideal language game of an ideal communication community is anticipated by anyone who follows a rule (implicitly by someone who claims to act in a meaningful way, explicitly by someone who argues) as a *real possibility* of the language game in which he is participating, which is to say that it is presupposed as the *precondition for the possibility and validity* of his action as a meaningful action.[75]

This ideal language game thus betokens the ideal *conditions* for communication just as much as the ideal *result* of a historical process of communication, i.e. an ideal and unlimited state of being in agreement and understanding each other as the ultimate telos of humanity in its *efforts* to communicate at any given time. If this is so – and I cannot see how this conclusion might be avoided – then the idea of an ideal *communication* community must also betoken the idea of an ideal, an ultimate *language* which would enable the assumption of the possibility of intersubjective understanding which we make in any linguistic utterance to be fulfilled at any time. But this is nothing other than 'the original dream of logical empiricism' projected onto the frame of reference of a pragmatic philosophy of language. The ideal communication community would have passed beyond error, dissent, non-understanding and conflict, but only at the price of freezing language, of the extinction of its productive energies, and thus of suspending the very linguistic and historical life-form of humanity.

This is where the profound ambiguity in the notion of an ideal communication community becomes apparent. To the extent that it represents an attempt to identify the idea of the absolute as a 'highest point' within this world, the notion of an ideal communication community still has a strong affinity with that 'original dream of logical empiricism'. By trying to interpret the absolute as the ultimate limit of a potential infinite progress of theoretical, practical and hermeneutic reason, Apel converts it to the image of a reason emancipated from the vicissitudes of its linguistic condition. Adorno was still enough of a theologian to know that such an absolute – which for him, too, represented the condition of the possibility of truth – could only be conceived as an ultimate horizon for the history of reason if it were firmly associated with the idea of a radical *break* with historical continuity: reconciliation, for him, would be the complete obverse of reason as it existed. Apel, on the other hand, having quite rightly built his case against Adorno on the partial nature of reason as it exists and on the possibility of moral progress, cannot resist going one step further, a step which in reality takes him back to a position which Adorno (and Benjamin) had already surpassed. Whereas for Adorno the absolute was 'shrouded in black' (in theological terms it was the kingdom of God), Apel tries to fetch it back into the continuum of history. The messianic perspective is converted back into the perspective of a potential unlimited progress towards the absolute. In the context of the theory of science in Peirce's sense, this perspective does have a certain legitimacy, but when it is transposed onto the historical and moral world as a whole then it is clear that it lacks the redeeming force to which it lays claim. It is not by chance that, from the perspective of a perfected physics, history becomes degraded to prehistory, individuality to contingency, and living language to a mere passing phase; but at least a perfected physics is *conceivable* as a form of knowledge attained by moral beings. The *generalization* of a future-orientated concept of absolute truth, on the other hand, would actually have to delete historical time at the limiting point of the absolute, for a truth to which all eyes are opened is something that must also be shared by those long since dead: the reconciliation of all humanity would have to be something in which the dead, too, participate. But this can only be conceived in theological terms, as Adorno very well knew.[76] With respect to humanity and its history, the idea of a perfect truth to which *all* eyes are opened is prefigured, not in the idea of a perfected physics, but in the image of the Day of Judgement. And the image of the Day of Judgement includes the hope of resurrection and salvation. Judgement, salvation and resurrection are categories of a radical break with the historical world; this is precisely what makes them theological categories. To be sure, it would be for philosophy to decipher the power of the images which have crystallized in these categories, but the deciphering offered by the philosophy of the 'ideal communication community' is scarcely more convincing than what Adorno offers with his philosophy of reconciliation.[77] For regardless of whether the absolute, as the horizon of the history of reason, is conceived of as demanding a *break* with reason as it exists (Adorno), or whether it is conceived as the immanent telos of that history (Apel), in either case it is clearly not recuperable within the boundaries of the historical world.[78]

It is not inadvertently that I compare Apel's philosophy of the ideal communication community with Adorno's philosophy of reconciliation. The common element between the positions of Apel and Adorno is that they both believe that the notion of truth can only be saved if it is conceived from the perspective of a reconciled humanity – an 'ideal communication community'. In both instances the idea of the absolute betokens the precondition for the possibility of truth. For Apel this means that the idea of unlimited progress towards an ideal communication community (as the location of 'absolute truth') offers the only possible alternative to a relativistic dissolution of the notion of truth.[79] I do not believe that this diagnosis of Apel's is accurate. Rather, I wish to show that the whole problem presents itself in a new light if we put aside the view, which is axiomatic for Apel, that equates the anticipation of an infinite rational consensus with the notion of an ideal communication community.[80]

Apel expressly refers to philosophical statements for which in his view we must necessarily presuppose the anticipation of an ideal communication community in order to understand or raise a corresponding claim to general validity.[81] But validity-claims of the kind that are expressed in philosophical statements are tied to the medium of ordinary language, and to their own context of explication. The argumentative dynamic of philosophizing which is crystallized in philosophical statements, and which is what really lends weight and significance to philosophical theses, is thus something which cannot be 'solidified' once and for all in the form of philosophical statements or systems of statements. In this sense Adorno was quite correct when he asserted that philosophy cannot be reduced to theses.[82] But if this is so, then philosophical truths are forever having to be discovered, acquired, thought through and formulated *anew*. Even the great philosophical texts, to which we constantly refer as the paradigm of a written, objectified philosophical truth, only contain a codified form of the truth; and this truth yields itself up to us only through a process of translation in which we, as it were, repeat the original process of their formulation with the means available to us. This is why the interpretation of philosophical texts plays such an important part in philosophy – quite independently of the fact that the interpretation of philosophical texts always implies separating out what is true and false in them, and independently of the fact that it is also possible to have *progress* in philosophy. The crucial point is that any philosophical truth, once uttered, would be lost without the incessant efforts of others to translate it and make it their own. The conservation of philosophical truths is a productive process. Even if it were possible to condense the *entire* truth of philosophy within a single text, we should only be able to preserve it by providing this text with innumerable commentaries; as a mere container of truth, the text would be dead as soon as we ceased to rewrite it.

But if this is the case, then the anticipation of an infinite consensus in this particular instance cannot have the meaning that Apel gives it. Apel's model for the anticipation of an infinite consensus is in the final analysis that of physics, whereby the *ultimate opinion* of the investigators would find expression in an ultimate language and in a stable system of statements. But if every philosophical statement carries an indication of the historical time and place in which it is made, and if the meaning of philosophical statements is a function of the context of which they are a part, then the possibility of an infinite consensus can in this instance really only mean the possibility of an infinite repetition in the sense of reacquiring, reformulating or hermeneutically reconstructing philosophical insights. But in this context the idea of an ultimate limit of *ideal* understanding makes no sense at all, for the 'obstacles to communication' here share the same origins as the preconditions for the possibility of communication itself: both are founded in the dependence of philosophical thought on language. A communication situation could only be 'ideal' in Apel's sense if linguistic signs had become a completely transparent medium for the communication of intended meanings, so that communication itself had acquired the quality of immediacy. But this would be a state of affairs exceeding the bounds of language.

In the instance of philosophical statements, it is thus not possible to conceive of an 'infinite consensus' as an ultimate and, as it were, 'stable' consensus. Precisely because in this instance there are no rules governing the logic of inquiry which would guarantee truth *in the long run*, it makes no sense to situate the truth at the end of history. It is rather the case that past, present and future are all equally possible 'locations' for philosophical truth. A consensus about philosophical truths among persons of sufficient competence to judge would naturally have to be one that was susceptible to constant renewal, even if mediated through a productive reinterpretation of philosophical texts. But we do not need the idea of an ideal communication community in order to be able to conceive this thought, not even in the form of a regulative principle. There can be no possibility of philosophical insights being 'ultimately' borne out, any more than there can be an 'ultimate' foundation of philosophical truths. This has nothing whatever to do with relativism. The problem of relativism is only produced by the angle of vision from which the philosophy of the absolute perceives the problems of validity. What is needed is a change in the angle of vision, and the problem of relativism would disappear.[83]

So far I have admittedly only dealt with the problem which Apel emphasizes concerning the possible validity-claim of philosophical statements. It seems to me, however, that it is sufficicent to demonstrate with reference to *one* element in the argument that we are not obliged to define our notion of truth in relation to Apel's conception of an ideal communication community. For if it is possible to demonstrate at only *one* point that the immanent criticism of idealizing concepts in Apel's transcendental pragmatics does not necessarily lead to the 'relativistic' or 'historicist' dissolution of the concept of truth which Apel fears, then it is legitimate for us to conclude from this that the problem of relativism had been wrongly posed. We might easily suspect, moreover, that the problem of relativism is merely the abiding shadow of an absolutism which would like to anchor the truth in some Archimedean point lying outside the world of our actual discourse. Relativism, in this connection, would be the reminder that there can be no such Archimedean point. But if it is true that we can hold fast to the idea of truth *without the aid* of such an Archimedean point, then at the same time as we take our leave of absolutism, we can also bid farewell to its shadow, relativism.

It ought by now to be clear that the 'weaker' version of consensus theory, which I earlier distinguished from Habermas's stronger version (cf. Section VII, above), is not sufficient to justify the strong underlying assumptions which lie at the foundations of the reformulation of the universalization principle proposed in discourse ethics. For if the idea of an infinite rational consensus can be explained independently of the idea of an ideal communication community, then this shows that the idealizing concepts which lie at the foundations of the consensus theories of both Habermas *and* Apel cannot represent a compelling conceptual reconstruction of inescapable presuppositions involved in speech and argument.

At this point it also becomes clear to what extent discourse ethics has remained *too Kantian.* Just as Kant had to resort to the idea of a kingdom of ends in order to explain the idea of practical reason, so too must Apel and Habermas resort to an ideal communication situation in order to explain the connection between rationality and truth, and with it the concept of practical reason. In either case, the problem lies in the idealizing concepts themselves, or in the fact that they are taken as 'ideals of reality' itself. For if this is how we understand them, then their inherently illusory quality ensures that they immediately become elusive. Just as the kingdom of ends not only betokens a state of affairs in which moral conflicts can no longer exist, but also one where an unbroken unity and communication among subjects would be realized (a state of affairs in reality, then, in which a plurality of subjects would no longer even be conceivable), so too do the formal structures of the ideal speech situation or the conditions of an ideal communication community (if we take them as an ideal telos of a linguistic reality) betoken not only an ideal condition of rational communication, but in reality also an ideal state of mutual understanding and intersubjective agreement – and thus a state of affairs in which, again, the darkness that lies between subjects and within them has been finally dispelled. But without this darkness there would also be no language – unless, of course, it be the ideal language of the constructive semanticists, which would, however, turn day to night.

IX

In the course of the last two sections, I have already implicitly repudiated the claim of discourse ethics to provide a fundamental grounding for practical reason. But in so far as this repudiation is directed at the arguments of Apel and Habermas, it still stands in need of justification itself. My thesis is that a universalistic moral principle cannot be derived from what Habermas calls 'normatively substantial presuppositions' of argument. I shall here ignore the distinction between a 'strong' and a 'weak' version of fundamental grounding (Apel versus Habermas[84]), since this appears to be only of secondary significance for my own considerations. I shall not discuss Habermas's sketched derivation of a universalization principle from presuppositions of argument because it seems to me self-evident that this derivation is false. Habermas introduces a supplementary 'semantic' premise at a crucial stage (the premise that 'the sense we associate with justified norms is that these regulate social matters in the common interests of those who may be affected': cf. DE 103); in this way the central content of the universalization principle is introduced illicitly through a side door. In this section I should like to tackle the problem *directly* by questioning the sense in which presuppositions of argument can have a universalistically understood moral content. My answer will be that this would only be possible if we presuppose a (strong) consensus theory of truth, something which I have already shown to be false.

I proceed on the understanding that Apel and Habermas are correct in their grounding of inescapable presuppositions of argument, and thus that anyone who tries to contest the validity of these presuppositions involves himself in a performative contradiction.[85] Being involved in a discourse, I cannot consistently contest the proposition that I am obliged to be sincere towards those with whom I am arguing, that only the better argument should prevail, or that none of the participants may be prevented from advancing their own arguments. But I maintain that the general norms for arguing, which we are dealing with here, do not amount to universalistic moral norms or meta-norms for morality. I wish to justify this thesis in two steps:

1 It is self-evident that the norms for argument which we are discussing here cannot govern the initiating or breaking-off of arguments. But if these norms leave me free to decide whether or not to become involved in particular arguments, and whether or not to break off a dialogue, then it is prima facie not plausible to understand them as having any moral content. Apel and Habermas believe it is possible to circumvent this difficulty by pointing to the general orientation of speech or even, in Apel's case, of solitary thought towards validity. We might say that if I have genuinely understood this orientation of speech and thought, then I have also understood that I may not suppress arguments – least of all those which speak against me – quite regardless of who voices them. In a certain sense this is of course correct: we call people irrational if they prove impervious to arguments or experiences which would shatter the opinions they hold, and thus if they 'suppress' arguments or experiences, not because the arguments are in reality bad ones or the experiences irrelevant, but merely as a *defensive reaction*. The concept of a good argument, however, implies that we disregard the question of who is voicing it. It appears, then, that what is demonstrated here, at last as far as controversial validity-claims is concerned, is a kind of implied obligation to *proceed* from speech, action and thought to argument, precisely as if it would be *irrational* in a fundamental sense for us not to involve ourselves in a discourse with any being capable of speech and action whenever they required us to do so. I believe that this is more or less the fundamental intuition which provides the bridge, so to speak, in Apel and Habermas from the presuppositions of argument to universalistic morality. But it is a bridge that will not hold up. The requirement not to suppress any argument, which we have recognized as fundamental to any rational approach to one's own opinions, is by no means identical in meaning with the requirement that we should not refuse to take part in arguments with others – whoever they may be. Such a refusal would only be irrational if, for instance, we refuse because we are afraid of the arguments of others. It may be that such a refusal could be *immoral* because we are denying to someone else a right which, other things being equal, we might very well claim for ourselves. But this moral dimension of arguing cannot be explained in

terms of the fact that speech is orientated towards validity, together with the presuppositions of argument – although it can be explained by means of a universalization principle in Kant's sense. I maintain, therefore, that the obligation not to suppress any argument, which is grounded in the validity-orientation of speech, has no *direct* consequences for the question of when and with whom I am obliged to argue, nor of what I am to argue about.[86] It is only the assumption of a consensus theory of truth that makes it appear that there is any such consequence, for the precise reason that, in the nature of this assumption, the achievement of consensuses by means of argument is *defined* as the basic form of a rational approach towards one's own validity-claims.

2   These deliberations might lead us to suspect that the unavoidable presuppositions of argument do not in themselves constitute *moral* obligations. Let me emphasize that I am not disputing that the practice of arguing is, so to speak, imbued with moral obligations. But this might be explained by the fact that a maxim of refusing to take part in dialogue is not generalizable. What is questionable, however, is whether those norms of argument which we cannot dispute without committing a performative contradiction actually betoken obligations of a moral nature. To put it another way, it is questionable whether the 'must' entailed in the norms of argument can be meaningfully understood as a *moral* 'must'. The moral 'must' certainly comes into play at the 'edges' of argument, at those points where a dialogue is being initiated or continued or declined. But if the norms of argument say nothing about whether I should permit the discussion partner to whom I must accord equal rights of speech actually to *exercise* these rights in the very next instant, as it were, then the 'must' entailed in the norms of argument can scarcely be interpreted as a morally substantial one. We seem here to be dealing rather with a 'must' of the kind that is associated with *constitutive* rules: I am unable to dispute this 'must' in my capacity as participant in an argument because it is constitutive of the practice of arguing.

Now norms of argument are of course not rules of a game in which we can participate or not participate as the mood takes us. They are *inherently* connected with norms of rationality such as that which says that we may not suppress any argument that is relevant to the point for which we are claiming validity, and in our capacity as speaking and arguing beings we are unable to escape such norms (this much in the intuitions of Apel and Habermas is correct). But precisely the fact that the inescapability of obligations to rationality can be expressed through a 'principle of avoiding performative contradictions' also shows that the most general norms of rationality are not directly capable of having a moral content. Obligations to rationality refer to the acknowledgement of arguments, moral obligations to the acknowledgement of persons. It is a requirement of rationality to acknowledge even the arguments of my enemy if they are good ones; it is a requirement of morality to permit even those people to speak who are not yet capable of arguing well. Overstating the point a little, we might say that obligations to rationality are concerned with arguments regardless of who voices them, whereas moral obligations are concerned with people regardless of their arguments. It is of course undeniable that requirements of rationality and moral obligations are frequently interwoven in complex ways, but only from the imaginary perspective of the 'highest point' of an ideal communication community can it appear as if the two would ultimately coincide.

I should like to clarify my fundamental arguments against the attempt at a fundamental grounding of discourse ethics with reference to the clear and carefully elaborated arguments of Wolfgang Kuhlmann.[87] Kuhlmann's attempt at a fundamental grounding starts, like that of Apel and Habermas, by considering the 'rules and presuppositions of meaningful argument'[88], but he then goes on to interpret these as norms of co-operation obtaining within the medium of discourse.[89] These norms of co-operation are the counterpart of the 'norms of' discourse mentioned by Habermas (cf. DE 99); they oblige us, as Kuhlmann puts it, 'to co-operate as *equal* partners, acknowledging and treating each other in the course of argument as possessing equal rights.' They demand 'that in the course of argument each participant is accorded the same right to contradict, to interrupt, to begin afresh, to demand that the argument continue, to put questions, to insist that points are justified, to adduce fresh viewpoints, etc.'[90] By way of these norms of co-operation, which are implicit in the presuppositions of argument, Kuhlmann attempts to derive a fundamental norm for communicative ethics. He formulates it as follows: 'Endeavour in all cases where your interests might collide with those of others to achieve a rational practical consensus with them.'[91] But Kuhlmann is only able to make the connection between the obligations inherent *within* discourse and a moral principle that *goes beyond* discourse by neutralizing the difference between solitary reflection and genuine discourse from the outset. He uses the word 'argument' in such a way that it includes solitary reflection in so far as this is itself orientated towards the assertion of validity.[92] Because he interprets solitary reflection from the viewpoint of genuine argument in this way, he feels entitled to *equate* the endeavour to arrive at 'consensual' – in the sense of 'true' – solutions with the endeavour to bring about a rational consensus at crucial stages in his exposition. Thus in fundamental norm N2, for example, which is intended to express 'the impossibility of going behind the will to a rational consensus', he says:'If we are seriously interested in the solution of a problem, then we must endeavour to find a solution to which all can agree, i.e. a rational consensus.'[93] In elucidation of this, Kuhlmann writes:

> The thing that we want if we really want to know something, if we really want to have the solution to a problem, is a solution *in favour of* which all good reasons can be adduced, and *against* which no justified objection is made or can be made, a solution to which everyone could justifiably *agree*. What we want is a rational consensus.[94]

If the will to truth is identical in meaning with the will to achieving rational consensuses, then universal norms of a genuine co-operation on equal terms with *all* others are indeed built into the validity-orientation of speech from the outset. If this were the case, then the fundamental norm of communicative ethics would be nothing more than a specification of the most general obligations to rationality defined for the special case of conflicts of interest.

My objections are not actually directed at the interpretation of solitary reflection as a virtual dialogue. On the contrary, if in our reflection we take various points of view into consideration, raise objections to our own arguments etc., then this process can hardly be understood other than as an internal dialogue. In the same way, we could understand the endeavour to achieve 'correct' solutions as an endeavour to arrive at an agreement with ourselves which might substitute for an agreement achieved in public dialogue, the voices of others being allowed to speak on the stage of the solitary subject. It is for this reason that genuine 'public' dialogues invariably also have the function of a test which is to show whether we have really represented the *possible* arguments, viewpoints or objections of others accurately in our solitary reflections. But then these others whose voices are heard in our solitary reflections are always 'representative' others; their claim to be heard is the claim that their arguments make on our consideration. The obligation to enter into genuine discourse can therefore only stretch as far as the obligation not to suppress any relevant argument, or not to evade possible objections. But this obligation is not *identical in meaning* with the obligation to achieve a genuine and universal rational consensus, and it is therefore also not identical in meaning with universalistically conceived obligations to co-operation. It is rather the case that the requirement not to suppress any argument leaves open the question of which persons I am obliged to argue with, and what about, and on what occasion; it therefore also leaves open the question of the specific instances in which I am obliged to pursue a genuine consensus. It is only if we *presuppose* a strong version of consensus theory as providing a criterion of truth that we can interpret elementary obligations to rationality *directly* as an obligation to direct our efforts towards the achievement of a rational consensus on controversial issues. If we do not make this presupposition, on the other hand, then general obligations to rationality, or even general presuppositions of argument, are manifestly too weak to serve as vehicles for a universalistic moral principle *on their own*.[95]

These last considerations suggest a new possibility for interpreting the notion of an 'ideal communication community'. We might say that the real communication community is present as an ideal within the process of solitary reflection, which is to say that it is present in the form of all the possible arguments that might be articulated by the members of an unlimited communication community. But this virtually present communication community is 'ideal' in a double sense: it is ideal *firstly* because it is only present in the form of possible *arguments* which *might* be articulated by real persons and from a multiplicity of perspectives; thus it is present as a community of arguers in which the only form of compulsion that obtains is that of superior argument. And *secondly* this community is ideal because the unlimited communication community we are referring to is envisaged ideally as assembled in one place and at one time. Now in this sense it is easy to concede that the assumption of an ideal communication community is constitutive even of real situations in which arguments take place. This idealization genuinely does elucidate a precondition for what we call 'rational argument' or 'rational reflection'. It is an idealizing abstraction of the empirical persons who articulate arguments – considering arguments *qua* arguments entails thinking of them as detached, as it were, from the persons who voiced them or who might voice them. When it is understood in this way, the assumption of an ideal communication community may well be *necessary*; but we should be deceiving ourselves about the *possible sense* of this assumption if we were to understand it as the anticipation of an *ideal state of affairs* to be realized by a real communication community, just as we are deceiving ourselves about the sense of the assumption of intersubjectively shared meanings if we understand them as the anticipation of an ultimate, an ideal language. That is to say, we deceive ourselves about the *sense* of the *necessity* of these assumptions if we hypostatize them as ideals attainable in reality, even if, as I indicated earlier, the roots of this deception are perhaps to be sought in language itself. It is of course possible to understand the presence of the ideal communication community within the real one as an expression of the inescapable validity-orientation of human speech, as Apel would have us do, but the stuff of which this ideal is made is not suited to designing an ideal life-form. The idealizing assumptions of argument contain neither an ultimate foundation for morality nor the promissory glimpse of an ultimate reconciliation.[96]

III Towards a Mediation betwen Kantian and Discourse Ethics

X

In section VI, above, I tried to show that Habermas's formulation of the universalization principle contains an unfortunate conflation of a universalistic moral principle with a procedural legitimation principle. This conflation is grounded in a consensus theory of truth which cannot be defended as a substantial theory in the sense that Apel and Habermas intend it. But as far as the conflation of moral principle and legitimacy principle in

Habermas is concerned, I have so far presumed a distinction between questions of moral rightness and questions of the justice of norms rather than elucidating the matter. For the sake of simplicity I shall begin here by elucidating the distinction between moral and legal *norms*. As far as so-called moral norms are concerned, the thing we always have to bear in mind is that these are either unspecific like the moral principle itself ('Human dignity is inviolate') or like ethical obligations of a 'broadly' binding nature ('help the needy'), *or else* they are so constructed as to admit of exceptions.

This last point is connected with the fact that moral judgements are primarily concerned with ways of acting in particular situations (in Kant's terms, with maxims); only in a derived, albeit *psychologically* important sense are they concerned with universal *norms*. If we may take this reservation as read, I should now like to proceed to a discussion of three characteristic distinctions between moral and legal norms.

(1) Legal norms are distinguished from moral norms firstly by the fact that they are brought into force or set aside, and that they hold, *if* they are in force, for a particular group of people who are affected by them. Legal obligations are a function of the legal norms that are currently in force. Moral norms and moral obligations, on the other hand, hold, if they hold at all, independently of any act that might bring them into force. The essential distinction here can be easily illustrated with reference to article 1.1 of the Basic Law of the Federal Republic of Germany. The principle of the inviolacy of human dignity holds, as a moral command, independently of the fact that it is enshrined in our constitution. The point of incorporating this moral command into our constitution as a legal norm was, of course, to bind the legislative and the judiciary powers, in the light of the experiences of German history, by means of a corresponding *legal* obligation. – Naturally, the analytical distinction between moral and legal norms is not applicable to the concrete ethical life of traditional societies. However, the transition to a post-conventional morality also means a *conventionalization* of law: to a certain extent the validity of laws becomes a matter of decision, subject of course to moral limitations. Some of these moral limitations have, with good reason, been incorporated *as* legal norms into the constitution of the Federal Republic.

The concept of moral obligation is connected with the grounding of a normative validity-claim; the concept of legal obligation is connected with the concept of the *social* (and thus in a certain sense factual) validity of a norm. Even if the validity of laws is scarcely conceivable without a moment of (social) recognition, it is never entirely subsumed by such recognition. It possesses a moment of pure facticity, if only in the form of a common resolution voluntarily made. It is only because moral and legal validity are not analytically identical that we can even raise the question of to what extent we are morally obliged to follow legal norms that are factually valid (in force). And even if we presuppose a morally grounded distinction between just and unjust norms, it nevertheless remains *meaningful* to ask to what extent we are morally obliged to respect even unjust norms, or whether under certain circumstances we might have the moral right or even the moral duty to offend against a just norm. It would be sheer nonsense, on the other hand, if someone were to ask whether we are morally obliged to follow moral norms which are not valid.

(2) Legal norms are secondly distinguished from moral norms by the fact that they are as a rule *constitutive* of a particular praxis: it is impossible to conceive of legal systems without a large proportion of constitutive rules. Legal norms are constitutive rules in so far as they do not simply lay down rights and duties, powers and sanctions, but also 'constitute' practices (such as 'parliamentary elections'), institutions (such as 'parliament' and, in the case of the Federal Republic, the 'Constitutional Court'), or offices (such as the 'Federal Chancellor'). Parliamentary elections, governmental decisions, proclamations of law, and even taxes owed, would not exist without the law which, whatever else it is, is *also* a system of mutually supporting definitions and constitutive rules. It is of course possible for such a system of institutions and practices to have evolved, as is the case in Britain, by a natural process, as it were, which is to say, historically; equally it is possible for new institutions and practices to develop spontaneously in revolutionary situations, in the form of a system of soviets, for example. But the constitutive character of rules is not crucially affected by the question of whether they are explicitly codified or only grounded in a general acceptance. As in the case of games, a praxis may persist without the written

codification of the constitutive rules for it (e.g. what counts as a 'goal', or as 'check', or what is a correct move in chess etc.). It is sufficient if in cases of disagreement such codifications can be effected as the need arises, whether they are intended to apply once and for all, or on an ad hoc basis.

It is inherent within the constitutive aspect of legal norms that they manifest themselves in the form of *systems*, which again makes them comparable with the rules of games: it is not possible to threaten imprisonment as the punishment for manslaughter without laying down what is to count as manslaughter, without laying down the rules of judicial procedure, and without rules for carrying out the sentence. It is not possible to lay down voting procedures in parliament without also determining what things parliament may decide, how it is to be elected, who is to watch over the implementation of laws that have been passed, etc. Moral norms do not have this systematic character for the reason that they concern the question of correct action in a *given* world, whereby what is given in reality includes legal norms amongst other things. From a moral standpoint, the social validity of legal norms is to start with one fact amongst others, so that, for example, I know that my vote does not 'count' if I fill out the voting slip incorrectly, or that I must expect to be punished if I break the traffic regulations or the tax laws. This brings me to my third point, the problem of sanctions.

(3) Legal norms are as a rule associated with the threat of external sanctions. In so far as constitutive rules are concerned, the sanctions consist quite simply in the fact that the non-observance of the rules renders the corresponding action legally invalid or ineffective. Voting or judicial verdicts, for instance, are invalid if the rules of procedure have been breached – just as a goal is no goal if it was scored from an offside position. In other cases the sanctions consist in legally established punishments such as imprisonment, fines, loss of civil rights, etc. We might even say that basic moral norms such as *'Neminem laede'*, 'Thou shalt not kill', 'Thou shalt not lie', etc. find their way into law in the form of penalties: anyone who does such and such will be punished by imprisonment for not less than . . . years. The penal code links particular states of affairs with punitive measures; it is, so to speak, the point of penal law that it introduces a graded system of sanctions for actions whose moral reprehensibility is as a rule (and not always with justice) simply presupposed. The necessity

of an analytical distinction between moral norms and corresponding legal norms becomes clear particularly when we bear in mind that the question of whether an action is morally reprehensible is quite different from the question of whether it ought to be punished. I might consider it morally repugnant for someone to claim that Auschwitz was all lies and yet be opposed to imposing a general punitive threat on such action.

In contrast to legal norms, moral norms are not linked in any *essential* sense with external sanctions; morally good action is not enforceable, by contrast with legally correct action. In the case of morality the essential sanctions are *internal* in nature:[97] feelings of guilt, remorse, self-reproach, self-contempt. Moral 'ought' can therefore not have the same sense as legal 'ought' or 'should'. The respective sense of 'ought' or 'should' cannot be independent of the answer to the question, 'And what happens if I do not do what I ought to do?' In the case of moral 'ought', the answer can only be of the kind, 'I shall not be at one with myself, shall not be able to look myself in the face.' In the case of legal 'ought', the typical answer consists in the threat of an external sanction.

The moment of facticity in the concept of the validity of laws, to which I drew attention above under point (1), naturally has something to do with the graded system of external sanctions which the law *also* represents, amongst other things. Legal systems cannot, of course, survive in the long term through sheer coercive authority: the social validity of the law implies, in addition to everything else, that at least a significant part of the legal system is acknowledged by those affected as legitimate ('just') and therefore as associated with moral obligations. But 'the law in force' does not *mean* the same as 'law that is acknowledged as valid (just)'.[98] It is rather the case that in the concept of the validity of laws, the moments of acknowledgement and enforcibility are interconnected in a complex fashion. The moment of a facticity that is associated with the expectation of external sanctions cannot be eliminated from the concept of the validity of laws, any more than can the moment of acknowledgement. If this were not so, then the question of whether and when and to what extent I am *morally* obliged to obey (or to apply) the existing laws would have no sense whatsoever. When the legitimacy of the law is linked with the idea of the freely given approval of all those affected, of course, (and thus ultimately with democratic procedures) then a state of law becomes *conceivable* in which physical sanctions would no longer be necessary because the form in which conflicts took place would be non-violent. A society without prisons is conceivable. But it seems to me uncertain whether it would be meaningful to assume the possibility of a legal system without external sanctions, for the 'externalization' of morality in the form of positive law and its external sanctions also contains an element of emancipation from internalized normative compulsion.

I have tried to clarify the distinction between morality and law with reference to three characteristic aspects of law. I should now like to elucidate more precisely why and in what sense a universalistic moral principle should be distinguished from a democratic principle of legitimacy. In *either* case the way of distinguishing between 'right' and 'wrong' involves an appeal to the idea of a common will formed in the absence of coercion, whether it is the will of rational beings or of those affected. But the nature of this appeal to a common will should be understood differently in each case. In the case of moral judgement we are concerned with finding a way of acting in concrete situations which we should be able, in B. Gert's terminology, to 'publicly advocate' as a generalizable one. I shall show below what function argument fulfils in this connection. The question that arises in each specific instance is whether we – as rational beings – are able to will that a particular way of acting should become universal. And only the *negative* answer to this question constitutes a moral 'ought'. Norms therefore fulfil a derived function in morality, important as they may be from a psychological point of view.

In law, by contrast, we really are dealing with norms and rules. As I pointed out earlier, the 'de-conventionalization' of morality in the course of a transition to post-traditional society has also meant the *conventionalization* of law. With law and morality developing in contrary directions like this, the law has also become subject to the demands of morality: morality becomes an authority existing beyond and 'above' the law. Connected with this process is the development of a procedural, a democratic concept of legitimacy, according to which a legal system is legitimate if it can be understood as an expression of the common will of those subjected to it. The modern tradition of natural law, right down to Kant, has tried to develop a corresponding concept of the legitimacy of law. But the appeal to a common will of those affected by a legal system means something structurally different here from what is implied in the case of morality. For here we are dealing with the *positive* common will of those affected to subject their lives to certain rules – which necessarily also means subjecting them to these rules and not to others – and to the sanctions associated with them. The common will is to be conceived here in action, as it were, in the form of a resolution or formal agreement; the act of bringing-into-force or setting-aside is analytically a part of positive law. This concept of the legitimacy of law also has a *counterfactual* application; it is in this sense, for example, that Kant says that the legislator may only make laws which the people would have been *capable* of imposing on themselves. Admittedly, it lies within the logic of the modern concept of legitimacy that the common nature of any decision-making process must as far as possible be realized *in actual fact* – that is, in so far as all those affected are ultimately to be accorded an equal right to participate in the collective processes by which the common will is formed: this is the idea of democracy. But if legitimate laws are to be such that all those affected would have been capable of passing them collectively, and if all those affected are – in principle – to have an equal right to participate in the collective decision-making process, then it goes without saying that the settling of normative questions by means of public argument must play a central part in any attempt to realize the possibility of legitimate law in the sense of the modern concept of legitimacy and to ensure that the law is acknowledged as legitimate. To argue in favour of a legal norm – or a system of legal norms – means in this case the attempt to provide reasons which convince all other affected persons why all people of good will and discernment should necessarily be able to deem it to be equally in the interests of all that this norm or these norms should prevail in society. When it comes down to it, Habermas, as we have seen, makes this *particular* case of the connection between normative validity and real argument into a model case for normative validity in general. But in this way his universalization principle falls behind the differentiation of moral and legal questions which is already clearly articulated in Kant (even if Kant does not clarify the issue satisfactorily). In particular this means that Habermas, because in structural terms he starts out on the level of the justice of norms, necessarily fails to come to grips with the problem of *moral* validity. It is no mere coincidence

– on the contrary, it lies in the very nature of the subject – that the contract theorists of modern natural law from Hobbes to Kant have treated questions of *moral* validity either in the context of their *preliminary* discussion or else as the very *foundation* of questions of the legitimacy of laws. The aim of discourse ethics to 'sublate' Kant's ethics and modern natural law by binding the law to a universalistic morality – *against* the trend of the moral counter-enlightenment – is an entirely justified one; but it can only be realized if we do not fall behind the degree of differentiation that has been achieved in earlier discussions of the problems.

XI

The thoughts expressed in preceding sections already contain the most important elements of a fallibilistic reconstruction of discourse ethics. The task now is to assemble these elements into a whole. I shall do this in an indirect way, by showing in what way the discursive clarification of moral validity-claims can be put into effect within the quasi-Kantian perspective which I have so far adopted. I call this perspective 'quasi-Kantian' because I have tried from the outset to separate the fruitful basic idea that Kant has from the formalistic husk in which he has concealed it. This selective reading of Kant rests on a critique of him which is entirely analogous with my critique of discourse ethics. In both cases my criticism is aimed at a philosophical architectonics which depends on an *ideal* as its keystone – the kingdom of ends in Kant's case, an ideal situation for communication in the case of Apel and Habermas. But just as the arch and the keystone can only maintain their position by virtue of mutual interdependence, so it is also the case here that the criticism of idealizing concepts necessarily also has implications for the overall construction. What this means in Kant's case I have only indicated so far, and not yet fully explained in its implications. My thesis is that the formalism and rigorism of Kant's ethics are directly connected with the attempt to ground ethics *sub specie aeternitatis*, i.e. from the point of view of a kingdom of ends. Kant's moral norms are maxims of action for the members of a kingdom of ends. That is why there can be no exceptions, disagreements, insoluble conflicts or irresolvable issues for Kant, and it is also why the faculty of judgement cannot play any significant part in Kant's ethics. For the kingdom of ends, the 'form of universality' is sufficient, and this is something that tolerates no muddying of the picture. But then it is only with the problem of *mediating* between the particular and the universal that the real problems of morality begin; to this extent at least, Hegel was correct. Now it is true that discourse ethics addresses precisely this problem, but it is unable to solve it because in one central respect it clings to Kantian architectonics: discourse ethics, too, describes morality *sub specie aeternitatis*.

The interpretation I should like to set against one that is guided by the idea of the perfection of moral sense, is one that rests on the idea of eliminating nonsense. My thesis is that the elimination of nonsense is conceivable even if we do not relate it to the idea of perfected sense, of ultimate reconciliation, of a final truth. I believe, moreover, that Kant's basic idea can in this sense be interpreted fallibilistically (and at the same time dialogically).

I have chosen an indirect way, as I say, showing the precise significance that arguments and ways of arguing have, in the context of forming moral judgements and of moral learning processes, if they are understood in a 'Kantian' sense as I have explained it above. As soon as it is made clear in what sense argumentative and communicative clarifications of moral questions are *possible*, incidentally, it will not be difficult to ground a norm for dialogue in Kantian terms. For in so far as dialogic clarifications are *possible* at all, and perhaps also *important* for those affected, it is easy to see that a maxim of *refusing* to take part in dialogue is not generalizable. The fact that a corresponding *norm for dialogue* must largely remain unspecific and can, so to speak, only assume a specific content in the context of specific interpretations of situations (which themselves remain subject to revision) is something that I consider rather to be an advantage by comparison with the quasi-transcendental norms for argument offered by discourse ethics, which of necessity promise more than they can deliver.

I shall argue here initially on the basis of a simplifying assumption, which I shall then retract in the second stage of my argument. My assumption is that the logic of moral arguments is already determined by a universalistically understood moral principle. This should not be understood in the sense of an empirical assumption about all members of our society, but in the (methodical) sense of bracketing out arguments and convictions in which competing sources of normative validity such as the will of God, the natural order of things, or the authority of tradition are presupposed. We are thus limiting ourselves to moral arguments in which the generalizability of ways of acting is presupposed as a criterion of what is morally correct or as a measure of moral value. My thesis is that, given this presupposition, moral argument is concerned almost exclusively with the interpretation of the situations attendant upon actions and needs, as well as with the way that those who act or suffer the consequences of actions see themselves – with the result that if we have reached agreement about the interpretations of situations and the way people see themselves, moral controversies will as a rule dissolve. This means that the question whether *we* are (rationally) able to will that *my* maxim should become a universal law becomes more or less identical in meaning with the question whether *my* understanding of situations, the way I see *my*self, *my* interpretations, are appropriate, accurate or truthful. The 'we' that so disquiets discourse ethics resides, so to speak, in the validity of my descriptions of situations, my understanding of reality, and the way I see myself. For the same reason, this is also the point at which to begin any critique or argumentative clarification.

This thesis could be elucidated by means of examples on two distinct *levels*: *firstly* that of the collective matrix of interpretation, *secondly* that of moral judgement in complex situations. As far as the level of the collective matrix of interpretation is concerned, relevant examples could be drawn from changes in traditional views of homosexuality, the role of women, education, abortion or the rights of children. Of course, the proponents of a universalistic morality (and it is with them that we are concerned here) never did believe that morality stops when it comes to homosexuals, women or children. They believed rather that homosexuality was corrupting, that women were not capable of rational self-determination, or that children must learn obedience above all in order to become decent human beings. In proportion as such views become questionable, which is to say that it is no longer possible to advance good reasons in their defence, so, too, do the *moral* views change that are associated with them. Physical chastisement of children becomes morally questionable if we recognize that it represents a senseless injury and not a necessary pedagogic measure. Legal prosecution and social discrimination against homosexuals becomes morally questionable if we recognize that the condemnation of homosexuals is unfounded. It becomes morally questionable to prevent women from realizing their personal potential if we recognize that the traditional views on the nature of women are untenable. In other words, socially prevailing moral orientations determining behaviour, for example, towards homosexuals, women or children, are anchored in collective matrices of interpretation; collective moral learning processes take place when reasons are brought forward which call such matrices of interpretation into question and prompt their revision, although it should immediately be added that such revision does not as a rule take place only in the medium of argument, but under the *pressure* of a struggle for recognition and under the *influence* of new experiences. Such learning processes result in a new way of talking about and behaving towards homosexuals, women and children (keeping to the examples we have already mentioned). They also result in those affected seeing themselves and behaving towards themselves in a new way. But from a *moral* viewpoint, what we are dealing with here is the *elimination* of inequalities and unequal ways of treating people which have had the floor pulled from under them, as it were, once the dogmatism of traditional views has been shown to be without foundation. Looked at in this way, collective moral learning processes consist in the extension of relationships of mutual recognition through the critical undermining of socially inherited attitudes and matrices of interpretation. What is involved here are *specific negations* rather than advances towards some ideal, as can be seen from the fact that the false or ideological inequalities of treatment conform, as it were, to an archetypal image – by which I mean those cases of *grounded* inequality in which human beings are not *yet*, or no *longer* accorded an equal possibility of *factual* self-determination. Small children, cases of severe mental handicap, and criminals are three examples. I do not want to be misunderstood: precisely children, the mentally handicapped and criminals are also examples of the idea of self-determination remaining in force well beyond the boundaries of traditional interpretations of it. But this only means that the demand that we behave towards every human being in the light of their *possible* self-determination must become more radical in meaning in proportion as false views about the socialization of children or the nature of psychic illnesses or the causes of crime are dissipated. Kant's insight that freedom can only be learned by training for it has acquired a whole new field of application today, for example, in the sphere of democratic psychiatry. But we are not even able to conceive an ideal ultimate goal for such changes: the principle of moral progress is not the perfection of sense, but the elimination of nonsense.

The second level on which I should like to illustrate my thesis is that of moral judgement in complex situations. I should like to start by distinguishing between three different forms of morally relevant complexity. I call those situations *morally complex* in which different moral demands, as it were, collide with each other and there is no easy or unambiguous possibility of choosing between them. I call situations *morally inscrutable* if the moral *significance* of actions in those situations is unclear, either because the agents are mistaken about their motives or because the communication situation as a whole is distorted. And finally I call situations *practically inscrutable* if the *consequences* of our actions in those situations are unclear. A situation would be morally *complex* if it prompts the question, '*Should* (or may) I (really) help him?' A situation would be morally *inscrutable* if it prompts me to ask, 'Do I really *want* to help him?' A situation would be *practically inscrutable*, finally, if it prompts me to ask, '*Can* I help him *in this way*?' All three forms of morally relevant complexity clearly have to be considered if we are asking about the logic of moral arguments concerning the correct way of acting in concrete situations. Now we could, at least for the purposes of crude orientation, classify *morally inscrutable* situations under the validity-dimension of *truthfulness* and *practically inscrutable* situations under the validity-dimension of empirical *truth*. And we could then label the corresponding dimensions of moral discourse, along the lines that Habermas proposes, 'therapeutic' and 'empirical–theoretical' discourse respectively. I use these classifications here merely in order to separate out that dimension of *specifically normative* argumentation which the moral principle of discourse ethics has in mind and which occupies a distinct *category* of normative discourse alongside therapeutic and empirical–theoretical discourse. Beyond this, we must make one further qualification. We have already dealt with *one* important aspect of moral discourse, namely the one concerned with general moral orientations and ultimately with socially prevailing modes of interpreting reality and needs. What remains as the essential core of moral discourse, after we have made all these qualifications, ought to enable us to make clear the logic of moral argumentation.

It might at first seem improper to limit discussion to morally complex situations. But I am proceeding on the understanding that, as far as elementary moral doctrine is concerned (e.g. cases of wilful lying, injury, killing, or even leaving others in the lurch), this causes no problems for the quasi-Kantian perspective I am propounding here. That is to say, I proceed on the understanding that – rationally – *we* cannot will that corresponding ways of acting should become universal. That is how we arrive at prima facie norms like '*Neminem laede*' or a prohibition on telling untruths. The problem of morally complex situations concerns the question how, in the case of a *conflict* of norms, for example, we are to understand the justification of *exceptions*. When formulated in this way, however, our statement already contains a misleading element. If norms, when looked at logically, do not have primary status in morality, but a derivative one, then the grounding of a moral judgement in morally complex situations does not mean the grounding of an exception, but ultimately, once again, the grounding of the generalizability – or non-generalizability – of a way of acting. I refer back here to the thoughts contained in section III. There I showed that the so-called exceptional moral situations cannot be made to conform to rules in a strict (Kantian) sense. Let us remind ourselves of this by looking at two examples, choosing the following two maxims for this purpose:

'If need be I shall try to preserve an unjustly persecuted (or accused) person from arrest (or sentence) by telling a lie,' and
'I shall assist a terminally ill patient to die if that is their wish.'

In the case of either maxim it seems clear that, as they stand, they *cannot* be called generalizable. In either case I have no difficulty in imagining situations in which I should consider it disastrous or at least wrong for these maxims to be acted upon. The person I assisted to die might only *believe* themselves to be terminally ill; or I might equally well want to get rid of them before they made a will, and be using this convenient moment etc. And where the innocent victim is concerned, I might be mistaken about their innocence, it might be that my lie would put another innocent person at risk, etc. Notice that we are not here dealing with the question of whether what I am able to will to be a universal law can also be willed by everyone else as a universal law. Rather it is possible that, if I think the matter through carefully, I am not myself able to will the corresponding maxim to be a universal law, even if I might perhaps consider a corresponding *action* to be correct in a specific situation. It thus transpires that so-called exceptional moral situations, as opposed to morally elementary situations, really cannot be made to conform to rules. If we wanted to formulate corresponding 'norms of permission' they would have to take the form, 'In situations that are sufficiently similar to *this* one, one may . . .' (or perhaps even 'one must').

This is where we encounter once more the curious asymmetry between morally elementary and morally complex situations. In the case of the first example, there is a norm which results from the non-generalizability of ways of acting such as might bring about a wilful injury to others, and that norm runs as follows: '*Neminem laede*, unless you have a good reason, one that can be "publicly advocated".' But our analysis of the second example shows that reasons which can be publicly advocated may only be formulated in the form of *norms* for exceptions if we think of them *either* as carrying an indexical element *or* as qualified by some unspecific limitation clause such as 'Under certain circumstances it is morally correct to . . .' All this applies, as I have said, quite independently of the question of any possible congruence between *my* 'being able to will' and that of everyone else. But on the other hand, if my analysis is correct, since the problem is a purely conceptual one, it poses itself in the same way for each individual making a moral judgement.

This brings me to the final step in my reflections. We have seen that the moral judgement that is made in morally complex situations cannot be expressed as a judgement about the generalizability of a maxim (in the strict sense of the term). But this means that a judgement about the generalizability or non-generalizability of ways of acting in particular situations – and I should like to stick to this interpretation of moral judgement – can ultimately only be grounded by means of the analysis of concrete situations. In other words, moral arguments are concerned in this case above all with the *appropriateness* and the relative *completeness* of descriptions of situations, including the various alternative ways of acting that are available in a given situation. This becomes even clearer if we remind ourselves of the 'negatory origins' of moral 'ought' or 'should' to which I pointed in section II, above. For it follows from these negatory origins of moral 'ought' or 'should' that the primary element in the formation of moral judgements and in moral arguments is not the generalizability, but the *non*-generalizability of ways of acting. Ways of acting are generalizable (permitted, legitimate) if they are not non-generalizable. There is no tautology here because we are dealing with a conceptual or cognitive primacy of negation – a cognitive primacy because it is, as it were, the elementary operation of moral judgement to establish the *non*-generalizability of ways of acting in a given situation. Now it seems to me clear that any judgement to the effect that a way of acting is *non*-generalizable is a function of understanding that way of acting *as* a way of acting in a given situation. Whether I judge the act of handing a fugitive over to the police to be non-generalizable or not depends entirely on whether I understand such a way of acting as an act of co-operation with legitimate state authority or as leaving a helpless and innocent victim of persecution in the lurch (or indeed as an act of complicity with a system of terror). But in a given situation, only one of these two interpretations can be correct. As soon as the question of a correct understanding of the situation is clarified, however, it will as a rule be the case that the question of the generalizability of specific ways of acting is also resolved. In this way we could understand moral judgement as the ability to grasp those aspects of situations upon which the non-generalizability (or the generalizability) of ways of acting depends. Moral discourse, however, would above all be a discourse about the correct way of understanding reality from a moral point of view.

My thesis is, therefore, that as a rule moral controversies are dissolved when agreement is achieved in those various dimensions of moral discourse which I have so far discussed – general interpretations, the way those affected see themselves, descriptions of situations and the understanding of the consequences of actions as well as the alternative ways of acting that can be discerned within a situation. In this sense we might say that the question of whether we are – rationally – able to will that a way of acting should become universal is above all a question about whether we have adequately understood the concrete situation in which action takes place. This also explains how the question of what we – as rational beings – are collectively able to will is reduced in practice to the question of how we – the persons affected – can achieve an adequate understanding of the situations in which we act. But as far as this question is concerned, a consensus among a few individuals who are sufficiently close to the concrete situation to be able to judge it is often more important for the process of assuring ourselves that a moral decision is correct than any actual general accord on the subject.

The preceding reflections force us to reconsider the distinction we previously made between 'therapeutic', 'empirical–theoretical' and (in the narrow sense) 'normative' aspects of moral discourse. It ought to be clear by now that we cannot bracket questions of truthfulness and empirical truth (in the broadest sense) out of moral discourse without robbing it of its substance. It is clearly not the case that what remains once we have bracketed out such questions is a problem of the grounding of moral *norms* honed down, so to speak, by analytical means to a fine point. What I have called the 'essential core of moral discourse', i.e. what remains after bracketing out those subsidiary aspects, seems rather to represent that aspect of moral judgement which is *either* self-evident (in the sense in which, according to Kant, it is self-evident that in the light of the categorical imperative I may not tell lies in order to secure my own advantage) *or else* no longer admits of any intersubjectively binding decision. This is less paradoxical than it sounds; we only have to abandon the premise that moral *judgements* can only be grounded with recourse to norms in order to see that moral *arguments* do not have to be normative in character. 'You promised him that you would' is a (simple) moral argument. But the proposition that, other things being equal, promises should be kept, is not really the premise of the conclusion 'Therefore you must do it' – i.e. it is not the kind of 'premise' about which we would begin to argue on a higher level of discussion if the case is controversial. It is much rather the case that this 'premise' really only expresses our understanding of corresponding situations for action in the form of a prima facie norm.

I do not, of course, wish to dispute that moral judgements carry an index of normative generality; in *this* sense it is easy to concede that moral arguments are always concerned with the grounding of norms. But the crucial point is how we understand this connection between the grounding of norms and the evaluation of ways of acting. Habermas understands this connection as a form of derivation: the moral command to act in a particular way is seen as following from the fact that this way of acting corresponds to a valid norm. By contrast, the view that I am propounding here is that the validity of moral norms only stretches as far as the validity of the moral judgements that can be – not grounded, but – expressed through these norms. The norms themselves carry, so to speak, a situational index which binds them to the situations in which they have their origins. This is the only reason why there is a problem in *applying* moral norms – and this is the only sense in which it can be understood. In other words, it is not possible in the case of moral norms to separate discourses concerning the justification of norms and discourses concerning the application of norms categorically from each other. Only if we bear this in mind can we interpret the problem of moral judgement in concrete situations meaningfully as a problem of the 'application' of moral norms.

I believe that the interpretation of moral argumentation that I am proposing here tends to strengthen the plausibility of the basic idea of discourse ethics. Moral dogmatism and moral self-deception barricade themselves as a rule behind interpretations of situations (including interpretations of needs and interest) which are kept out of the discussion itself. When reality is warded off like this, there is always a potential danger that some injury may be done to individuals. The command to seek communicative or discursive clarification of interpretations of situations, and of the way we see ourselves, therefore has the status not only of an obligation to be rational, but of a moral norm – at least in so far as it is a matter of letting those affected speak for themselves. Of course, what I said earlier about other moral norms goes for this one, too; for this reason alone, it cannot provide a foundation for everything else.

Excursus   Contrary to the position I have expounded here, Habermas insists on a sharp analytical distinction between the problems of justification and the problems of application.[99] In the distinctions drawn between these two sets of problems, Habermas even sees a new level of differentiation which Kant was the first to attain, and below which 'we must not allow ourselves to fall'.[100] I have argued, against this, that Kant systematically *neglects* the problem of application for reasons connected with his rigorism on the point of 'laws'. What Kant is doing in reality is differentiating the problems of grounding norms *at the expense of* the problems of application. Moreover, Habermas's differentiation thesis seems to me in itself unclear. As far as the grounding of moral norms is concerned, we have already seen that the norms we are talking about here can only be 'prima facie' norms (such as 'Thou shalt not lie'). But if that is the case, then the problems of application largely coincide with the problems of exceptional situations or situations of conflict (which means much the same as morally complex situations). But if, as I have also shown, morally complex situations cannot be reduced to rules in the same sense as morally elementary situations, and if what is actually being grounded is the generalizability or non-generalizability of ways of acting in situations of a particular sort, then it is no longer possible to separate the problems of grounding from the problems of application in the sense that Habermas means it. Not to put too fine a point on it, we might say that the problem we are dealing with in the process of moral grounding *is* a problem of application; what is being 'applied' is the moral principle itself. I have already shown what this means in the case of morally complex situations, but it would also be possible to understand the grounding of general moral orientations in the same way. Returning to the examples we used before, we were looking there at principles like 'Human dignity is inviolate' or 'Every person has an equal right to the free development of his or her personality' – principles which are, as it were, not very far removed from the 'ends formula' of the categorical imperative – and asking what they *mean* in connection with behaviour towards women or children or homosexuals. In contrast to Habermas, then, I am of the opinion that in the case of morality, the problem of grounding has the character of a problem of application; what moral discourse is concerned with is the 'application' of the *moral point of view*, whether to concrete social problem areas or to the situations in which individuals act.

If Habermas's response to this is to say that 'no norm [contains] the rules of its own application',[101] then this may be true, but it does not justify the separation of the problems of grounding from the problems of application in this case. It seems to me rather that he is conflating two different problems of application. *One* of these is the kind of problem that presents itself when prescribed rules, codes of behaviour or norms – such as the norms of penal law – are to be applied to concrete cases, in which case the *grounding* of norms and the *application* of norms are two different things: the grounding of a norm (or at least the 'promulgation' of it) precedes its application. But precisely because moral consciousness becomes emancipated from the dogmatism of *substantial* prescribed norms in the process of differentiation between justice and morality and in the transition to a post-conventional sense of morality, the problem of application that emerges for morality is a problem of a *different* kind. This *second* kind of problem of application is concerned with the question of the correct way to bring the 'moral point of view' to bear in the case at issue. *This* is the question with which moral discourse is concerned; only in a derived sense is it concerned with the grounding of norms. In an essential sense it is therefore a *discourse of application*. Moral discourse and moral judgement thus do not differ in their *object*; practical reason expresses itself as moral judgement. (This seems to me to be the real point of Hannah Arendt's reflections, too, in her essay 'Thinking and Moral Considerations'.[102] But then again, Hannah Arendt only deals with an aspect of the matter which complements Habermas's approach. Whereas Habermas marginalizes the problem of application by comparison with the problem of grounding, Arendt does not make it clear what moral judgement has to do with the possibility of moral *discourse*.)

   In the interview to which I referred earlier, Habermas gives a further peculiar reason for separating the problem of grounding off from the problem of application. He says there that moral theories which follow Kant are 'typically restricted to the question of the *justification* of norms and actions', and that they 'have no answer to the question of how justified norms can be *applied* to specific situations and how moral norms can be *realized*'. But he accounts for this position by saying that 'one should not place excessive demands on moral theory, but leave something over for social theory, and the major part for the participants themselves – whether it be their moral discourses or their good sense.'[103] This is a curious way to account for the 'differentiation thesis' because the question of 'leaving the major part for the participants themselves' is not at issue. Habermas himself argues that the *grounding* of norms is not part of the business of moral theory, but is a matter for moral discourse among the 'participants'. What is at issue, then, is not the drawing of correct boundaries for moral theory, but the correct understanding of what should be left for the participants themselves, namely moral discourse.

I have so far proceeded on the assumption that the logic of moral argument is determined by a universalistic moral principle. As I indicated earlier, I wish to drop this assumption in the second stage of my argument. If Kant asserts that the categorical imperative is a universal and inescapable 'fact of reason', then this thesis clearly makes little sense if we understand the categorical imperative as a universalistic moral principle in itself. We could, however, also understand it to be saying, in a weaker sense, 'Act according to your normative convictions,' which is to say, 'Make no exceptions for yourself,' or 'Do what you (believe that you) ought to do.' When understood in this way, the categorical imperative *is* a fact of reason, for it is merely formulating an elementary condition of consistency for human action. When we understand it like this, of course, the categorical imperative is compatible with the most diverse systems of norms, which might be particularist or feudal in nature, or based in religion. I believe, however, that even when its meaning is thus restricted the categorical imperative contains no *trivial* requirement – at least, not if we may assume that the tendency to moral self-deception and to making exceptions for oneself is a feature of all known human societies.

The 'minimal' interpretation of the categorical imperative which we are considering here rests, of course, on the assumption that a dimension of moral judgement and self-judgement is constitutive of all forms of human community.[104] That is to say that a categorical 'ought' is built into the structure of reciprocity that characterizes human social relations, and that the commands of this 'ought' can only be violated at the price of moral condemnation and self-condemnation (feelings of guilt). We are unable to withdraw from this dimension of moral judgement *as such*, and this implies that we are unable to withdraw from the conditions of living in mutual recognition of each other. Nevertheless, the fact that a categorical 'ought' might (perhaps) obtain universally does not, of course, make it as such a fact of *reason*. It is rather the case that particularist, traditionalist or religious ways of viewing and grounding this categorical 'ought' must first have disintegrated before it is even possible to ask about the possible *rational* sense of it. Now, I think that the Kantian moral principle gives us an answer, if not to the question about the rational *sense* of categorical 'ought', then at least to the question about its *rationalizable core*. The rationalizable core of categorical 'ought' – which is in itself less a fact of reason that a fact of human natural history – is the thing that ought to be done as the negation of what *we* are unable to will as a universal way of acting. *In retrospect* this also holds for traditional societies or even for the particularist moralities of tribes, although moral commands were not understood in this way at the time, but rather as divine commandment, for example, or as the expression of a natural order of things. The rationalizable core of categorical 'ought' is thus anchored in the structure of reciprocity as such. The development of a universalistic morality can then be understood as the successive elimination of the foundations of a particularist understanding of such structures of reciprocity. *In retrospect* we can identify that common feature which constitutes a universal core of morality in all structures of reciprocity – in terms of content it can be expressed in commands like 'Do not lie', 'Do not kill', 'Do no wilful injury', etc. But on the other hand it is only through the discovery that the traditional categorical 'ought' is without foundation that this 'ought' becomes accessible to reason, that it becomes 'rationalizable'. Universalistic morality itself owes its being to an elimination of what is false, without the possibility that it might be able to completely recover its foundations by means of some fundamental grounding. It retains a moment of mere facticity which is connected with the fact that we are not able to become the persons we are, nor to live, outside the structures of reciprocal recognition. But this fact, which is not a fact of reason, but something fundamental to all possibility of reason, can *retrospectively* be included among the preconditions of reason. In *this* sense it is true that reason recovers its own foundations in universalistic morality. But the impossibility of a fundamental grounding of morality in terms of a pragmatic philosophy of language is connected with the fact that the impossibility of leading a morally good life if we cannot look ourselves straight in the eye is something for which we cannot in the final analysis provide a grounding, but which we simply have to accept. It is impossible to conceive of any process of successful individuation which does not involve a confrontation with others as, in Kantian terms, 'ends in themselves', or which is not, in Hegelian terms, bound into structures of reciprocal recognition. The medium of such mutual recognition is language. It is in language that mutual recognition is represented in the form of normative validity-claims, and as linguistic utterances, such validity-claims are always implicitly orientated towards the possibility of concurrence among all beings capable of speech. This is precisely where the attempt to look for universalistic morality in the foundations of speech finds its legitimation. But it would be inconceivable that we could work away in the medium of language at eliminating the original particularism of forms of mutual recognition if there were not some pre-existing basis for an affectively anchored moral 'ought' connected with the conditions of the possibility of our being ourselves. In the power of this moral 'ought' it is still possible to discern weak traces of a real power which accompanied the process of individuation in the form of a threat. In universalistic morality, this real power is sublated within a state of affairs in which the only form of compulsion that obtains is that of superior argument. But it is sublated only if the mere awareness of a 'necessitation' by the moral law is replaced by an awareness of the price that has to be paid if structures of reciprocity are infringed by a self that owes its existence to the internalization of such structures of reciprocity. Then, and only then, is the categorical 'ought' of moral validity-claims sublated within a practical knowledge of the preconditions of a good life. Moral validity-claims are claims in two senses: they contain an expectation of general concurrence, and they *demand* a certain way of behaving. Kant's categorical 'ought' is the expression of this character of morality as a demand. From Schopenhauer to MacIntyre, the rational sense of this categorical ought has been repeatedly challenged;[105] but for Kant it was quite simply an expression of the state of tension prevailing in finite rational beings *between* reason and the sensual. Only of a 'perfectly good will' would it be possible to say, as Kant does, that it 'could not . . . be conceived as *necessitated* to act in conformity with law,'

since of itself, in accordance with its subjective constitution, it can be determined only by the concept of the good. Hence for the *divine* will, and in general for a *holy* will, there are no imperatives:

'*I ought*' is here out of place, because '*I will*' is already of itself necessarily in harmony with the law.[106]

Kant conceives the sublation of 'I ought' within 'I will' as the ultimate goal of a potential moral progress. But since the 'perfectly good will' can really only be imagined in Kantian terms as the will of a totally disembodied subject, and thus not as a will at all, his sublation formula remains aporetic. It could be converted – contrary to Kant's intention – into worldly terms, not by secularizing the idea of a perfectly good will, but by identifying the worldly aspect of the categorical ought itself by which it still belongs *outside* the sphere of reason, namely external compulsion which has become internalized. The sublation of 'I ought' within 'I will' – which would also represent the sublation of the opposition between deontological and teleological ethics – could be conceived as the form of a moral consciousness for which there no longer existed any opposition between self-love and solidarity for others, between self-assertion and the acknowledgement of others. *This* scheme of sublation does not force us to assume a 'perfectly' good will (of which it would not even be possible to say how it would have to be constituted), rather it expresses a potential enlightenment of moral consciousness about itself, the sublation of (mere) virtue in (practical) knowledge.

It is in *this* sense that a universalistic morality is cognitive. But at the same time, a 'lack of moral sense' is not a cognitive deficiency, but rather an expression of the fact that the person concerned has not been adequately trained in reciprocal recognition, and this is something against which mere arguments are powerless. If it were the case, however, that a moral consciousness had already developed, then the development of a *universalistic* moral consciousness is the only alternative, under the conditions of enlightenment, to withdrawing from the language game of morality altogether. To withdraw in this way, and thus to rupture the bonds of solidarity with others rather than extending them, would, moreover, involve the individual in doing injury to himself, in extreme cases it would imply his self-destruction.[107] It was an insight of this kind, I believe, that Kant was expressing when he called the necessitating of the will through a moral law a 'fact of reason'. It would be less misleading to speak of the fact of a life lived under *conditions* of reason. This is a fact of which we can *remind* ourselves and others, but to remind ourselves in this way is not identical in meaning with demonstrating the inescapability of the obligation to rationality. This act of reminding, which certainly cannot take the form of a fundamental grounding, is perhaps the only possible foundation upon which morality can be grounded.

XII

In section VI, above, I mentioned Habermas's attempt to interpret moral ought as a predicate of a higher order (analogous to the predicate 'is true'). This is how Habermas tries to resolve the problem of moral ought in cognitivistic terms by interpreting ought as one of three types of universal validity-claim. As I have tried to show, the difficulties which arise from this attempt when the discourse–ethical approach is put into practice are virtually irresolvable. Now, I believe that these difficulties are apparent in the very grammatical reconstruction that Habermas proposes, precisely because he relates it from the outset exclusively to *moral* validity-claims. The point of the reconstruction he proposes is, as we have just noted, to make it possible to explain moral demands as one of exactly three types of universal validity-claim (truth, truthfulness, normative rightness), of which Habermas asserts that they are present in *every* linguistic utterance, direct or indirect. If it were possible to explain moral ought in this way, this would mean that it was so deeply anchored in universal linguistic structures that it would be unnecessary to ask about its possible rational sense. But this is also the reason why so much depends on the successful fundamental grounding of a moral principle, for only such a fundamental grounding could bridge the gap between the *general* grammar of normative validity-claims and the *particular* demands of a universalistic morality. Now it seems to me that we already run into problems if we load the *general* concept of a normative validity-claim from the outset with the particular sense of *moral* validity-claims. The moral use of words like 'ought', 'must', 'may', 'is commanded', 'right, 'good', etc. is a very special one. But since the general (non-moral) use of these words is also linked with validity-claims, it might have seemed an obvious step not to relate the grammatical reconstruction of this basic normative vocabulary from the outset to the special case of moral validity-claims. In other words, if the reconstruction proposed by Habermas is correct, then it ought to be equally applicable to hypothetical imperatives in Kant's sense, to grammatical prescriptions ('here one must use the infinitive'), and even to aesthetic 'must' statements ('here there must be a sudden *forte*'). In all these cases we are dealing with validity-claims which can be grounded and criticized every bit as much as moral statements, and in a general sense they are certainly also normative validity-claims (in contradistinction to claims to truth or truthfulness). Normative validity-claims in the general sense of the word are distinguishable from moral validity-claims, however, in that they only yield prima facie reasons for doing something without expressing an *unconditional* (categorical) obligation in the way that moral validity-claims do. The obligatory character is clearly connected with the kind of reasons that one can put forward, from case to case, for normative validity-claims of a particular type. But this means that the categorical sense of moral ought can only be elucidated in connection with the reasons that one can adduce for moral validity-claims. It is for this reason that, in Kant, categorical ought appears in the moral principle itself. But since the concept that appears in Habermas's principle (U) is only that of a 'valid' (just) norm, we should have to understand the connection between his grammatical reconstruction of 'ought' statements and his formulation of principle (U) as meaning that the words 'right' or 'commanded' only assume the sense of 'morally right' or 'morally commanded' in connection with principle (U). What he is saying, therefore, is something like this: 'In circumstances S, it is morally (*unconditionally*) commanded (right) to do p if p corresponds to a valid norm.' But here we can see that the grammatical reconstruction of normative validity-claims has not disposed of the problem of moral ought; rather it remains a *particular* problem which consists in the fact that there is an *unconditional* command in this particular case to do, not what is right, but what is in a *certain* sense right, so that there can be no possibility in this case of finding good reasons for refusing to do what is in *one* sense right by appealing to alternative criteria of rightness. (I leave aside the question of whether this is a totally adequate picture of the priority of moral validity-claims over other normative validity-claims; at least it is a picture that Habermas shares with Kant.) Because the priority of moral validity-claims over other normative validity-claims is not made clear in Habermas's recon-

struction, I think that his use of the insights of linguistic pragmatics has not in reality neutralized the problem of moral ought,
but merely off-loaded it, so to speak, into a grey area which lies
between his grammatical reconstruction of normative validity-
claims and his formulation of principle (U).

The most that could be said against this is that moral ought is
so deeply anchored in the way that communicative action is
orientated towards the pursuit of validity that even the truth-
claim of assertoric utterances could be elucidated in categories
of a claim to rightness analogous to that of moral ones. If we
understand 'truth' as 'warranted assertibility', then we are interpreting the act of assertion itself as an act of both claiming a
right and entering into an obligation: the claim that is raised in
the assertoric utterance is one that could be redeemed by means
of argument, and if I assert something, then I commit myself to
redeeming such a claim by means of argument, as the need
arises. We might be tempted, therefore, to invert the priority of
propositional truth over other modes of validity that is characteristic of the philosophical tradition, and give priority to normative
rightness instead. If it were possible to ground a primacy of
practical reason in this sense, then the problem of moral ought
would dissolve into nothingness, being, as it were, an expression
of the 'logocentric' prejudices of Western thought.[108] The
acknowledgement of moral or analogous obligations would turn
out to be a precondition of the possibility of participating in
any kind of communicatively orientated action, and thus also a
precondition of the possibility of assertoric utterances.

The consensus theory of truth is indeed itself an expression of
such a radical inversion of traditional priorities. Habermas has
also tried to justify this inversion 'genealogically' in his *Theory
of Communicative Action*. Following Durkheim, he sees the
validity of moral ought as having origins in a pre-rational, symbolically structured sacred sphere – as it were, the sphere of a
primordial normative consensus that is not yet conscious of
itself.[109] In this way, a still pre-rational understanding of the
validity of norms is constituted, which performs a crucial
mediating function in the grammatical differentiation of human
speech. This process of differentiation takes the form of a 'linguistification of the sacred'.[110] The reason why the sphere of the
sacred is able to take on this mediating function is that it occupies
a special position among the 'three roots of communicative

action'.[111] These three roots are the pre-linguistic roots of linguistically articulated cognitions, obligations and expressions,[112] which should be seen as the basic building-bricks, so to speak, of *every* grammatically differentiated linguistic utterance. Grammatically differentiated speech is nothing other than the integration of these moments into a whole made up of propositional, illocutionary and expressive components.[113] Now, only the propositional and the expressive components of speech can be derived from a pre-linguistic order that is not itself already symbolically structured. The pre-linguistic correlate of the propositional component of linguistic utterances is to be found in perceptions, mental images, and adaptive behaviour; that of the expressive component in bodily gestures.[114] The illocutionary components of speech, on the other hand, which are what really lend assertoric and expressive statements their power 'to motivate a hearer to accept a speech-act offer',[115] point towards a pre-linguistic root of a different kind, namely that sphere of the sacred which, though pre-linguistic, is nevertheless not natural, but already symbolically structured.

> What is puzzling about this root is that it is from the very beginning symbolic in nature. Cognitive dealings with perceptible and manipulable objects, and expressions of subjective experiences, are in contact with external or internal nature through stimulation of our senses or through our needs and desires. They are in touch with a reality that not only transcends language but is also free of symbolic structures. Human cognitions and expressions, however shaped by language they may be, can also be traced back to the natural history of intelligent performances and expressive gestures in animals. Norm consciousness, on the other hand, has no equally trivial extralinguistic reference; for obligations there are no unambiguous natural-historical correlates, as there are for sense impressions and needs. Nevertheless, collective consciousness, the paleo-symbolically supported normative consensus, and the collective identity supported by it secure for experiences of obligation contact with a reality that is, if not free of symbols, at least prelinguistic [in the strict sense of propositionally differentiated language] – they are 'older' than interaction mediated by grammatical speech.[116]

The 'binding effects' of the illocutionary component of linguistic utterances are due to the fact that its pre-linguistic root is itself already a symbolically, or rather 'paleo-symbolically' structured normative consensus. If this were the end of the matter, then, as Habermas states, 'constative and expressive speech actions could not achieve binding effects *on their own* but only in virtue of their normative content. The illocutionary component of such speech acts would then have no motivating force; the burden of coordinating action would have to be borne instead by the prior consensus supporting the normative context.'[117] Now, at this point Habermas reasserts his point about the parallel between

> (1) 'It is right that a in S'

and

> (2) 'It is the case (is true) that p',[118]

and expresses the following assumption: let us assume that the assertion of truth-claims with the help of constative utterances of type (2) only became possible by virtue of the fact that an already available concept of norm-validity migrated, as it were, into the illocutionary mode of assertion, and that it did so in such a way that a type of claiming of right was thus constituted in which, by contrast with the case of genuine norm-validity, the grounding of such claims coincided from the outset with their redemption.

> It may be the case that the claim to propositional truth originally borrowed the structure of a validity claim that can be *justifiably* redeemed from the kind of claim that rests on valid norms, but it had at once to appear in a radicalized version geared to the giving of reasons in its support. This suggests that the concept of a criticizable validity claim derives from an assimilation of the truth of statements to the validity of norms (which was, to begin with, not criticizable).[119]

As Habermas explains, following Durkheim, the concept of norm-validity is already linked with the assumption of an ideal-ized agreement among all members of a society, which is how the primordial, symbolically structured normative consensus can become the point of departure for a grammatical differentiation of speech, which is to say that it becomes the model for *all* concepts of validity, and for the concept of truth-validity in particular.

> The normative consensus that is expounded in the semantics of the sacred is present to members in the form of an idealized agreement transcending spatiotemporal changes. This furnishes the model for all concepts of validity, especially for the idea of truth.[120]

The normative consensus, articulating itself as the sphere of the sacred, is the prototype of an idealized agreement, 'of an inter-subjectivity related to an ideal communication community',[121] and thus the prototype of potential intersubjective validity. Through the linguistification of the sacred, this prototype of all validity is released from its paleo-symbolic shell and becomes available as a foundation for potential rational validity. And finally, the concept of norm-validity itself loses the privileged status it originally possessed in the context of the sacred, and is transformed by way of the differentiation of the modes of validity into the form of a discursively redeemable validity-claim analogous to the validity of truth.[122] In this way we end up with 'the binding force of moral agreement grounded in the sacred' replaced by 'moral agreement that expresses in rational form what was always intended in the symbolism of the holy: the generality of the underlying interest'.[123]

With this fascinating sequence of thoughts, Habermas does indeed appear to have succeeded in anchoring moral ought so deeply in the general structures of linguistic communication that the question about its rational sense becomes redundant. If it turned out that an awareness of moral obligation represented, as it were, the core of all possible rationality of linguistic communication, then the problem of moral ought in the form which troubled Kant could finally be seen to be a pseudo-problem. Now, Habermas's 'genealogical' reconstruction of a grammatically differentiated concept of validity draws on theoretical assumptions which need to be substantiated as the reconstruction proceeds. Habermas uses the concepts of an 'idealized agreement' or an 'ideal communication community' in the sense of a presupposed consensus theory of truth. Only if the reconstruction could be clarified at crucial points independently of such presuppositions would it be possible to derive from it an *independent* argument for the theoretical premises of discourse ethics. But in its crucial aspects Habermas's reconstruction seems to me far from clear. If Habermas is interpreting the symbolism of the sacred as the expression of a *moral* agreement, then this might perhaps be justified in the sense of a functionalist way of looking at things; but it does not seem to me justified as a thesis about the priority of moral validity over the other modes of validity in terms of linguistic pragmatics. A more obvious course, it seems to me, would be to assign the concept of the sacred, as Habermas uses it, to a way of thinking for which the modes of validity that later became differentiated are not yet clearly distinguishable from one another, so that the boundaries between moral validity and truth-validity, for example, were still fluid. If we adopt a perspective such as this, then the problem of differentiation presents itself in a different light than it does in the context of Habermas's development of the thoughts of Durkheim. It presents itself, in fact, rather more in the shape that Habermas himself gives it in volume 1 of his *Theory of Communicative Action*, in the section entitled 'Some Characteristics of the Mythical and the Modern Ways of Understanding the World'.[124] Habermas there establishes a connection between the 'closedness' of mythical ways of thinking and the absence of fundamental differentiations of the kind that are characteristic of modern ways of thinking. Moreover, he does not only mean differentiation between various modes of validity, but also differentiation between causal and symbolic connections, between culture and nature, between language and world. The absence of such differentiations makes it quite impossible to envisage the sphere of symbolic validity as a sphere of criticizable validity-*claims*. The mythical way of thinking is, so to speak, still encapsulated in itself because it has not yet developed the linguistic resources that would allow it to look upon itself reflexively.

> Evidently there is not yet any precise concept for the nonempirical validity that we ascribe to symbolic expressions. Validity is confounded with empirical efficacy. I am not referring here to special validity claims – in mythical thought diverse validity claims, such as propositional truth, normative rightness, and expressive sincerity are not yet differentiated. But even the diffuse concept of validity in general is still not freed from empirical admixtures. Concepts of validity such as morality and truth are amalgamated with empirical ordering concepts, such as causality and health. Thus a linguistically constituted worldview can be identified with the worldorder itself to such an extent that it cannot be perceived *as* an interpretation of the world that is subject to error and open

to criticism. In this respect the confusion of nature and culture takes on the significance of a reification of worldview.[125]

If we present the problem of differentiation like this, then for a start it becomes understandable why the sphere of the sacred has been interpreted in the course of the history of anthropology not only as a sphere of primordial *norm-validity* (an antecedent form of morality), but also as a sphere of primordial explanation of the world (an antecedent form of science), as a sphere of mimetic–expressive actions (an antecedent form of art), or even as a sphere of still crude attempts to master the world (magic as an antecedent form of technology).[126]

In reality it seems impossible to consign the interplay of symbolism and ritual in the sphere of the sacred definitively to *one* of these functions.[127] Habermas himself points to the connection that Durkheim emphasizes between the moral binding function of the sacred and its function as a mirror and external fixation of a collective identity. The collective identity of the group is the consciousness of a 'we' that becomes capable of experiencing itself in sacred symbols and rites, and which simultaneously discharges and regenerates itself in these symbols and rites.[128] From the functional point of view of keeping the group together, this means 'that the motivational makeup of the associated individuals is taken hold of symbolically and structured through the *same* semantic contents.'[129] But the sacred is capable of fulfilling this normative binding *function* precisely because cognitive, mimetic–expressive and moral contents are not separated from each other within its *semantics*. Even if we accept Habermas's thesis that it is possible to understand those forms of affective ambivalence that surround the sacred (the close involvement of a sense of salvation with a sense of terror, of respect with horror, of attraction with repugnance) as primordial forms of the emotional ambivalence associated with moral obligations,[130] we could not really speak of *moral feelings* because a concept of moral obligation, however rudimentary, would still be missing. And such a concept seems to *presuppose* that differentiation of spheres of validity which Habermas wants to use it to explain.

Against this, of course, it would be possible to say that there is a concept of norm-validity already *available* in the sphere of the sacred that is sufficient to bear the weight of Habermas's argument (consider for example prescribed rituals and taboos).

If the authority of the sacred means that *every* prescription, *every* rule is surrounded, as it were, with the aura of an unconditional 'must' and charged with the affective forces that this implies, then we might conclude from this that the norm-consciousness assigned to the sacred is, by virtue of its structure, moral.[131] This would mean that a norm-consciousness was only able to constitute itself *as* a moral consciousness, even if its most important contents – ritual and taboo – were perhaps not moral in our sense. Seductive as this idea is, it seems to me psychologically and conceptually implausible. For it is surely possible to see from the fragmented remnants of ritual and taboo-dominated practices that extend into our own culture that the unconditional ought that is connected with the prescription of rituals and taboos not only does not need to possess any moral *content*, but can also express constraints of a quite different nature from those of a moral ought – and needs of a quite different nature from the need for personal recognition or self-respect. I can only attempt to substantiate these thoughts conceptually here, not anthropologically or psychologically. When a child, for example, insists on a particular order of things or actions, such as a ritual of story-telling or reading aloud that is precisely fixed right down to the last word, then there is certainly an unconditional sense of 'right' and 'wrong' implied in this insistence, and thus an unconditional 'ought'; but with this 'ought', this sense of 'right' and 'wrong', the child's ego is defending the particular order of a world in which it feels at home. An infringement of this order is a threat to the ego. When the child says 'You must,' what is really meant is 'This is the way *it* must be.' This does, of course, constitute a genuine moral claim on others, but it is a moral claim which can only be recognized by someone who recognizes the non-moral character of the 'right' and 'wrong' in question. The *moral* claim is the claim for the needs of the child to be respected; but to express the point paradoxically, what the child is demanding is not that its moral claim be respected, but that the right order of things be respected. This right order of things is not a moral order, it is much rather an order of the world without which not only the child, but – in an expanded sense – ultimately nobody can feel at home with themselves.

What I want to show with this example is the possibility of a categorical 'ought', of a norm-consciousness, that cannot be called moral, even though it is affectively highly charged, because it is not moral from the point of view of its *function*. This becomes clear if we were to try – retrospectively, as it were – to provide it with a moral *grounding*. It would not then turn out to be the case that the demand was morally unfounded; it would rather turn out to be the case that the demand was not a moral one. But if this is correct, we could not simply ascribe the existence of an affectively highly charged norm-consciousness in archaic societies to morality. We should have rather to assume that this norm-consciousness is of a 'mixed' nature. *We* cannot distinguish the moral from the non-moral elements of these norms by considering whether the norms are well founded; we can only do so by considering what sort of grounding would be conceivable once the 'grounding game' had been introduced. Thoughts along these lines are indeed to be found in the literature of anthropology, where the realm of the taboo is discussed. Robin Horton, for example, has followed Mary Douglas[132] in connecting the taboo with the 'protective' attitude of archaic societies towards a system of classification, which means that they experience any challenge to that system as a threat.[133] If the anthropological observations are correct, then here, too, the affectively highly-charged distinction between 'right' and 'wrong', between 'good' and 'evil', would be connected with the stabilization of a collective identity – but it would not be possible to call it 'moral'.

Finally we could also remind ourselves of the 'quasi-sacred' character that the rules of games, and even rules of etiquette can assume in our society in certain contexts – and not only among children. This is *shown* by the high affective charge that such rules possess. Now, the claim that we should abide by the rules of the game or of etiquette is, of course, always a moral claim *as well*. But the rules *themselves* are not moral in nature, even if they contain a categorical 'ought'.[134] The rules say we ought to (or may not) do a certain thing in certain situations, or that we ought to (or may not) do something in a certain way. This 'ought' or 'may' is not a moral 'ought' or 'may', it is rather the 'ought' or 'may' of rules which are constitutive of the playing of a game, or at least constitutive of a certain way of playing a game. We might suppose that under conditions of scant cognitive and social differentiation the categorical 'ought' of *any* rule has the aura of a *moral* 'ought' conferred upon it; but this could only mean that the moral rules only become distinguishable from the non-moral ones as the differentiation grows. And what this implies is not only that conventional moral norms are replaced by moral principles, but also that conventional norms split up, so to speak, into moral and non-moral rules (which include grammatical, aesthetic, juridical rules, and constitutive rules of all kinds). What I mean to say is this: there are conceptual as well as empirical reasons for supposing that the normative consensus of archaic societies cannot be *equated* with a moral consensus. I believe that the only reason why we easily lose sight of this fact is because the concept of 'conventional' moral consciousness, as it has come to be commonly used in the wake of Kohlberg, carries the inherent suggestion that all 'conventional' norms are precursors of moral norms or norms that can be morally grounded, as if they had the same *point* (or the same function) as moral norms. But even if we argue on the premise that the common norms of an archaic society *express* the 'generality' of an 'underlying interest', it is not possible to infer from this that they always carry the *intention* of asserting a common – as opposed to an individual – interest, as Habermas says that they do.

In other words, even if the concept of norm-validity that is already available in the sphere of the sacred can be characterized as having an affectively highly-charged unconditional ought, it does not follow from this that this concept of norm-validity may be equated with a primordial concept of *moral* validity. Rather it is to be expected that the concept of moral validity is encapsulated within this primordial concept of norm-validity in precisely the same way that the scientific explanation of the world is encapsulated within the mythical interpretation of the world, namely as *one* of several things it might signify. Which potential *rational* sense is expressed by the unconditional ought of 'conventional' norms would then depend on which kinds of justification become available when the 'conventional' way of understanding the world opens itself up to reflection. But if it is not the case that every ('conventional') categorical 'ought' is, in the meaning of the term, a moral 'ought', then the problem of differentiation becomes transferred onto that very primordial concept of norm-validity that Habermas presupposes. This would mean that it might well be permissible to interpret the validity of ought as a universal type of validity, but that precisely *as such* it could not be equated with moral validity. And this exactly corresponds with what I had to say about Habermas's grammatical reconstruction of normative validity-claims at the beginning of this section.

I am very well aware of the tentative character of these reflections, but I hope that I have shown that Habermas's suggestive
and imaginative development of Durkheim's interpretation of
the sacred throws up conceptual problems which are hardly fewer
in number than those it is intended to solve. This is why I
cannot at any rate see in Habermas's reconstruction any *additional*
argument for the consensus-theoretical premises of discourse
ethics which I earlier subjected to a purely immanent critique.
But if, as I suspect, the concept of moral obligation is the result
of a differentiation of spheres of validity (including precisely
normative spheres of validity), then this would in turn suggest
that (universal) obligations of rationality should be distinguished
from (specific) moral obligations, as I have distinguished them
above. As I see it, the real point of this distinction for a theory
of rationality is that it alone enables us to think in terms of a
'plural' and open concept of rationality which neither depends
on fundamental groundings nor looks for ultimate reconciliations.
It seems to me that the consensus-theoretical premises of discourse ethics, which are closely associated with the interpretation
of moral ought as a pragmatic universal in linguistic terms, is an
obstacle to the development of such a plural and open – but in
no way relativistic – concept of rationality. Moreover, I believe
that this is also the concept of rationality that Habermas himself
always has in mind when he 'translates' the meta-theoretical
premises of universal pragmatics into an analysis of the normative content of modernity. The thing that particularly becomes
clear whenever he does this is that there is absolutely no need
for strong consensus-theoretical premises in order for us to be
able to conceive of 'the rationalization of the life-world' (in
general) or a dialogic 'opening-up' of ethics (in particular). In his
latest book, *The Philosophical Discourse of Modernity*,[135] Habermas
defines the historical goals or 'vanishing points' of a potential
rationalization of the life-world as follows: 'for culture, a condition of the constant revision of traditions that have been
unthawed, that is, that have become reflective; for society, a
condition of the dependence of legitimate orders upon formal and
ultimately discursive procedures for establishing and grounding
norms; for personality, a condition of the risk-filled self-direction
of a highly abstract ego-identity'. For there arise through the
rationalization of the life-world 'structural pressures toward the
critical dissolution of guaranteed knowledge, the establishment

of generalized values and norms, and self-directed individuation (since abstract ego-identities point toward self-realization in autonomous life projects)'.[136] The 'vanishing points' of a rationalization of the life-world to which Habermas refers are not the structures of an ideal communication community, but the 'structural pressures' of a life-world imbued with a commonality of universalistic values and the consciousness of universal obligations to rationality. What he is characterizing is not an *ideal condition* for society, but a set of *problems and possibilities as they actually exist* in modern societies, which cannot rationally be circumvented. The 'vanishing points' of the rationalization of the life-world are actually vanishing points of an *understanding* of rationality from which we can only retreat at the cost of regression, suppression or terror. It is only on the basis of this understanding of rationality that appropriate ways can be found to process the substantial problems of the social order and the good life, and that the 'potential for negation inherent in the process of reaching agreement in language'[137] can be developed in such a way as to leave open the possibilites of a good life, the possibilities of critical revision, and the possibilities of innovatory change.

> Rationalization of the lifeworld means differentiation and condensation at once – a thickening of the floating web of intersubjective threads that simultaneously holds together the ever more sharply differentiated components of culture, society, and person. The reproductive mode of the lifeworld does not change linearly in the direction indicated by the catchwords 'reflexivity', 'abstract universalism', and 'individuation'. Rather, the rationalized lifeworld secures the continuity of its contexts of meaning with the discontinuous tools of critique; it preserves the context of social integration by the risky means of an individualistically isolating universalism; and it sublimates the overwhelming power of the genealogical nexus into a fragile and vulnerable universality by means of an extremely individualized socialization.[138]

But if this suggestive image of a rationalized life-world cannot signify a potential ideal state of affairs, if it is rather the case that it contains a description of structural changes which are to some extent going on before our very eyes, then it also becomes clear that the concept of a rationalization of the life-world is too unspecific a term with which to describe the *particular* problems of *specific* societies and the ways in which they are deficient in rationality. The rationalization of the life-world is after all not a process at the end of which it would even be possible to *conceive* of a *perfectly* rational life-world (which would indeed be an idea without any clear sense); it is much rather a process in which the consciousness that there are no secure foundations for potential validity is put into effect socially, and with it the consciousness that the only means by which it is possible to secure a network of underlying common orientations and values and to ensure that this network is repeatedly established anew are those of communicative and argumentative praxis. This process is *directed* in the sense that 'the development of the potential for negation inherent in the process of reaching agreement in language' can only be conceived as a process of learning and innovation. But the point of reference for this process is not an ideal communication community conceived as situated in the future, but the present with all those pathologies, irrationalities, psychological blocks and inhumanities which may be empirically observed.

I think that the two models of differentiation which I have distinguished above imply two alternative possibilities for conceiving of the unity of reason in conjunction with the differentiation of its separate moments. The first model, that of 'consensus theory', remains tied to a perspective of reconciliation which will be formulated in either romantic–utopian or rationalistic terms, depending on the emphasis adopted. The unity of reason is here conceived from the perspective of an ideal final situation in which understanding has been reached, and in which the separated moments of reason would have arrived at a constellation of definitive reconciliation. The second model, on the other hand, is comparatively conventional, linking *directly* with that sense of problems which predominates in modern European philosophy, namely that, among the modes of validity that have become differentiated in the course of time, the one that is more difficult to understand is not the validity of truth, but that of moral ought. Undoubtedly this is *also* connected with deep-seated 'logo-centric', i.e. scientist preconceptions of modern philosophy. But that is not the whole story. The puzzling aspect of moral ought is rather that it is here that the linguistification of the sacred encounters resistances which have no equivalent in the area of truth-validity. The fear that moral consciousness must lose its firm footing if it is not supported by the authority of the sacred is, of course, a topos of the counter-enlightenment, but the fact that the effectiveness of moral arguments remains dependent on preconditions which are not only cognitive, but also affective in nature shows that this fear does have a foundation in fact. A rational equivalent to a moral agreement supported by sacred or religious authority is only possible in so far as a successful adaptation to conditions of mutual recognition between persons – in both cognitive *and* affective terms – has taken place. To the extent that this is not the case, moral arguments lose their point of purchase, although this need not necessarily also be the case with arguments of an empirical or technical nature. There *is* a lack of moral sense – that is a fact. But we can only interpret this as a deficiency in rationality if we assume conditions which can precisely not be fulfilled wherever this lack of moral sense manifests itself.

In the second of the two models of differentiation which we have distinguished, we find *on the one hand* that the autonomy of the differentiated modes of validity is treated seriously; that is what makes it impossible to conceive of the unity of reason from the perspective of an ideal communication community in which the partiality of the separate moments of reason would finally have been sublated in the unity of a moral ideal. *On the other hand* this second model of differentiation enables us to give sharper contours to the internal *connection* between the differentiated modes of validity. As I tried to show earlier, moral discourse can be understood to a large extent as discourse about 'facts' – in the broadest sense – or about the appropriateness and completeness of interpretations of situations. This is why, in the sphere of morality, the transition from 'is' to 'ought' is always preordained, not by any ultimate normative *premises*, but by the 'moral point of view' itself.[139] But in the interpretation of the facts that are relevant to moral judgements, aesthetic experiences are always brought to bear – there is a fluid boundary also between moral discourse and aesthetic discourse. But then discourse about facts is not impervious to moral or aesthetic viewpoints either. Not only is the language in which we speak about the human life-world and history impregnated with value-judgements, the facts also present themselves differently in the light of various possible orientations within the life-world – and within these orientations it is always the case that moral attitudes and empirical convictions are already linked together. This appears to point towards a circular process, and thus ultimately towards relativism. This circle is not a theoretical problem, however, but a practical one, representing factual boundaries to rational discourse which repeatedly become apparent. We can break the circle only from within, through the application of a reason which does not withhold *any* validity-claim from critical scrutiny. The reason why we are not confronted with a circular problem in theoretical terms is that the mesh of practical orientations and empirical convictions is not secured at any point by ultimate premises which would not be amenable in principle to immanent criticism or to criticism in the light of new experience.

In the life-world at least, then, there are always interconnections between moral, practical and technical, and aesthetic perspectives or modes of discourse, as well as those concerned with truth. Rationality manifests itself here both in the ability to *distinguish* between various perspectives, and also in the ability to *connect* them with each other in the right way. But to a greater or lesser degree, much the same is true of the institutionally differentiated 'value-spheres' of science, art and law. In the case of law this seems to me self-evident. Where art is concerned, Martin Seel has shown[140] that it is possible to explain the sense of aesthetic validity with reference to the interrelationship between empirical, moral, and expressive validity-claims in aesthetic discourse. And in the case of science, finally, the problem presents itself in different ways, depending on the type of science in question. Human and social sciences participate by their very nature in the interrelationship between spheres of validity that is characteristic of the life-world, even when they specialize in questions of empirical or theoretical truth. Perhaps the natural sciences in their mathematical aspect are the only paradigm of an empirical science which is only affected at its 'edges' by normative, let alone aesthetic issues – they are affected by moral issues where they are concerned with the aims and applications of research, and by methodological and 'grammatical' issues where the *foundations* of scientific inquiry are concerned. It is precisely the mathematical language of the natural sciences that has become the true paradigm for the differentiation of spheres of validity in all modern philosophy, i.e. the paradigm of pure truth-validity.

This is still true of Habermas and Apel. And if this is the point of reference one takes, then of course the question of the sense and possibility of moral validity stands out with great clarity, but I doubt whether it is possible to achieve an adequate reconstruction of the internal *connection* between the spheres of validity using this point of reference. It is true that knowledge derived from the natural sciences is playing an ever greater part in moral controversies (the most recent example is the Aids question), but it hardly makes sense to assume that natural science also provides the measure of what is *real*, in the sense of what is or is not an empirical fact, for the purposes of moral argument – as Sellars once argued that it did.[141] The difference between 'is' and 'ought' can be easily illustrated in terms of the contrast between 'He told a lie' and 'One ought not to tell lies', or between 'He is innocent' and 'Innocent persons must not be condemned'. Sellars, as an empiricist through and through, would not *ultimately* be able to accept the possible truth of the factual statements we have just cited because they are not recognizable in the terms of natural science as factual statements.[142] But if we measure the concept of an empirical fact by Sellars' yardstick as, curiously enough, Apel and Habermas do, then the sphere of social facts becomes a puzzling entity which has, so to speak, to be 'reconstituted' from the spheres of validity as they have become historically differentiated.[143] Perhaps this also explains why, in universal pragmatics, the *one* (extreme) concept of truth-validity is only opposed by *one* (extreme) concept of normative validity. It would then be the case, as I suggested earlier, that consensus theory is the complement of a covert scientistic residue in the theories of Apel and Habermas.

Against this I would argue that while 'is' is fundamentally different from 'ought', there are various criteria of 'ought', just as there are of 'is', depending on the sense of the statement in either case, and that there are therefore various possible forms in which 'is' or 'ought' statements can be grounded or criticized, as well as various possible relationships between the two. Since it is in any case not possible to allocate aesthetic validity to *one* validity-claim in Habermas's sense,[144] it seems logical not to distinguish between spheres of validity along the lines of a typology of dimensions of validity grounded in speech-act theory and thus to allocate them to 'theoretical', 'practical' or 'aesthetic' discourse, but rather to distinguish between various types of validity-claim, and of forms of arguing to be allocated to them, *within* theoretical and practical discourse. Theoretical discourse is concerned with the validity of statements and theories, practical discourse with the correctness of actions. Theoretical discourse might, for example, be concerned with the truth-claims (assertions, theories, explanations, interpretations, reconstructions) of mathematics, physics, historiography, literary hermeneutics or moral philosophy, to which quite different forms of argument, criteria of validity, or testing procedures may correspond. 'Science as such' is a conglomerate of individual sciences, their common feature consisting solely in a specialization in the pursuit of truth independent of practical action. Such a pursuit of truth need not be independent of questions of moral or aesthetic validity, but this does not imply that theoretical discourse necessarily has to turn into practical discourse or the discourse of art criticism where such questions arise. We are concerned here, moreover, not in the first instance with the truth of *individual* statements, but with the validity of 'concatenations' of statements (theories, explanations, reconstructions, interpretations, etc) which may be *internally* articulated in a complex way; the validity of these concatenations (which allows for a certain latitude, a 'more' or 'less') cannot be equated either with the truth of individual statements or with the adequacy of language systems.

This is why 'propositional truth' is not an adequate term for what theoretical discourse is about. Theoretical discourse is concerned above all with the validity of propositional structures of a higher kind (which can themselves, under certain circumstances, take the form of interconnections between arguments), and in this connection, of course, it is also concerned with the truth of individual statements. Practical discourse, on the other hand, is concerned with the grounding and evaluation of *actions*, i.e. with questions of whether actions are politically, juridically, economically, technically, aesthetically or morally correct, with different forms of argument and criteria for validity again corresponding to various perspectives on correctness. Whereas in theoretical discourse standards of rationality are provided by the meaning of the validity-claims which are being discussed in each particular instance, or by the internal connection between validity-claims and their presuppositions, with practical discourse we encounter the additional problem that competing standards of rationality have to be related to each other and relativized with respect to each other. Practical reason expresses itself not least as the ability to relate the various dimensions of rationality implied in action – such as technical, economic, moral or aesthetic rationality – to each other in an appropriate fashion, and to relativize them with respect to each other. As Seel puts it, it expresses itself as an 'interrational faculty of judgement'.[145] The term 'faculty of judgement' carries the implication that the correct (i.e. justified) solutions which it is possible to find for the 'mediation of the moments of reason'[146] are only ever valid here and now; they are not universal or ultimate solutions. 'Unreason' should be understood in this connection as a partial insensitivity towards whole realms of experience and dimensions of validity, and thus as an inability to relate the various dimensions of experience and validity to each other in an appropriate fashion.[147] *Aesthetic* discourse, finally, is concerned neither with the validity of statements, nor with the correctness of actions, but with the meaning of aesthetic objects and whether they are successful or not, i.e. with the (aesthetic) 'validity-claims' of these objects. As with theoretical and practical discourse, interpretations, empirical assertions, and claims to moral correctness are interlinked in aesthetic discourse, but they are not the *themes*, but rather the *arguments* of aesthetic discourse, just as expressive validity-claims are. What is grounded through aesthetic discourse are aesthetic value-judgements; but these point beyond themselves to the validity-claim of the aesthetic objects on which the judgements are made, and that is something which can only be redeemed in aesthetic experience.

Theoretical, practical and aesthetic discourse are interrelated in many ways, but each is concerned with something different. Theoretical discourse aims at valid statements, explanations and interpretations; practical discourse at correct actions, attitudes and decisions; aesthetic discourse at appropriate ways of perceiving aesthetic objects. But within each of these forms of discourse, too, the various forms of argument are always – potentially at least – interlinked in many ways, because the sense of particular arguments is derived from the presence of perspectives and premises which can make it necessary *in a case of doubt* for the discussion to move to a different form of argument. But precisely these internal links between different forms of argument are not capable of explanation by means of a typology of validity-claims (propositional truth, moral correctness, [expressive] truthfulness) grounded in universal pragmatics. To put it another way, distinctions based on speech-act theory are not in themselves sufficient to render understandable either the *difference* between 'spheres of validity' or the internal *connection* between them. The reconstruction of the unity of reason with recourse to universal pragmatics and consensus theory simultaneously pitches its theoretical argument too low and too high; that is why *on the one hand* it remains committed to foundationalist figures of thought and ones that relate to the philosophy of reconciliation, while *on the other hand* it remains peculiarly encumbered with distinctions of a scientistic nature. It is distinctions of this kind which ultimately obscure the very thing which ought to be made clear, namely that the partial moments of reason communicate with each other even after they have become separated from each other.

The unity of reason can now be seen as a network of connecting lines and interchanges between theoretical, technical, moral and aesthetic issues and ways of arguing. Wherever these connections and interchanges are blocked or severed, quite specific pathologies and one-sided usages of reason result. If a form of behaviour offends against elementary requirements of consistency, or if this consistency can only be maintained at the price of a rejection of arguments and experiences, then we can call such behaviour 'irrational'. If, on the other hand, rational behaviour is reduced in such a way that *one* dimension of rationality is treated as absolute at the expense of the others, then we can call such forms of behaviour 'unreasonable', as Seel has suggested.[148] The term 'reasonable' might then be accorded the position currently occupied in Habermas's theory by the term 'communicative competence' which, after all, also means an *integration* of the moments of reason – except that it will no longer be possible to elucidate what is meant by 'reasonable' with reference to an ideal structural model that can be characterized in formal procedural terms. The 'steadfast pursuit of the tortuous routes along which science, morality, and art communicate with one another', as Habermas puts it,[149] requires discernment, imagination *and* good will; these are elements of 'reasonableness' for which there is no ideal state of affairs to be realized, but which aim rather to keep open and to extend latitude for freedom and possibilities for living. The unity of reason is realized in the interaction between partial moments of reason, and this interaction is something for which there can be no ultimate foundations or ultimate yardsticks, nor even ultimate reconciliations. Of course, reason does have a foundation – that foundation is the existence of a 'culture of reason'.[150] Where such a foundation once exists, the postulate of the freedom of *all* must become a postulate of (practical) reason. This is the indispensable (practical) chiliasm of reason,[151] which Apel and Habermas, following Kant, rightly wish to preserve. But this postulate only acquires its precise sense against the background of a *lack* of freedom as it exists and as it may be experienced in concrete situations. It does not mean the attainment of any ultimate reconciliation or ideal understanding. If it were ever so that there was no longer any reason to engage in a political struggle for freedom, then freedom would still have to be preserved, transmitted, and acquired anew. But this would not even be *conceivable* within a mode of seeking to attain an ideal understanding, for any such ideal understanding would be disrupted by each new generation in turn. On the other hand, without the element of being able to begin anew there could be no freedom.[152]

Notes

1 Truth, Semblance, Reconciliation: Adorno's Aesthetic Redemption of Modernity

1 In C. Dahlhaus et al., 'Was haben wir von Adorno gehabt?', *Musica* 24 (1970).

2 See esp. H. K. Metzger, 'John Cage oder die freigelassene Musik' and 'Anarchie durch Negationen der Zeit oder Probe einer Lektion wider die Moral. Hebel-Adorno-Cage (Variations I)', both in H. K. Metzger and R. Riehn (eds), *Musik-Konzepte, Sonderband John Cage*, Munich 1978; also the same author's 'Musik wozu', in R. Riehn (ed.), *H. K. Metzger, Musik wozu. Literatur zu Noten*, Frankfurt 1980. – Of course, Adorno's authority as a music theorist was never undisputed even in the circles of the post-war musical avant-garde. Cf. e.g. H. Eimert, 'Die notwendige Korrektur', in *Die Reihe* 2 (Anton Webern), 2nd edn, Vienna 1955, where Eimert presents a sharp opposition to Adorno's sceptical appraisal of Webern's disciples. – As far as the more strictly 'technical' side of Adorno's musical analyses is concerned, too, serious objections have been raised: cf. D. la Motte, 'Adornos musikalische Analysen', in O. Kolleritsch (ed.), *Adorno und die Musik*, Graz 1979. By comparison, the well-known controversy between Metzger and Adorno on the subject of serial music, the terms of which were incidentally drawn from Adorno's own philosophy of music, has diminished in importance as it recedes in time (see H. K. Metzger, 'Das Altern der Philosophie der neuen Musik', in R. Riehn (1980), pp. 61ff, and 'Disput zwischen Theodor W. Adorno und Heinz-Klaus Metzger', ibid., pp. 90ff).

3 Cf. T. Baumeister and J. Kulenkampff, 'Geschichtsphilosophie und

philosophische Ästhetik. Zu Adornos *Ästhetischer Theorie'*, *Neue Hefte für Philosophie*, vol. 5, 1973; R. Bubner, 'Kann Theorie ästhetisch werden? Zum Hauptmotiv der Philosophie Adornos', in B. Lindner und W. M. Lüdke (eds), *Materialien zur ästhetischen Theorie. Th. W. Adornos Konstruktion der Moderne*, Frankfurt 1980.

4   The proximity of certain basic ideas in the *Dialectic Of Enlightenment* to the philosophy of Klages is something to which my attention was drawn by A. Honneth: see his '"Der Geist und sein Gegenstand". Anthropologische Berührungspunkte zwischen der *Dialektik der Aufklärung* und der lebensphilosophischen Kulturkritik', MS (1983). The important work of Klages in this connection is *Der Geist als Widersacher der Seele* (4th edn, Munich 1960). On the direct connections to Nietzsche, see J. Habermas, 'The Entwinement of Myth and Enlightenment', *New German Critique* 26 (Spring and Summer 1982), pp. 13–30.

5   Both lines of tradition have their origins in German Idealism. The connection may be seen above all in the early work of Hegel, where the subsequently diverging strains of cultural critique and Kant criticism are still closely associated.

6   Cf. Theodor W. Adorno, *Minima Moralia*, London 1974, p. 247 (*Gesammelte Schriften*, vol. 4, p. 281).

7   Adorno, *Ges. Schriften*, vol. 16, p. 254.

8   Ibid.

9   Ibid., p. 252.

10 Ibid.

11 Cf. Walter Benjamin, *Illuminations*, New York 1969, p. 253.

12 Adorno, *Minima Moralia*, p. 247 (*Ges. Schriften*, vol. 4, p. 281).

13 Jürgen Habermas, *The Theory of Communicative Action*, vol. 1, London and Cambridge, Mass., 1984, esp. pp. 366ff.

14 Ibid., p. 390.

15 Cf. H. R. Jauss, *Aesthetic Experience and Literary Hermeneutics*, Minneapolis 1982, pp. 15ff.

16 Cf. Peter Bürger, *Zur Kritik der idealistischen Ästhetik*, Frankfurt 1983.

17 Ibid., esp. pp. 67–72, 128–35.

18 Ibid., p. 67.

19 Cf. K. H. Bohrer, *Plötzlichkeit. Zum Augenblick des ästhetischen Scheins*, Frankfurt 1981, esp. pp. 111ff ('Ästhetik und Historismus: Nietzsches Begriff des "Scheins"') and pp. 180ff ('Utopie des "Augenblicks" und Fiktionalität. Die Subjektivierung von Zeit in der modernen Literatur').

20 Ibid., p. 211.

21 Cf. ibid., p. 95.

22 Gabriele Schwab, *Entgrenzungen und Entgrenzungsmythen. Zur Subjektivität im modernen Roman*, Stuttgart 1987.

23 Cf. F. Koppe, *Grundbegriffe der Ästhetik*, Frankfurt 1983, p. 88.
24 See Martin Seel, *Die Kunst der Entzweiung. Zum Begriff der ästhetischen Rationalität*, Frankfurt 1985.
25 Cf. Adorno, *Aesthetic Theory*, translated by C. Lenhardt, London 1984, p. 107 (*Ges. Schriften*, vol. 7, p. 281).
26 R. Bubner, 'Über einige Bedingungen gegenwärtiger Ästhetik', *Neue Hefte für Philosophie*, 1973, Heft 5.
27 Cf. Jauss, *Aesthetic Experience*, pp. 19, 39ff.
28 Cf. Peter Bürger, *Theory of the Avantgarde*, Minneapolis 1984.
29 Bürger, *Zur Kritik der idealistischen Ästhetik*, p. 189.
30 Bürger, *Theory of the Avantgarde*, p. 42.
31 Cf. Bürger, *Zur Kritik der idealistischen Ästhetik*, p. 187.
32 Ibid., p. 135.
33 Cf. ibid., pp. 128ff.
34 Cf. Pierre Boulez, *Wille und Zufall. Gespräche mit Célestin Deliège und Hans Meyer*, Stuttgart and Zurich 1976, p. 131.
35 Quoted in D. Schnebel, 'Wie ich das schaffe?', in H.-K. Metzger and R. Riehn (eds), *Musik-Konzepte. Sonderband John Cage*, Munich 1978, p. 51.
36 On this point, cf. Jürgen Habermas, 'Modernity vs. Postmodernity', *New German Critique* 22 (Winter 1981), pp. 3–14.
37 Adorno, letter to Walter Benjamin, 18 March 1936, published in F. Jameson (ed.), *Aesthetics and Politics*, London 1977, p. 123.
38 Adorno, 'On the Fetish Character of Music and the Regression of Listening', in A. Arato and E. Gebhardt (eds), *The Essential Frankfurt School Reader*, New York 1978, p. 272 (*Ges. Schriften*, vol. 14, p. 17).
39 Ibid.
40 Cf. Walter Benjamin, 'Das Kunstwerk im Zeitalter seiner technischen Reproduzierbarkeit', *Ges. Schriften*, vol. 1.2, Frankfurt 1974, p. 460. [*Translator's note*: The passage in question is not included in the English edition; see Walter Benjamin, *Illuminations*, pp. 217–52.]
41 Cf. ibid., p. 462.
42 Ibid.
43 On this point, cf. T. Kneif, *Einführung in die Rockmusik*, Wilhelmshaven 1979.

2 The Dialectic of Modernism and Postmodernism: The Critique of Reason since Adorno

1 Jean-François Lyotard, *Intensitäten*, Berlin 1978, p. 104 [original title: *Des dispositifs pulsionnels*, Paris 1973].
2 Ihab Hassan, 'The Critic as Innovator: The Tutzing Statement in X Frames', *Amerikastudien* 22 (1977), Heft 1, p. 55.

3   Ibid., p. 57.
4   Interview with Frederic Jameson, *Diacritics*, vol. 12 (Fall 1982), p. 82.
5   Ibid., p. 83.
6   Ibid.
7   Cf. Lyotard, *Apathie in der Theorie*, Berlin 1979, p. 36 [original title: *Instructions païennes*, Paris 1977].
8   Lyotard, *Essays zu einer affirmativen Ästhetik*, Berlin 1982, p. 17 [originally in *Des dispositifs pulsionnels*, Paris 1973 and 1980].
9   Ibid., p. 21.
10 Ibid., p. 121.
11 *Tod der Moderne. Eine Diskussion (Konkursbuch)*, Tübingen 1983, p. 25.
12 Ibid., p. 103.
13 Lyotard, *The Postmodern Condition: A Report on Knowledge*, translated by G. Bennington and B. Massumi, Minnesota and Manchester 1984, p. 65.
14 Cf. ibid., p. 66.
15 Conversation between J. F. Lyotard and J. P. Dubost, in Jean-François Lyotard, *Das postmoderne Wissen*, Bremen 1982, p. 131.
16 Cf. Lyotard, *Postmodern Condition*, pp. 37ff.
17 Ibid., p. 79.
18 Theodor W. Adorno, *Aesthetic Theory*, translated by C. Lenhardt, London 1984, p. 34.
19 Lyotard, *Postmodern Condition*, p. 79.
20 Cf. ibid., p. 79f.
21 Ibid., p. 81f.
22 Cf. Charles Jencks, *The Language of Post-Modern Architecture*, New York 1977; Albrecht Wellmer, 'Art and Industrial Production', in this volume, pp. 95–112.
23 Cf. Jencks, p. 87.
24 Peter Bürger, 'Das Altern der Moderne', in L. v. Friedeburg and J. Habermas (eds), *Adorno-Konferenz 1983*, Frankfurt 1983, pp. 177ff.
25 Adorno, *Aesthetic Theory*, p. 303; cf. Bürger, 'Das Altern der Moderne', p. 186.
26 Cf. Bürger, 'Das Altern der Moderne', pp. 191, 194.
27 Cf. Albrecht Wellmer, 'Truth, Semblance, Reconciliation', in this volume, pp. 18–29.
28 Lyotard, *Postmodern Condition*, p. 77.
29 Ibid., p. 74.
30 Cf. ibid., p. 76.
31 Cf. ibid., p. 81. [The formulation of Lyotard's argument is rendered more precisely here than in the published English translation.]
32 Ibid., p. 78.
33 Cf. ibid.

34   On this point, cf. Wellmer, 'Truth, Semblance, Reconciliation', in this volume, pp. 18–29.

35   Lyotard, 'Das Erhabene und die Avantgarde', *Merkur* 38 (1984), Heft 2, pp. 151ff.

36   Ibid., p. 159.

37   Ibid.

38   Adorno, 'Voraussetzungen', in *Noten zur Literatur* (*Ges. Schriften*, vol. 11), Frankfurt 1974, p. 433.

39   R. M. Adams, 'Scrabbling in the "Wake"', *New York Review of Books*, 31 May 1984, p. 43.

40   Cf. K. Reichert, 'Von den Rändern her oder Sortes Wakeianae', in L. Dällenbach and C. L. Hart Nibbrig (eds), *Fragment und Totalität*, Frankfurt 1984, p. 306.

41   Quoted in ibid., p. 302.

42   'The ageing of works of art is only a process of destruction in a very superficial sense, namely from the point of view of the restorer. In its best sense, ageing means that habituation neutralizes and compensates for the demanding challenge that any work of art presents to the viewer. The process by which works of art become forgotten, pigeon-holed, or cast onto the scrap heap of things that have become dispensable represents a creative force which makes it possible for old forms to convey new meanings.' Bazon Brock, 'Die Ruine als Form der Vermittlung von Fragment und Totalität', in L. Dällenbach and C. L. Hart Nibbrig (eds), *Fragment und Totalität*, p. 138.

43   Walter Benjamin, *The Origins of German Tragedy*, translated by J. Osborne, London 1977, p. 182.

44   Brock, 'Die Ruine', p. 138.

45   Ibid.

46   Axel Honneth, *Kritik der Macht. Reflexionsstufen einer kritischen Gesellschaftstheorie*, Frankfurt 1985, p. 129.

47   Max Horkheimer and Theodor W. Adorno, *Dialectic of Enlightenment*, translated by John Cumming, London 1973.

48   Cf. Theodor W. Adorno, *Negative Dialectics*, translated by E. B. Ashton, New York 1973, p. 26.

49   Cf. ibid., p. 9.

50   Horkheimer and Adorno, *Dialectic of Enlightenment*, p. 234.

51   Ibid., p. 28.

52   Cf. Michel Foucault, *Discipline and Punish. The Birth of the Prison*, translated by Alan Sheridan, London 1979, pp. 170ff.

53   Cf. Horkheimer and Adorno, *Dialectic of Enlightenment*, p. 13.

54   Adorno, *Negative Dialectics*, p. 15.

55   Horkheimer and Adorno, *Dialectic of Enlightenment*, p. 33.

56   This is the nub of the so-called 'private language' argument, as Saul

A. Kripke demonstrates in his *Wittgenstein on Rules and Private Language*, Oxford 1982.

57 Cornelius Castoriadis, *The Imaginary Institution of Society*, translated by Kathleen Blamey, Cambridge 1987.

58 Ibid., p. 248.

59 Ibid., p. 250.

60 Manfred Frank, *Was ist Neostrukturalismus?*, Frankfurt 1984, p. 511.

61 Derrida is too complex an author for me to do justice to him here. I am referring here to only *one* figure of thought, but it is one which I believe Frank has represented accurately. Cf. especially Jacques Derrida, 'Signature Event Context', in *Glyph. The Johns Hopkins Studies*, 1 (1977); 'Limited Inc', in *Glyph. The Johns Hopkins Studies*, 2 (1977). I have no wish, incidentally, to defend Searle's position against Derrida: cf. J. R. Searle, 'Reiterating the Differences. A Reply to Derrida', in *Glyph. The Johns Hopkins Textual Studies*, 1 (1977).

62 Kripke, *Wittgenstein on Rules*, p. 55.

63 I am speaking of *radical* hermeneutic scepticism. I am not denying, of course, that it makes good sense to say that the meaning of the texts an author writes has eluded him. In other words, I am not advocating an intentionalist theory of interpretation. But does it mean the same thing when I say that the meaning of a particular word eludes me? The point is, I think, that it is appropriate to say this in some cases, but not in others. If we now say that there can be no case where it is *not* appropriate, then we are introducing a new criterion of appropriateness. But I think the reasons for this do not arise from a self-criticism of language so much as from the self-criticism of intentionalist *theories* of meaning.

64 L. Wittgenstein, *Philosophical Investigations*, translated by G. E. M. Anscombe, Oxford 1953, p. 81[e] (§199).

65 Adorno, *Negative Dialectics*, p. 5.

66 Ibid., p. 9.

67 Ibid., p. 15.

68 Cf. Horkheimer and Adorno, *Dialectic of Enlightenment*, p. 39. [*Translator's note*: The English edition translates the imagery very loosely here.]

69 Cf. ibid., p. 40.

70 This is also the central thought of Jürgen Habermas's critique of Adorno: see J. Habermas, *The Theory of Communicative Action*, vol. 1, London and Cambridge, Mass., 1984, pp. 366ff., esp. pp. 389ff. Habermas describes the limits of the philosophy of the subject as follows: 'Under "object" the philosophy of the subject understands everything that can be represented as existing; under "subject" it understands first of all the capacities to relate oneself to such entities in the world in an objectivating attitude and to gain control of

objects, be it theoretically or practically. The two attitudes of mind are representation [*Vorstellen*] and action. . . . These two functions of mind are intertwined: knowledge of states of affairs is structurally related to the possibility of intervention in the world as the totality of states of affairs; and successful action requires in turn knowledge of the causal nexus in which it intervenes.' (Ibid., p. 387) It is possible, in contrast, to characterize the disclosure of a *communicative* dimension in language in formal terms, as Habermas does, by speaking of the symmetrical–performative relationship between *subject* and *subject* attaining parity with the asymmetrical relationship between *subject* and *object*. The objectivation of reality relates back to an agreement *in* the language. In this way, a more complicated *dialogic* structure becomes apparent behind the monologic structure of a subject that represents [*vorstellt*] and acts instrumentally. Two subjects agree *with each other about something* that exists. The grammar of first and second person personal pronouns reflects the symmetrical–performative relationship between the speaker and the listener in the speech-act that is 'orientated towards understanding'; objective facts can only exist in an arena of such relationships between potential speakers and listeners – whereby the *particular* conditions of an objectivation of *social* facts are simultaneously reflected in the grammatical relationships between first, second *and* third person.

71   Adorno, 'Fragment über Musik und Sprache', *Ges. Schriften*, vol. 16, Frankfurt 1978, p. 252.
72   Adorno, *Negative Dialectics*, p. 15.
73   Thomas Bernhard, *Wittgensteins Neffe*, Frankfurt 1982, pp. 13f.
74   Cf. note 70. Habermas's theory of communicative action is the systematic development of this idea. My own case against Adorno is, however, independent of the systematics of Habermas's theory of language.
75   Cf. Adorno, *Negative Dialectics*, p. 23.
76   On this point, cf. Mary Douglas, *Purity and Danger*, London 1966.
77   Cf. Adorno, *Negative Dialectics*, p. 26. Adorno's thought revolves incessantly around the idea of a *non-violent* unity – as a form of cognition, as a form of individuation, as a form of social solidarity. This idea is what expressions like 'coherence of the non-identical' or 'non-violent synthesis' stand for. What is surely Adorno's most profound problem lies in the question of how to relate the two figures of unity to each other, namely the compulsion towards system and identity of the 'concept' and the 'ego-principle' on the one hand, and the non-violent coherence of the non-identical on the other. In two characteristic formulations from his *Negative Dialectics* we read: 'But unity and unanimity are at the same time an

oblique projection of pacified, no longer antagonistic conditions upon the co-ordinates of supremacist, oppressive thinking.' (p. 25) And: 'What the conception of the system recalls, in reverse, is the coherence of the non-identical, the very thing infringed by deductive systematics.' (p. 26) Phrases such as these are part of Adorno's aporetic *defence* of discursive reason against *irrationalism* (cf. ibid., p. 8). But Adorno's philosophy lacks the categorial 'degrees of freedom' which would enable him to give a genuine answer to the question I have raised.
78 Cf. ibid., p. 9.
79 Cf. Ludwig Wittgenstein, *Tractatus logico-philosophicus*, with an English translation by D. F. Pears and B. F. McGuiness, London 1961, proposition 5.632 (p. 117).
80 Adorno, *Negative Dialectics*, p. 15.
81 Ibid., p. 18.
82 Ibid., p. 33.
83 Cf. ibid., pp. 22ff.
84 This was indeed the title of a special volume of *Konkursbuch*, cf. note 11, above.
85 See my own essay, 'Truth, Semblance, Reconciliation', in this volume, p. 19.
86 Cf. Jürgen Habermas, 'Können komplexe Gesellschaften eine vernünftige Identität ausbilden?', in J. Habermas and D. Henrich, *Zwei Reden*, Frankfurt 1974, pp. 68ff.
87 Lyotard, *Postmodern Condition*, p. 67.
88 Ibid., p. 81.
89 Jürgen Habermas, *Die Moderne – ein unvollendetes Projekt*, Frankfurt 1981. This is Habermas's speech on the occasion of being awarded the Theodor W. Adorno Prize of the city of Frankfurt am Main for the year 1980.
90 Cf. Wellmer, 'Truth, Semblance, Reconciliation', in this volume, p. 29f.
91 Cf. Martin Seel, *Die Kunst der Entzweiung. Zum Begriff der ästhetischen Rationalität*, Frankfurt 1985.
92 Cornelius Castoriadis, *Crossroads in the Labyrinth*, translated by K. Soper and M. H. Ryle, Brighton 1984, p. 224.

3 Art and Industrial Production: The Dialectics of Modernism and Postmodernism

1 Octavio Paz, *Convergences. Essays on Art and Literature*, translated by Helen Lane, London 1987, p. 51.
2 Ibid., p. 52.

3   Ibid., pp. 57, 59.
4   Joan Campbell, *The German Werkbund*, Princeton 1978; Kurt Jung-
    hans, *Der deutsche Werkbund. Sein erstes Jahrzehnt*, (East) Berlin 1982;
    Lucius Burckhardt, *Der Werkbund in Deutschland, Österreich und der
    Schweiz*, Stuttgart 1978. There is a fine documentation of the history
    of the Werkbund in the book that accompanied the Werkbund
    Exhibition in the Staatliches Museum für angewandte Kunst in
    Munich, 1975: see Wend Fischer (ed.), *Zwischen Kunst und Industrie.
    Der deutsche Werkbund*, Munich 1975.
5   I am leaving out of account those chauvinistic undertones which
    were not absent from the early phase of the Deutscher Werkbund.
    (For references, see note 4, above.)
6   Adolf Loos, 'Kulturentartung', in *Sämtliche Schriften*, vol. 1, Vienna
    and Munich 1962, p. 274.
7   Julius Posener, 'Le Corbusier', in *Aufsätze und Vorträge 1931–1980*,
    Braunschweig and Wiesbaden 1981, p. 188.
8   W. J. Siedler, E. Niggemeyer, G. Angress, *Die gemordete Stadt*, Berlin,
    Munich and Vienna 1964, p. 13.
9   Jane Jacobs, *The Death and Life of Great American Cities*, New York
    1961, chap. 22.
10 Theodor W. Adorno, 'Funktionalismus heute', *Ges. Schriften*, vol.
    10.1, Frankfurt 1977, p. 389.
11 Ibid., p. 387.
12 Ibid., p. 388.
13 For what follows, cf. Jürgen Habermas, 'Moderne und postmoderne
    Architektur', in *Die andere Tradition* (Catalogue to exhibition no. 3
    in the series 'Erkundungen'), Munich 1981, which I was able to
    read only after the present text was completed. The affinities with
    my own argument are readily apparent and by no means coinciden-
    tal.
14 Charles Jencks, *The Language of Post-Modern Architecture*, New York
    1977.
15 Jürgen Habermas, *The Theory of Communicative Action*, 2 vols, Cam-
    bridge, Mass., 1984 and 1987.
16 Cf. K. Frampton, *Modern Architecture*, Oxford and New York 1980,
    p. 293.
17 Ludwig Wittgenstein, *Philosophical Investigations*, translated by
    G. E. M. Anscombe, Oxford 1958, p. 46ᶜ.
18 Jencks, *Language of Post-Modern Architecture*, pp. 128ff.
19 Ibid., p. 14.
20 Adorno, *Aesthetic Theory*, translated by C. Lenhardt, London 1984,
    p. 167.
21 Alexander Schwab, 'Zur Abteilung Städtebau und Landesplanung',

Die Form, 1930, Heft 3, quoted in F. Schwarz and F. Gloor, *'Die Form'. Stimme des Deutschen Werkbundes 1925–1934*, Gütersloh 1969, p. 157.

22 Ernst Bloch, *The Principle of Hope*, translated by Neville Plaice, Stephen Plaice and Paul Knight, 3 vols, Oxford 1986, p. 735.

23 Ibid., p. 737.

24 Ibid., p. 735. Cf. also A. M. Vogt, 'Entwurf zu einer Architekturgeschichte 1940–1980', in Vogt, Jehle and Reichlin (eds), *Architektur 1940–1980*, Berlin 1980, p. 12.

25 Lucius Burckhardt, 'Design ist unsichtbar', in *Design ist unsichtbar*, Vienna 1981.

4 Ethics and Dialogue: Elements of Moral Judgement in Kant and Discourse Ethics

A note on the references to Kant. For passages quoted from the works of Kant, those translations have been selected which yielded the greatest conceptual clarity in the English. They are the translations by Abbott (for the *Critique of Practical Reason*), Meredith (for the *Critique of Judgement*), and Paton (for the *Groundwork of the Metaphysic of Morals*). Alternative references to other English translations are given where these conveniently combine various relevant works of Kant in a single volume. The references to the collected works of Kant in German (*Werke in sechs Bänden*, ed. W. Weischedel, Darmstadt 1956–64, hereafter cited as *WSB*) are retained for readers who may wish to refer to the original wording of Kant's arguments.

1 On this subject, cf. Peter Sloterdijk, *Critique of Cynical Reason*, London 1988.

2 Jürgen Habermas, 'Diskursethik – Notizen zu einem Begründungsprogramm', in Habermas, *Moralbewusstsein und Kommunikatives Handeln*, Frankfurt 1983.

3 Cf. Marcus G. Singer, *Generalization in Ethics*, New York 1971, pp. 37ff.

4 Cf. Richard M. Hare, *Moral Thinking*, Oxford 1981, pp. 8ff.

5 Singer, *Generalization in Ethics*, p. 38.

6 This is where I see the decisive weakness in what is in certain respects a throughly convincing reconstruction of Kant's ethics, or of a 'Kantian' ethics, by Singer. Cf. Singer, *Generalization in Ethics*, pp. 63ff.

7 H. J. Paton, *The Moral Law. Kant's Groundwork of the Metaphysic of Morals. A New Translation with Analysis and Notes*, London 1961, p. 91; Immanuel Kant, *Ethical Philosophy*, translated by James W.

Ellington, Indianapolis 1983, p. 32. (*WSB*, vol. IV, 1956, p. 54 (BA 57).)

8 Bernard Gert, *The Moral Rules*, New York 1973.

9 Ibid., pp. 60ff; cf. also Georg Henrik von Wright, *The Varieties of Goodness*, London 1963, pp. 197ff.

10 Cf. Julius Ebbinghaus, 'Die Formeln des kategorischen Imperativs und die Ableitung inhaltlich bestimmter Pflichten', in Ebbinghaus, *Gesammelte Aufsätze, Vorträge, Reden*, Hildesheim 1968, vol. I, section 7, pp. 140–60.

11 Singer, *Generalization in Ethics*, p. 240: 'If the maxim of an action *cannot* be willed to be a universal law, then it is wrong to act on it, we have the duty or obligation not to, and it can be said that we ought not to. However, if a maxim *can* be willed to be a universal law, it does not follow that it is obligatory to act on it or that it would be wrong not to. What follows is that it is permissible to do so, or not wrong (and thus right in the *permissive* sense), and hence that it cannot be said that we ought not to – which is not the same as saying that we ought to.' This is also the approach taken by Joachim Aul: 'Aspekte des Universalisierungspostulats in Kants Ethik', *Neue Hefte für Philosophie*, Heft 22, 1983, esp. pp. 85ff. Such an interpretation is not entirely foreign to Kant himself, as the following passage from notes of one of his lectures shows: 'In all moral judgements we ask ourselves: how is this action constituted if it is taken as universal? If the intention of the act is in harmony with itself when it is made into a universal rule, then the act is morally possible; if the intention of the act is not in harmony with itself when it is taken as universal, then the act is not morally possible.' Cf. Kant, *Gesammelte Schriften*, ed. Akademie der Wissenschaften der DDR, vol. XXVII (Kants Vorlesungen, vol. IV: Vorlesungen über Moralphilosophie), Berlin 1979, pp. 1276f. I am obliged to Henry Gerlach for drawing my attention to this passage.

12 Cf. also William K. Frankena, *Analytische Ethik*, Munich 1972, p. 52.

13 Cf. Paton, *The Moral Law*, pp. 89f; Ellington, p. 31. (*WSB*, vol. IV, p. 53 (BA 54).)

14 See for example *Kant's Critique of Practical Reason and Other Works on the Theory of Ethics*, translated by Thomas Kingsmill Abbott, London 1927, pp. 114f. (*WSB*, vol. IV, p. 136 (A 49).)

15 Cf. Paton, *The Moral Law*, p. 91; Ellington, p. 32. (*WSB* vol. IV, pp. 54–5 (BA 56–7).)

16 Cf. ibid., p. 92; Ellington, p. 33. (*WSB*, vol. IV, p. 55 (BA 58).)

17 This is Schopenhauer's 'principle of justice'. Cf. Arthur Schopenhauer, *On the Basis of Morality*, translated by E. F. J. Payne, Indianapolis 1965, p. 149. I shall not be discussing Schopenhauer's critique of Kant here, but I should like to mention Schopenhauer's thesis

that 'the concept of *ought*, the *imperative form* of ethics, applies solely to theological morality, and that outside this it loses all sense and meaning' (ibid., p. 130). A similar 'sense-criticism' (in Apel's terminology) of the concept of an unconditional moral ought also occurs in recent discussions on ethics; see, for example, G. E. M. Anscombe, 'Modern Moral Philosophy', in *Philosophy* 33 (1958), and A. MacIntyre, *After Virtue*, Notre Dame, Indiana, 1981 (p. 57); cf. also P. Foot, 'Morality as a System of Hypothetical Imperatives', in *Virtues and Vices*, Berkeley 1978, pp. 163ff, and U. Wolf, *Das Problem des moralischen Sollens*, Berlin 1984, pp. 3ff. I think that we cannot ignore 'Schopenhauer's problem', as I should like to call it, even if the critique of Kant within which Schopenhauer's thesis has its context is not itself convincing. I shall touch on this problem indirectly in section XI.

18 Kant, *Ethical Philosophy*, translated by James W. Ellington, Indianapolis 1983, p. 48 (*WSB*, vol. IV, p. 520 (A 20).)
19 Cf. Gert, *The Moral Rules*, pp. 128ff.
20 Kant, *Ethical Philosophy*, translated by James W. Ellington, Indianapolis 1983, p. 52. (WSB, vol. IV, p. 524 (A 27).)
21 On the term 'prima facie principles', cf. Hare, *Moral Thinking*, p. 38.
22 Ibid., pp. 25ff.
23 Ibid., p. 41.
24 Cf. ibid., p. 46.
25 Ibid., p. 33.
26 *Kant's Critique of Practical Reason*, translated by T. K. Abbott, pp. 119, 114f. (*WSB*, vol. IV, pp. 140, 136 (A 54, 49).)
27 Ibid., pp. 114f (p. 136 (A 49)).
28 Cf. Richard M. Hare, *The Language of Morals*, Oxford 1952, pp. 68f.
29 Cf. Gert, *The Moral Rules*, chap. 2, esp. p. 37.
30 Cf. von Wright, *The Varieties of Goodness*.
31 John Rawls, *A Theory of Justice*, Cambridge, Mass., 1971.
32 Cf. the thoughts of Gert in *The Moral Rules*, chap. 10: 'Why Should One Be Moral?'
33 Cf. ibid., pp. 204ff.
34 A representative selection can be found in Friedrich Kambartel (ed.), *Praktische Philosophie und konstruktive Wissenschaftstheorie*, Frankfurt 1974. See also Oswald Schwemmer, *Philosophie der Praxis*, Frankfurt 1971; Paul Lorenzen and Oswald Schwemmer, *Konstruktive Logik, Ethik und Wissenschaftstheorie*, Mannheim 1973.
35 John R. Silber, 'Procedural Formalism in Kant's Ethics', *Review of Metaphysics*, vol. XXVIII, no. 2 (1974).
36 Kant, *The Critique of Judgement*, translated by J. C. Meredith, Oxford 1952, p. 152. (*WSB*, vol. V, 1957, p. 390 (B 158).) The maxims in question are: '(1) to think for oneself; (2) to think from the stand-

point of everyone else; (3) always to think consistently.'
37 Silber, 'Procedural Formalism', p. 216.
38 Ibid., p. 199.
39 Ibid., p. 221. Cf. Immanuel Kant, *Religion within the Limits of Reason Alone*, translated by T. M. Greene and H. H. Hudson, La Salle, Illinois, 1960, p. 62. (*Werke in sechs Bänden*, vol. V, p. 722.)
40 See for instance K.-O. Apel, D. Böhler and G. Kadelbach (eds), *Funkkolleg Praktische Philosophie/Ethik: Dialoge 2*, Frankfurt 1984, esp. units 18–20. K.-O. Apel, 'Ist die Ethik der idealen Kommunikationsgemeinschaft eine Utopie?', in W. Vosskamp (ed.), *Utopieforschung*, vol. 1, Stuttgart 1982, and 'Kant, Hegel und das aktuelle Problem der normativen Grundlagen von Moral und Recht', in Arno Werner (ed.), *Filosofi och Kultur*, Lund 1982. On the question of fundamental grounding, see esp. K.-O. Apel, 'The Problem of Philosophical Fundamental Grounding in the Light of a Transcendental Pragmatic of Language', in *Man and World* 18 (1975), pp. 239–75, and 'Sprechakttheorie und transzendentale Sprachpragmatik zur Frage ethischer Normen', in K.-O. Apel (ed.), *Sprachpragmatik und Philosophie*, Frankfurt 1976; also 'The *a priori* of the communication community and the foundations of ethics', in *Towards a Transformation of Philosophy*, translated by G. Adey and D. Frisby, London 1980.
41 Habermas, *Moralbewusstsein und Kommunikatives Handeln*, Frankfurt 1983, p. 136.
42 Ibid., pp. 136f.
43 Thomas McCarthy, *The Critical Discourse of Jürgen Habermas*, Cambridge, Mass., 1978, p. 326.
44 Paton, *The Moral Law*, p. 91; Ellington, p. 32, (*WSB*, vol. IV, p. 54 (BA 57).)
45 Cf. above, section III (Excursus), pp. 131–5.
46 This description first appears in Jürgen Habermas, 'Wahrheitstheorien', in Helmut Fahrenbach (ed.), *Wirklichkeit und Reflexion. Festschrift für Walter Schulz*, Pfullingen 1973, esp. pp. 252ff. The critique that follows has some elements in common with the comprehensive and trenchant critique of consensus theory by R. Zimmermann in *Utopie – Rationalität – Politik*, Munich 1985, pp. 303ff.
47 See for example 'A Philosophico-Political Profile', in Jürgen Habermas, *Autonomy and Solidarity*, London 1986, pp. 162–3. Habermas here adds the qualification, however, that the consensus or discourse theory of truth simultaneously 'undermines the clear distinction between meaning and criterion' (p. 163).
48 Personal letter.
49 Ludwig Wittgenstein, *Philosophical Investigations*, Oxford 1963, p. 88^e (para. 242).

50 Habermas, 'Wahrheitstheorien', p. 244.
51 Ibid., p. 249.
52 This comes close to the approach taken by Apel. For full formulations of it cf. Karl-Otto Apel, 'Scientism or Transcendental Hermeneutics', in *Towards a Transformation of Philosophy*, translated by
G. Adey and D. Frisby, London 1980, pp. 105, 116f. The approaches
of Apel and Habermas differ only in their initial point of departure
and their emphasis; the difference in the results they achieve is not
always easy to determine. Apel appeals to the authority of Habermas, for example, when he postulates the necessity of assuming
an 'ideal speech situation' as a precondition for the possibility of
argument. (Cf. K.-O. Apel, 'Sprechakttheorie und transzendentale
Sprachpragmatik zur Frage ethischer Normen', in Apel (ed.), *Sprachpragmatik und Philosophie*, Frankfurt 1976, p. 121.) On the other
hand, Habermas views the *rational* consensus (i.e. a consensus
achieved under the conditions of an ideal speech situation) as eo
ipso a possible *infinite* consensus. (Cf. Habermas, 'Wahrheitstheori-
en', p. 239: '. . .the meaning of truth is not the circumstance that a
consensus has been reached, but that whenever we enter into a
discourse, at whatever time and in whatever place, a consensus
can be achieved under conditions which distinguish it as a fully
grounded consensus.') There is a simple reason why I have not
included what is for Habermas the self-evident precondition of the
infinite repeatability of rational consensuses in my considerations
from the outset, and that is that as long as the presence of the
formal conditions of an ideal speech situation is understood as a
criterion of truth (cf. Habermas, 'Wahrheitstheorien', pp. 239f), then
the possibility of an infinite consensus is merely a *consequence* of
the *rationality* of consensuses as defined by formal conditions. The
explicatum of the truth concept is not the infinite consensus, but
the rational one. This was what prompted my initial objections: I
tried to show that the – formally characterized – structural features
of an ideal speech situation cannot represent an appropriate criterion for truth; *either* the criterion is false, *or* it is inherently
vacuous and thus no criterion at all. If we now take into consideration the connection that Habermas assumes between the rationality and the infinite repeatability of consensus, then it becomes
clear that the ideal speech situation is conceived from the very
beginning rather in terms of a vacuous criterion. For if the infinite
repeatability of consensuses *follows analytically* from their rationality, then by the same token it follows that a consensus which
subsequently turns out to be false and unable to stand up to
criticism *cannot* have come about under the conditions of an ideal
speech situation (cf. 'Wahrheitstheorien', pp. 257f). But then the

permanence of consensuses would in reality be the criterion of their rationality (their truth). This is the second variant of consensus theory, which corresponds rather to the fundamental intuitions of Apel.

53 Habermas, *Autonomy and Solidarity*, pp. 162ff.
54 Ibid., p. 162.
55 Ibid., pp. 162f. [*Translator's note*: I have rendered Habermas's term 'Voraussetzungen' as 'preconditions'; in *Autonomy and Solidarity* it is translated – wrongly for its context – as 'presuppositions'].
56 Apel does, however, say that this is a regulative idea which can never be 'fully realized'. Cf. K.-O. Apel, D. Böhler and G. Kadelbach (eds), *Funkkolleg Praktische Philosophie/Ethik: Dialoge 2*, Frankfurt 1984, p. 136; also 'Kant, Hegel und das aktuelle Problem der normativen Grundlagen von Moral und Recht', in Arno Werner (ed.), *Filosofi och Kultur*, Lund 1982, p. 85.
57 The reflections of C. F. von Weizsäcker on the possibility of achieving a unity, and thus a final perfection, of physics are of relevance here: see C. F. von Weizsäcker, *Die Einheit der Natur*, Munich 1971, esp. pp. 207ff. Von Weizsäcker here advances the ambitious hypothesis that it must ultimately be possible to derive all the fundamental principles of a perfected physics from an analysis of the preconditions for the possibility of experience (ibid., p. 217). The idea of a 'final' (in the sense of totally adequate) language of physics occurs in a different form nowadays in the tradition of American pragmatism, where it finds its subtlest elaboration in Wilfrid Sellars' philosophy of 'scientific realism'. For Sellars, scientific progress represents a process of continual language criticism, much as it did for Peirce; according to this conception of things, 'reality' would be the correlate of those physical theories which had ultimately been found to be true. Cf. Wilfrid Sellars, *Science, Perception and Reality*, London 1963, esp. pp. 119, 126; 'Scientific Realism or Irenic Instrumentalism. Comments on J. J. C. Smart', in R. S. Cohen and M. W. Wartofsky (eds), *Bostom Studies in the Philosophy of Science*, vol. II, New York 1965, esp. p. 204; 'Counterfactuals, Dispositions, and the Causal Modalities', in H. Feigl, M. Scriven and G. Maxwell (eds), *Minnesota Studies in the Philosophy of Science*, vol. II, Minneapolis 1958, esp. p. 263; also 'Theoretical Explanation', in Sellars, *Philosophical Perspectives*, Springfield, Ill., 1967.
58 Karl-Otto Apel, *Towards a Transformation of Philosophy*, pp. 93ff.
59 Cf. Apel, 'From Kant to Peirce', ibid., p. 87.
60 Apel, 'Scientism or Transcendental Hermeneutics', ibid., p. 125.
61 See for example 'From Kant to Peirce', ibid., p. 87.

62   Charles Sanders Peirce, *Collected Papers*, 5.311 (quoted by Apel, ibid., p. 87).
63   Ibid., pp. 87f.
64   Ibid., p. 88.
65   Cf. 'Scientism or Transcendental Hermeneutics', ibid., p. 113.
66   Ibid., pp. 125f.
67   Cf. ibid., p. 123.
68   Ibid., p. 112.
69   Ibid., p. 125.
70   Ibid., pp. 120f.
71   Cf. ibid., p. 123.
72   Ibid., p. 125.
73   Ibid.
74   Ibid.
75   K.-O. Apel, *Transformation der Philosophie*, vol. II, Frankfurt 1973, p. 348 ('Der transzendentalhermeneutische Begriff der Sprache').
76   Adorno's 'Meditations on Metaphysics' in part three of *Negative Dialectics* are a sustained attempt to rescue the theological motif which in Kant's case entered into the construction of the connection between the concept of the intelligible and the postulates of pure practical reason. It is true that Adorno attempts to release this theological motif – in materialistic fashion – from the rigid opposition of immanence and transcendence; but by taking it literally, i.e. as an expectation of the resurrection of the body, he also precludes for himself the possibility of merely levelling out the difference. He sees the ambiguity and the aporetic quality of Kant's construction as ultimately justified by the fact that the absolute is *for us* veiled in black, as he puts it elsewhere. 'That no reforms within the world sufficed to do justice to the dead, that none of them touched upon the wrong of death – this is what moves Kantian reason to hope against reason. The secret of his philosophy is the unthinkability of despair. Constrained by the convergence of all thoughts in something absolute, he did not leave it at the absolute line between absoluteness and existence; but he was no less constrained to draw that line. He held on to the metaphysical ideas, and yet he forbade jumping from thoughts of the absolute which might one day be realized, like eternal peace, to the conclusion that therefore the absolute exists. His philosophy – as probably every other, by the way – circles about the ontological argument for God's existence; but his own position remained open, in a grandiose ambiguity. There is the motif of *"Muss ein ewiger Vater wohnen –* must live an eternal father," which Beethoven's composition of Schiller's Kantian Hymn to Joy accentuated in true Kantian spirit,

on the word "must". And there are the passages in which Kant – as close to Schopenhauer here as Schopenhauer later claimed – spurned the metaphysical ideas, particularly that of immortality, as imprisoned in our views of space and time and thus restricted on their part. He disdained the passage to affirmation.' (Theodor W. Adorno, *Negative Dialectics*, translated by E. B. Ashton, New York 1973, p. 385.)

77   Cf. Albrecht Wellmer, 'Adorno, Anwalt des Nicht-Identischen', in Wellmer, *Zur Dialektik von Moderne und Postmoderne*, Frankfurt 1985, pp. 160f.

78   Kant, too, considers the idea of an infinite approximation to a condition of moral perfection and thus to the kingdom of God as a practically necessary idea. (Cf. *Religion within the Limits of Reason Alone*, pp. 29f, 42, 54, 60f, 113; (*WSB*, vol. V, pp. 682f, 697, 713, 720f, 786f.) But he considers it precisely as a *practically* necessary idea; it is really the idea of a potentially endless progress 'from a deficient to a better good' (ibid., p. 60). As far as the ideal 'ultimate goals' of moral perfection or of the 'ethical state' (the 'kingdom of virtue') are concerned, Kant's thoughts remain extraordinarily ambiguous; for it is impossible to overlook Kant's remarks to the effect that a realization of these ultimate goals is something which a finite reason under finite conditions is scarcely capable of conceiving adequately (cf. ibid., pp. 58 (footnote), 60, 126). The theological motif of which I spoke earlier (note 76) asserts itself precisely at those points where Kant tries to look beyond the duty to moral progress and imagine its ultimate goals (moral perfection or the kingdom of God) as having been realized by creatures of finite reason. At any rate, Kant was aware of the difficulty of *conceiving* a kingdom of ends, which belongs to the sphere of the intelligible, as something empirically realized. Apel tries to avoid this difficulty by calling into question, as Peirce does, the Kantian distinction between *noumena* and *phainomena* and also that between regulative principles and moral postulates (cf. Apel, 'From Kant to Peirce', p. 90). But in this way the idea of an ideal communication community is accorded, in addition to its regulative function, a *constitutive* function not only for empirical cognition, but also for moral judgement. This means that Kant's difficulties with the sphere of the intelligible are carried, with all ambiguities eliminated, right into the centre of epistemology and moral philosophy. At heart, these difficulties arise from the fact that a subject in the singular is the 'highest point' of (Kant's) transcendental philosophy. My objection to Apel is that the ideal communication community still occupies the position of a subject in the singular – a subject, admittedly, which is now conceived as something *in the process of becoming* within this world. (Apel speaks

explicitly of a *single* transcendental subject which 'on the one hand must always be anticipated, and on the other hand is always yet to be realized': cf. 'Sprechakttheorie und transzendentale Sprachpragmatik', p. 127.)

79   Cf. Apel, 'Scientism or Transcendental Hermeneutics', p. 124.

80   It would of course be possible to *equate* the anticipation of an infinite consensus with the idea of an ideal communication community. In fact this would appear to offer *one* possible sense of the concept of an ideal communication community that would not be suspect; it is my belief that Habermas, for example, occasionally uses the concept in this sense (cf. Habermas, 'Moral und Sittlichkeit. Treffen Hegels Einwände gegen Kant auch auf die Diskursethik zu?', *Moralbewusstsein und kommunikatives Handeln*, p. 13). In this instance the ideal communication community is simply the community of *all* beings capable of speech whom we imagine, as it were, ideally assembled at one time But within this meaning of the concept, it is not possible to speak meaningfully of even an approximate *realization* of the ideal.

81   Apel, 'Scientism or Transcendental Hermeneutics', p. 126.

82   'The crux is what happens in it [philosophy – A. W.], not a thesis or a position – the texture, not the deductive or inductive course of one-track minds. Essentially, therefore, philosophy is not expoundable. If it were, it would be superfluous; the fact that most of it can be expounded speaks against it.' Adorno, *Negative Dialectics*, pp. 33f.

83   This is also, if I understand it correctly, the basic idea of Richard Bernstein in *Beyond Objectivism and Relativism*, Oxford 1983.

84   Cf. also the literature cited in footnote 40, above.

85   Apel has formulated the principle of fundamental grounding for the normative foundations of argument as follows: 'If I cannot dispute something without contradicting myself in the immediate circumstances, and if I can also not justify it deductively without falling into a logical petitio principii, then it belongs to those transcendental–pragmatic presuppositions of argument which we must always have acknowledged if the language game of argument is to retain its *sense*. We can therefore call this transcendental–pragmatic mode of argument the *sense-critical form of fundamental grounding*.' (K.-O. Apel, 'The Problem of Philosophical Fundamental Grounding in the Light of a Transcendental Pragmatic of Language', in *Man and World* 18 (1975), pp. 239–75.) Although I am arguing here on the premise that unavoidable presuppositions of argument, in the sense in which Apel and Habermas speak of them, do exist, I have so far been unable to find in either Apel or Habermas a stringent *exposition* of the argument for fundamental grounding. I

believe there is a connection between this and the fact that it has so far not become clear what the unavoidable presuppositions of argument really are. Here are two examples of an allegedly 'performative' or 'pragmatic' self-contradiction which is in reality no such thing. (1) Apel asserts that the following statement contains a pragmatic self-contradiction: 'I hereby assert (= I propose as a statement which can command a universal consensus in the ideal communication community) that not all discursively justified norms – including the pragmatically practical limitations on discourse – are necessarily able to command a universal consensus.' (Apel, 'Lässt sich ethische Vernunft von strategischer Zweckrationalität unterscheiden?', in *Archivo di Filosofia*, 1983, no. 1–3, p. 424.) The assertion we are dealing with states that not all norms that are discursively justified (and thus capable of commanding a consensus) are necessarily capable of commanding a consensus. This seems to me to be an assertion of the kind, 'Not all white elephants are necessarily white.' There may well be a contradiction involved, but it is a contradiction of the simple logical–semantic type. (2) The second example comes from Habermas's work on discourse ethics, where he says:

> Similarly it must be possible to demonstrate performative contradictions in the case of statements by a proponent who wished to justify the following proposition:

> (3)* After excluding A, B, C, . . . from the discussion (by silencing them or forcing our own interpretations upon them), we were finally able to convince ourselves that N is correct, where the following things are true of A, B, C, . . . : (a) they belong among those who would be *affected* by the implementation of norm N, and (b) they do not differ *as participants in the argument* from the others in any relevant respect. (DE 101)

In what sense, given conditions (a) and (b), could assertion (3)* contain a contradiction? I believe that the answer is once again simple. If those who have been excluded from the discussion do not differ in any relevant respect from the other participants, then this can only mean that their arguments are just as important and worth taking seriously as those of the people who do take part in the discussion. *Suppressing* these arguments therefore means suppressing arguments which might be important for establishing the truth. What assertion (3)* is saying, therefore, is that 'we' have convinced ourselves of something by not taking any notice of some of the possibly relevant arguments. It is thus tantamount to saying that there are possibly good arguments against the conviction we have formed, but that we shall not take any notice of them. It amounts to saying that our conviction is well-founded, but possibly not well-founded. And this, once again, appears to me to be not a *performative*, but a *logical* contradiction.

I have cited these two examples in order to make clear that everything depends on showing precisely *at which point* the fundamental grounding is really taking hold.

86 This can also be seen from the rules of discourse cited by Habermas (following Alexy), from which principle (U) is supposed to be derived. Rule 3.1 (cf. DE 99) reads as follows: 'Any subject capable of speech and action may participate in discussions.' I need not emphasize that I share the universalistic intuitions which are expressed in this rule. But it cannot be overlooked that the rule, as it is formulated, is either false or else says (relatively) little. Either the rule is saying that I am obliged to enter into a discourse with any being capable of speech and action whenever and upon whatever topic they wish, in which case the rule is quite evidently *false*. Or it is saying that no being capable of speech and action may *in principle* be excluded from discussions, in which case the rule would be far too *weak*.

87 Wolfgang Kuhlmann, *Reflexive Letztbegründung*, Munich 1985.

88 Ibid., pp. 22ff.

89 Ibid., pp. 196ff.

90 Ibid., p. 198.

91 Ibid., p. 208.

92 Cf. the discussion of the 'second objection', ibid., pp. 227ff.

93 Ibid., p. 189.

94 Ibid., p. 190.

95 But see section XI, below.

96 Following these reflections, it is possible to illustrate the error in Apel's idea for fundamental grounding with reference to a single short passage from one of his more recent texts (K.-O. Apel, 'Lässt sich ethische Vernunft von strategischer Zweckrationalität unterscheiden?', pp. 375ff). The passage appears in the context of a critique of Kant's transcendental solipsism which, in Apel's opinion, forced Kant to proclaim the moral law as a 'fact of reason' instead of providing a *grounding* for it. 'This situation is crucially altered,' Apel says, 'if it is shown that intersubjectively valid thought itself, being bound to the medium of speech, has the structure of discourse. Through transcendental self-reflection of the "I think", it is now possible to demonstrate that, together with the structure of discourse, an (in principle unlimited) *community of finite rational beings* and the similarly generalizable *mutuality of*

claims (of interests or needs for which arguments may be advanced) *and of the competence to evaluate arguments*, in short, an *ideal communication community* is presupposed, which is anticipated within the real communication community. The *capacity of an argument to command a consensus* within the ideal, unlimited community of argument is thus acknowledged as a regulative idea of the intersubjective validity of arguments, whether these are of theoretical or of practical ethical relevance.' (Ibid., p. 421) It is immediately apparent from this passage that the supposed fundamental grounding of ethics is directly connected with the transformation of a necessary *presupposition* into a necessary anticipation (a necessary regulative idea), whereby the crucial point is, of course, that the sense of the presupposition itself has been misinterpreted.

97   This is something to which Ursula Wolf draws attention in her critique of Ernst Tugendhat: *Das Problem des moralischen Sollens*, Berlin 1984, pp. 23, 35ff. Tugendhat has assimilated this criticism and used it as a basis on which to propose a grounding of morality which comes closer to Kant; I shall take up the principal ideas of Tugendhat's proposal below. Cf. Ernst Tugendhat, *Probleme der Ethik*, Stuttgart 1984, pp. 132ff ('Retraktionen').

98   This is where H. L. A. Hart sees the moment of truth as conceived by the positivistic tradition to reside. Hart recognizes morality as an *evaluative standard* for legal norms, but rejects the reduction of the concept of legal validity to that of moral validity. 'There are thus two dangers, and it will help us to navigate between them if we insist on this distinction [i.e. the distinction between what is and what ought to be the case – A. W.]: on the one hand there is the danger that justice and its authority dissolves into what people think justice ought to be; and on the other hand there is the danger that prevailing notions of justice supplant morality in its function as the ultimate measure of behaviour, and thus elude criticism.' (Hart, *Recht und Moral*, Göttingen 1971, p. 19.)

99   Cf. Habermas, *Autonomy and Solidarity*, p. 171, and 'Moral und Sittlichkeit', pp. 21f.

100   'Moral und Sittlichkeit', pp. 21f.

101   Ibid.

102   In *Social Research*, vol. 38, no. 3 (Autumn 1971).

103   Habermas, *Autonomy and Solidarity*, p. 171.

104   The arguments that begin here follow, somewhat loosely, the thoughts of Ernst Tugendhat in *Probleme der Ethik*, Stuttgart 1984, pp. 132f.

105   Cf. note 17, above.

106   Paton, *The Moral Law*, p. 81; Ellington, p. 24. (*WSB*, vol. IV, pp. 42f (BA 39).)

107 This is the sense in which I would understand the words of Klaus Heinrich which Habermas quotes in his latest book: 'Keeping the covenant with God is the symbol of fidelity; breaking this covenant is the model of betrayal. To keep faith with God is to keep faith with life-giving Being itself – in oneself and in others. To deny it in any domain of being means breaking the covenant with God and betraying one's own foundation . . . . Thus, betrayal of another is simultaneously betrayal of oneself; and every protest against betrayal is not just protest in one's own name, but in the name of the other at the same time.' (Klaus Heinrich, *Versuch über die Schwierigkeit nein zu sagen*, Frankfurt 1964, p. 20, quoted in Jürgen Habermas, *The Philosophical Discourse of Modernity*, Cambridge 1987, p. 325.) In elucidation of this, Habermas develops an early statement by Hegel, commenting: 'In the restlessness of the real conditions of life, there broods an ambivalence that is due to the dialectic of betrayal and avenging force.' (Ibid.) Any infringement of a communal life is visited with 'avenging force' upon the person responsible for that infringement. But we can only speak of a 'dialectic' here if we can *simultaneously* think of the avenging force as a force sublated within judgements expressible in language, i.e. as condemnation or contempt on the part of others and – in view of the inescapable intersubjectivity of such judgements – as self-condemnation or self-contempt. But we have to think of it precisely as a *force* sublated within a judgement or self-condemnation expressible in language. The fact that such a condemnation or self-condemnation possesses the power to afflict the life of the 'condemned' person shows that moral condemnation and self-condemnation still contain a reflection of real external force. It would not be possible to account for this power of moral condemnation and self-condemnation to afflict a person's life if the 'avenging force' were not merely sublated within moral judgement but had completely disappeared in it.

108 Cf. Habermas, *The Philosophical Discourse of Modernity*, p. 310.

109 Habermas, *The Theory of Communicative Action*, vol. 2, Cambridge 1987, pp. 43ff, esp. p. 52.

110 Ibid., pp. 77ff.

111 Cf. ibid., pp. 62ff.

112 Ibid., p. 63.

113 Cf. ibid., pp. 62ff.

114 Ibid., p. 63.

115 Ibid., p. 68.

116 Ibid., p. 61.

117 Ibid., p. 69.

118 Cf. ibid.

119   Ibid., p. 70.
120   Ibid., p. 71.
121   Ibid., p. 72.
122   Ibid.
123   Ibid., p. 81.
124   Habermas, *The Theory of Communicative Action*, vol. 1, London 1984, pp. 72ff.
125   Ibid., p. 50.
126   For substantiating references see, for example, Bryan R. Wilson (ed.), *Rationality*, Oxford 1974.
127   Cf. Alasdair MacIntyre, 'Rationality and the Explanation of Action', in his *Against the Self-Images of the Age*, New York 1971, p. 252: 'For when we approach the utterances and activities of an alien culture with a well-established classification of genres in our mind and ask of a given rite or practice, "Is it a piece of applied science? Or a piece of symbolic and dramatic activity? Or a piece of theology?" we may in fact be asking a set of questions to which any answer may be misleading . . . For the utterances and practice in question may belong, as it were, to all and none of the genres that we have in mind.'
128   Habermas, *The Theory of Communicative Action*, vol. 2, pp. 52f.
129   Ibid., p. 55.
130   Cf. ibid., p. 49.
131   This is also how Freud interprets the taboo, stating that 'the prohibitions of taboo are to be understood as consequences of an emotional ambivalence' (Sigmund Freud, *Complete Psychological Works*, vol. XIII, London 1955, p. 67). He also interprets 'taboo conscience' as the oldest form of (moral) conscience (ibid.).
132   Mary Douglas, *Purity and Danger*, London 1966. Robin Horton, 'African Traditional Thought and Western Science', in Bryan R. Wilson (ed.), *Rationality*, pp. 131ff.
133   Horton, 'African Traditional Thought', pp. 164–6. Cf. also Edmund Leach, *Culture and Communication*, Cambridge 1976, pp. 37ff.
134   Philippa Foot has pointed out that it is not the categorical ought itself, but at best the way in which it is grounded that distinguishes moral rules from the rules of a club or the rules of etiquette. 'It is obvious that the normative character of moral judgement does not guarantee its reason-giving force. Moral judgements are normative, but so are judgements of manners, statements of club rules, and many others.' ('Morality as a System of Hypothetical Imperatives', in Philippa Foot, *Virtues and Vices*, Berkeley 1978, p. 162.)
135   Habermas, *The Philosophical Discourse of Modernity*, Cambridge 1987.

136 Ibid., p. 345.
137 Ibid., p. 346.
138 Ibid.
139 This is similar, as I have subsequently discovered, to the position adopted by William Frankena in his essay, 'Has Morality an Independent Bottom?', *The Monist*, vol. 63, no. 1 (January 1980), pp. 49ff.
140 Cf. Martin Seel, *Die Kunst der Entzweiung. Zum Begriff der ästhetischen Rationalität*, Frankfurt 1985. Cf. also Albrecht Wellmer, 'Truth, Semblance, Reconciliation: Adorno's Aesthetic Redemption of Modernity', in this volume, pp. 22ff.
141 Cf. Wilfrid Sellars, 'Empiricism and the Philosophy of Mind', in his *Science, Perception and Reality*, London 1963, p. 173.
142 Cf. ibid., esp. pp. 32ff. It is true that Sellars goes on to concede that the moral and thus also the social sphere possess a reality of their own. As with every philosopher of importance, it would therefore be possible to produce a critique of Sellars which largely consisted in reading him 'against the grain'. 'Thus the conceptual framework of persons is the framework in which we think of one another as sharing the community intentions which provide the ambience of principles and standards (above all those which make meaningful discourse and rationality itself possible) within which we live our own individual lives. A person can almost be defined as a being that has intentions. Thus the conceptual framework of persons is not something that needs to be *reconciled with* the scientific image, but rather something to be *joined* to it. Thus, to complete the scientific image we need to enrich it *not* with more ways of saying what is the case, but with the language of communal and individual intentions, so that by construing the actions we intend to do and the circumstances in which we intend to do them in scientific terms we *directly* relate the world as conceived by scientific theory to our purposes, and make it *our* world and no longer an alien appendage to the world in which we do our living.' (Ibid., p. 40)
143 Cf. Habermas, *The Theory of Communicative Action*, vol. 2, p. 398: 'In each of these spheres, differentiation processes are accompanied by countermovements that, under the primacy of one dominant aspect of validity, bring back in again the two aspects that were at first excluded. Thus nonobjectivist approaches to research within the human sciences bring viewpoints of moral and aesthetic critique to bear – without threatening the primacy of questions of truth; only in this way is critical social theory made possible.' What I have just said about Sellars (note 142) applies also to Habermas. What I am criticizing – and this is what I am

aiming at in reading either author 'against the grain' – is the assumption that we have to conceive of social facts *in the first instance* in the same terms as physical facts.

144   Cf. Albrecht Wellmer, 'Truth, Semblance, Reconciliation', in this volume, p. 28.

145   Martin Seel, 'Die zwei Bedeutungen kommunikativer Rationalität. Bemerkungen zu Habermas' Kritik der pluralen Vernunft', MS (1985), p. 16.

146   Cf. Habermas, *The Theory of Communicative Action*, vol. 2, p. 398.

146   Here I am following a suggestion made by Seel. For what follows, too, cf. Seel, *Die Kunst der Entzweiung*, pp. 320ff.

148   Ibid.

149   Habermas, *The Theory of Communicative Action*, vol. 2, p. 398.

150   Cf. Friedrich Kambartel, 'Vernunft: Kriterium oder Kultur? Zur Definition des Vernünftigen', in F. Kambartel, *Philosophie der humanen Welt*, Frankfurt 1989.

151   An allusion to Kant, who speaks of a '*philosophical millennium*, which hopes for a state of perpetual peace based on a league of peoples, a world-republic', as distinct from a theological millennium, 'which tarries for the completed moral improvement of the entire human race'. Kant, of course, also defends this theological millennium as a practical idea. Cf. *Religion within the Limits of Reason Alone*, pp. 29f (*WSB*, vol. V, pp. 682f.)

152   This is the point of view which is emphasized by Hannah Arendt above all; it is what her concept of 'natality' refers to: Arendt, *The Human Condition*, Chicago 1958, pp. 175ff.

Index

Studies in Contemporary German Social Thought
Thomas McCarthy, General Editor

Theodor W. Adorno, *Against Epistemology: A Metacritique*
Theodor W. Adorno, *Prisms*
Karl-Otto Apel, *Understanding and Explanation: A Transcendental-Pragmatic Perspective*
Seyla Benhabib and Fred Dallmayr, editors, *The Communicative Ethics Debate*
Richard J. Bernstein, editor, *Habermas and Modernity*
Ernst Bloch, *Natural Law and Human Dignity*
Ernst Bloch, *The Principle of Hope*
Ernst Bloch, *The Utopian Function of Art and Literature: Selected Essays*
Hans Blumenberg, *The Genesis of the Copernican World*
Hans Blumenberg, *The Legitimacy of the Modern Age*
Hans Blumenberg, *Work on Myth*
Susan Buck-Morss, *The Dialectics of Seeing: Walter Benjamin and the Arcades Project*
Jean Cohen and Andrew Arato, *Civil Society and Political Theory*
Helmut Dubiel, *Theory and Politics: Studies in the Development of Critical Theory*
John Forester, editor, *Critical Theory and Public Life*
David Frisby, *Fragments of Modernity: Theories of Modernity in the Work of Simmel, Kracauer and Benjamin*
Hans-Georg Gadamer, *Philosophical Apprenticeships*
Hans-Georg Gadamer, *Reason in the Age of Science*
Jürgen Habermas, *On the Logic of the Social Sciences*
Jürgen Habermas, *Moral Consciousness and Communicative Action*
Jürgen Habermas, *The New Conservatism: Cultural Criticism and the Historians' Debate*
Jürgen Habermas, *The Philosophical Discourse of Modernity: Twelve Lectures*
Jürgen Habermas, *Philosophical-Political Profiles*
Jürgen Habermas, editor, *Observations on "The Spiritual Situation of the Age"*
Jürgen Habermas, *The Structural Transformation of the Public Sphere: An Inquiry into a Category of Bourgeois Society*
Axel Honneth and Hans Joas, editors, *Communicative Action: Essays on Jürgen Habermas's Theory of Communicative Action*
Hans Joas, *G. H. Mead: A Contemporary Re-examination of His Thought*
Reinhart Koselleck, *Critique and Crisis: Enlightenment and the Pathogenesis of Modern Society*
Reinhart Koselleck, *Futures Past: On the Semantics of Historical Time*
Harry Liebersohn, *Fate and Utopia in German Sociology, 1887–1923*
Herbert Marcuse, *Hegel's Ontology and the Theory of Historicity*
Guy Oakes, *Weber and Rickert: Concept Formation in the Cultural Sciences*
Claus Offe, *Contradictions of the Welfare State*
Claus Offe, *Disorganized Capitalism: Contemporary Transformations of Work and Politics*
Helmut Peukert, *Science, Action, and Fundamental Theology: Toward a Theology of Communicative Action*

Joachim Ritter, *Hegel and the French Revolution: Essays on the Philosophy of Right*

Alfred Schmidt, *History and Structure: An Essay on Hegelian-Marxist and Structuralist Theories of History*

Dennis Schmidt, *The Ubiquity of the Finite: Hegel, Heidegger, and the Entitlements of Philosophy*

Carl Schmitt, *The Crisis of Parliamentary Democracy*

Carl Schmitt, *Political Romanticism*

Carl Schmitt, *Political Theology: Four Chapters on the Concept of Sovereignty*

Gary Smith, editor, *On Walter Benjamin: Critical Essays and Recollections*

Michael Theunissen, *The Other: Studies in the Social Ontology of Husserl, Heidegger, Sartre, and Buber*

Ernst Tugendhat, *Self-Consciousness and Self-Determination*

Mark Warren, *Nietzsche and Political Thought*

Albrecht Wellmer, *The Persistence of Modernity: Essays on Aesthetics, Ethics and Postmodernism*

Thomas E. Wren, editor, *The Moral Domain: Essays in the Ongoing Discussion between Philosophy and the Social Sciences*

Lambert Zuidervaart, *Adorno's Aesthetic Theory: The Redemption of Illusion*